VICTORIAN IDENTITIES

Also by Julian Wolfreys

BEING ENGLISH: Narratives, Idioms, and Performances of
National Identity from Coleridge to Trollope

Victorian Identities

Social and Cultural Formations in Nineteenth-Century Literature

Edited by

Ruth Robbins

and

Julian Wolfreys

Foreword by

James R. Kincaid

First published in Great Britain 1996 by
MACMILLAN PRESS LTD
Houndmills, Basingstoke, Hampshire RG21 6XS
and London
Companies and representatives
throughout the world

A catalogue record for this book is available
from the British Library.

ISBN 0–333–63886–7

First published in the United States of America 1996 by
ST. MARTIN'S PRESS, INC.,
Scholarly and Reference Division,
175 Fifth Avenue,
New York, N.Y. 10010

ISBN 0–312–12850–9

Library of Congress Cataloging-in-Publication Data
Victorian identities : social and cultural formations in nineteenth
-century literature / edited by Ruth Robbins and Julian Wolfreys ;
foreword by James R. Kincaid.
p. cm.
Includes bibliographical references and index.
ISBN 0–312–12850–9 (cloth)
1. English literature—19th century—History and criticism.
2. Literature and society—Great Britain—History—19th century.
3. Politics and literature—Great Britain—History—19th century.
4. Great Britain—Intellectual life—19th century.   5. Women and
literature—Great Britain—History—19th century.   I. Robbins,
Ruth, 1965–   .   II. Wolfreys, Julian, 1958–   .
PR461.V53   1996
820.9'008—dc20
        95–14915
        CIP

10   9   8   7   6   5   4   3   2   1
05   04   03   02   01   00   99   98   97   96

Printed and bound in Great Britain by
Antony Rowe Ltd, Chippenham, Wiltshire

These to His Memory – since he held them dear,
Perchance as finding there unconsciously
Some image of himself – I dedicate
Alfred, Lord Tennyson

Contents

Notes on the Contributors

David Alderson studied at the Universities of Newcastle upon Tyne and Sussex. He is now Associate Lecturer in English at the University of Northumbria at Newcastle, and his other publications include a paper on Wilde in *Sexual Dissidence in Irish Writing*.

William Baker is Professor of English at Northern Illinois University. He is the author and editor of numerous books and articles on George Eliot and nineteenth-century literature; he is also a regular reviewer and contributor to several journals, and is the editor of *George Eliot–George Henry Lewes Studies* journal.

Claire M. Berardini currently teaches at Rutgers University. She has published an article on Tennyson in *Victorian Poetry*. She is currently writing a book on Tennyson titled *Victorian Resistance: Structure and Agency in the Poetry of Tennyson*.

Helen Debenham is a Senior Lecturer in English at the University of Canterbury, New Zealand.

Diana Gardner is Associate Lecturer in English Studies at the University of Luton. Her main areas of interest are children's literature and representations of gender in literature.

Geoffrey Hemstedt teaches English at the University of Sussex.

Nancy Henry received her degrees from Stanford University and the University of Chicago. She is currently Assistant Professor of English at the State University of New York at Binghamton. She has recently published the first annotated edition of George Eliot's *Impressions of Theophrastus Such* and is working on a book entitled: *Originating Fiction: George Eliot and Harriet Beecher Stowe*.

James R. Kincaid is Aerol Arnold Professor of English at the University of Southern California. He is the author of numerous articles and books on Victorian literature. His most recent publications are *Annoying the Victorians* and *Child Loving: The Erotic Child and Victorian Culture*.

Carolyn Lesjak is a graduate student at Duke University where she teaches English Literature and Composition and is currently completing her dissertation on labour and pleasure in nineteenth-century British fiction and socialist thought.

Jessica Maynard is a visiting lecturer at the University of Luton. She is currently researching into discourses of terror and terrorism in nineteenth- and twentieth-century fiction, and representations of the city.

Robin Melrose is Principal Lecturer in English Studies at the University of Luton. His main areas of interest are literary stylistics and the relationship between ideology and language.

Ruth Robbins is a lecturer in literary studies at the University of Luton. She has research interests in late nineteenth-century literature and has published articles on Housman, Wilde and Vernon Lee.

Jenny Bourne Taylor teaches English at the University of Sussex. Her publications include *In the Secret Theatre of Home: Wilkie Collins, Sensation Narrative and Nineteenth-Century Psychology*. She is currently working on a study of the cultural significance of illegitimacy, *Illegitimate Fictions: Narratives of Bastardy in English Culture*.

Alexis Weedon is a lecturer with the Department of Media Studies at the University of Luton.

Julian Wolfreys is Senior Lecturer in English at the University of Dundee. He has published a number of essays on Victorian literature, James Joyce and feminist film theory, as well as being a regular reviewer for several journals. He is the author of *Being English: Narratives, Idioms and Performances of National Identity from Coleridge to Trollope* and *Affirmative Resistances*; he is currently working on two books, provisionally entitled *Writing London* and *Victoriographies*, a study of postmodern nineteenth-century pastiche.

Foreword

James R. Kincaid

Here in these essays Mr Podsnap meets Karl Marx and doesn't, on the whole, approve; George Eliot takes the measure of Michel Foucault; Lord Tennyson brings along some bastards to make the acquaintance of the famous, though French, lecturer on deconstruction. The encounter of Victorian studies and contemporary literary theory represented with such variety and sophistication in this collection is actually not, in form, unlike the powerful climactic moment in so many Victorian narratives, enacted in novels, on stage, and (we all feel sure) in life itself:

Charles: Why, then, if these documents speak true, you are not a stranger at all. You are –
Stranger: Yes, my boy, your long-lost –
Charles: Oh father! Can it be?
Stranger-No-Longer: It can. It is!
Charles: And then I am – Is it possible?
Marian: You are the heir, and all this we see is yours. Oh my darling!
Charles: My head reels! I am no stable boy at all. All this time I have been in error. I now look with other eyes, dream other dreams. Oh sweet new world!
[*Curtain*]

The final, throbbing speech given to Charles, with its allusive richness – the echoes are from *The Tempest* by William Shakespeare – suggests what is captured in these essays: not a reeling dizziness so much as a sense of sudden refiguring of who we are and where we stand. These essays reposition the Victorian subjects they treat of, certainly; but more important is the way in which they seek to understand in new terms where we stand, how we see, what it is we do.

xi

For these writers and scholars, then, theory has come to Victorian studies not as an interpretive tool but as a startling new geography. Little interested in producing new readings, these essays seem exciting, even strange, because they speak out of fresh landscapes. It's not that an entirely new language has been invented, of course; or even a new subject matter: the authors and even many of the topics for conversation are familiar and many of the ways of understanding the texts of literature, culture and history bear a strong resemblance to those of previous decades. What has changed most startlingly, whirled us about most ruthlessly, has been a new self-consciousness about the ways in which we participate in, contaminate, deploy to our advantage (or not), and have dictated to us the modes of our own understanding.

The most puzzling question is not so much what we see when we look at the past but why we see what it is we suppose we see. Why is that particular picture being produced? Who is grinding the lenses we look through when we read *David Copperfield* or the trials of Oscar Wilde? How are we complicit with the ideology of our own time and what hope can we have of gaining any distance from it? How can we be resistant or subversive readers? How can we read our own reading?

No longer satisfied with doing interpretations, with producing little memos to ourselves to reassure us that our way of thinking is akin to nature itself, we have become sceptical of our own practices, our own lethal knowingness. Knowingness: that is the way of ideological control hardest to detect, hardest to counter. Only by burrowing down to the roots of our own trusting natures, suspecting most deeply that which seems most obvious, can we hope to dislodge or at least disrupt the forms by which literary study maintains its conventional irrelevance, its smiling obedience to the *status quo*.

These essays, then, seem to me so sophisticated, so sly that they deserve to be called wonderfully, superbly stupid. None is willing to sell out to competence, to grind out smugly another good reading, to do 'a fine job'. Each one is so richly informed by theory and by the courage of bravado performance that it goes for much more than good criticism.

That these essays are not really 'bad', not so strange that we cannot hear them or join with their undertakings, is not a sign of compromise but of hospitality. If we have any hope of rebelling against the taken-for-granted, of keeping ourselves from settling down into knowingness, of being obtusely scandalous, then we need all the help we can get from one another. We don't want leaders, much less heroes; we want partygoers. It's not intrepid individualism we are after but a fluid, self-critical community.

Come to think of it, self-critical isn't the right word. What kind of a community would that be? Who likes criticism or is really very anxious to direct it toward one's own self, however inviting as targets others may be? Let's say the community of theorists and scholars we imagine, the community reflected in these essays, is alert, not self-critical, and playful rather than faultfinding. When Charles (the young heir, you remember) and Marian and the old squire (now declining fast but happily), settle in to enjoy the estate and invite all their many friends to join them for partying, what's needed is not criticism but motion. Keep the game going and don't stop – or the forces of knowingness will get you. These essays show us how to play, and then play some more.

JAMES R. KINCAID
Los Angeles and Sierra Madre

Introduction: A Moment, Recalled

Ruth Robbins and Julian Wolfreys

Nothing would happen, nothing would have taken place without this 'encounter'... .

Jacques Derrida

The moment or encounter out of which this collection of essays has arisen as the coming forth of a certain community was, as is usually the case with such heterogeneous collections, a conference. The conference was entitled, with all the ambiguity that could be mustered, 'Victorian Literature, Contemporary Theory', and took place, that is to say took place 'initially' and repeatedly, both at the time, during the time, of the event and, again, here, in another fashion, in different voices, during a weekend in July at the University of Luton in 1994. This is what is being recalled. Even at this point of recollection the title of the conference still retains its ambiguity, the four terms of the title holding together in uneasy, yet convivial, conference, as moments in overheard discourses, coming together, as if it were by chance or, as it turned out at the time, good fortune. Strangers at a party, with no one knowing who the host was. Whatever relationship is mapped between the terms 'Victorian', 'Literature', 'Contemporary', 'Theory' is kept at a remove from immediate comprehension; and this is, perhaps, best; for this illustrates, for the moment, that the field of Victorian literary studies is a diverse field, with no one theory mastering, appropriating, policing or dominating the proceedings. Nothing is reified, and all remains delightfully 'improper' – or even, on occasion, scandalous, to use a favoured word of one of the two keynote speakers, James R. Kincaid – in the interpretation of texts and the uses of 'theory'.

Forty-four papers were presented at the conference, all of which, on reflection, can be taken to be in some way scandalous or improper. William Baker's 'Afterword' to this volume comments on the chimerical presence of theoretical positions. It would not be going too far, we think, to suggest that no solidified positions were

1

ever announced; there was a refreshing lack of logocentrism and intellectual muscle-flexing. Instead, our various speakers cuddled up to texts and theories, quite often tickled them, frequently played fast and loose with ideas in a manner wholly (in)appropriate to the intellectually playful and exploratory nature of many 'Victorian' texts, and to what we understand by the concept 'Victorian'. And this is important to bear in mind, for what emerged at the time of the conference, and what emerges from this collection, is that there is not one Victorian Identity, there are no fixed Victorian values; rather there are disparate identities and values, many of which appeared – and still seem – modern or even postmodern. The Victorians our contemporaries? Maybe not, but perhaps our children's or, at least, our future, if we can bear to give up being old-fashioned and even somewhat prudish in our knowingness about what constitutes, constructs or performs the 'Victorian'. We may even find out about our own constructedness as readers of the Victorian. What exactly is it we desire from the nineteenth century? What do we look for as images, if not of the Victorians, then versions of the 'Victorian' which are really portraits of ourselves, kept in some attic, like the picture of Dorian Gray?

But the purpose of the conference was never to drag out musty, worm-eaten images for reverential adoration, or sober reflection; the intent was never to impose on nineteenth-century texts readings under the rubric of 'theory' or whatever is gathered together by that catch-all term. If any sense was made of the title of the conference ahead of the event, *avant la lettre*, then it was to see what 'theories' were available from Victorian writing, what could be read, returned to the present, to the scene of writing and reading today, through the voices that the situation of a conference made possible. At the same time, it was hoped that whatever it is that we choose to call 'theory' today might make equally possible and available resonances – or dissonances – in the reading of nineteenth-century textuality which would allow for a community of heterogeneous identities to emerge.

What emerged at the time, and what emerges from this collection, is a vitality in the most literal sense; to such a degree, in fact, that this collection of essays stands as being wholly distinct, as the other of the conference from which it has developed. This is not merely an outgrowth or continuation, not merely the register of an event (even though it is that also), but a network of divergent, though sometimes overlapping traces, always on the way to community, promising a community-to-come. What we have here are other headings, points of departure. This is an echo of the moment of the conference in itself, which moved from day to day, from voice to voice, from agreement to contradiction, and from contradiction to agreement: in short, like the conference of July 1994, this collection marks the space of a disparate, yet momentarily convergent plurality.

It has become a virtual commonplace in the discipline of literary studies to insist on the diversity of the Victorian age. As critics and scholars we work hard to demonstrate that the adjective 'Victorian' means not one thing – not a monumental set of values, moralities or beliefs – but many. The critical consensus has developed to suggest that the nineteenth century was in a constant state of flux where conflicting discourses struggled for pre-eminence. The movement away from an earlier twentieth-century perception that the Victorians were merely hypocrites and prudes began perhaps in 1966, with Steven Marcus's groundbreaking study of sexuality and pornography in mid-nineteenth-century England, *The Other Victorians*. In the introduction to that book, Marcus insists on the connections between the historical culture he seeks to excavate and the contemporary (1960s) audience for whom he writes. But, at the same time, while 'we' (in the twentieth century) are connected to 'them' (in the nineteenth), he asks us also to recognise that the sub-culture to be studied was '"foreign", distinct, exotic' (Marcus 1966, xx), thereby almost unconsciously enunciating a hierarchy of 'us and them', of 'self and other', in which 'we', with our more sophisticated knowledge and methodologies have a privileged view of a more ignorant past.

Nonetheless, despite its adoption of twentieth-century 'knowingness' and its anachronistic applications of Freudian analysis, Marcus's book remains important both as a source of fascinating information, and as a first attempt at breaking down the monolithic structures by which Victoria's reign was understood by the generations which succeeded her. Its significance is perhaps nowhere more apparent than in the adaptation of its title by Michel Foucault, whose first chapter of *The History of Sexuality* is entitled 'We "Other" Victorians'. In that introduction, Foucault launches a polemic against the fundamental ignorance of twentieth-century 'knowingness'. We, he argues, have adopted the language practices of our Victorian forebears – or rather, our own reconstructions of the language practices we assume them to have used – in order to maintain the possibility of transgression and taboo. We require our reconstruction of their ignorance in order to validate what we want to believe are our more enlightened historical, theoretical and methodological positions. We are guilty of making assumptions about our own superiority; we are 'other Victorians' because we have too easily accepted dominant discourses in our own age as well as adopting as our own those of the age of Victoria.

The distinguished international group of scholars who have contributed to this volume, as the diversity of their subjects implies, have taken seriously the challenge to examine more carefully what might be meant by the word 'Victorian'. And, as the diversity of their approaches also suggests, they have accepted the impossibility of finding definitive answers – whether in the Victorian era, or in ours – to the questions they have set themselves in their various chapters. What each chapter demonstrates is that limits and boundaries of whatever kind exist, then and now, as Foucault himself might have argued, as lines to be crossed as well as markers of containment.

The title of Helen Debenham's chapter signals this commitment from the outset. Her definition of sensation fiction as an 'art' speaks of generic and publishing boundaries which are insecure. Rhoda Broughton's insistent use of quotations from and allusions to the texts of 'high' culture in a text defined as 'low' or popular requires that her readers are competent interpreters of both high and low. The individual reader and the culture as a whole each contain both possibilities, suggesting that there is no necessary or fundamental distinction between them. All boundaries are/were shifting, as Nancy Henry's chapter shows in complicating our understanding of George Eliot's relationship to Jewish culture.

Victorian literature provides the reader with almost limitless possibilities of inclusion and exclusion – sometimes even within the same text. The very geography of Victorian England and its conception of itself as a nation both contained and excluded London Jews as Carolyn Lesjak demonstrates. London itself, the capital of empire, cloaked in mysterious fog, was itself simultaneously present and absent, inclusive and exclusive, as Julian Wolfreys and Geoffrey Hemstedt's respective essays on Dickens's London suggest. Even the most respectable Victorians were always already potentially 'other' Victorians. Claire Berardini takes the figure of the public poet – the nation's poet – Alfred Tennyson, and shows some of the dissident readings to which his work is open. And for Jenny Bourne Taylor, the legal situation of the bastard child defines corrupted values through its exclusion of this innocent cipher; at the same time, the representation of bastardy in Victorian fiction opens up the possibility for that same child to find acceptance and happiness within the very bosom of the same Victorian society whose laws have dispossessed him/her.

The evidence is always blurred. It is not possible to tell the whole truth, as Jessica Maynard's analysis of the 'not proven' verdict in Collins's *The Law and the Lady* suggests. There is no absolute truth about the past, and the attempt to impose one on history is a betrayal; Judas does indeed write the biography if the biography depends on a single, unchallenged and unchallengeable reading, says Ruth Robbins. The age which 'discovered' evolution was itself caught up in many processes of change. From the ways in which the Victorians defined masculinity in terms of nationhood, discussed by David Alderson, to questions of production – how books are made and disseminated – examined by Alexis Weedon, and reproduction (how children are or are not formed by their contacts with culture) analysed by Robin Melrose and Diana Gardner, the ground of Victorian studies is reassuringly unstable. Reassuring because the very fact that an age which is still seen (in the popular imagination at least) as an age of repression, was in fact seething with myriad possibilities, gives hope to our contemporary world. We too, perhaps, can claim to be pluralistic, diverse, evolving; like them, we too can resist being pinned down or framed. We can become 'other' Victorians as a form of celebration rather than as a penance.

It is always usual in places such as these to acknowledge all those near and dear, loved and cherished, and even a few of more ambiguous status. Such lists usually mean little, the proper name, to paraphrase Derrida improperly, marking the limit of the knowable, the limit of translation. And we certainly would not wish to translate those being named into any other form. Charmian Hearne of Macmillan has been a wonderful editor to work with; her energy and enthusiasm for this project is largely the reason for its coming to being; Tim Boatswain, Dean of Humanities at the University of Luton, helped in whatever manner he could to encourage and ensure the success of the conference. He balanced foresight and enthusiasm with good humour and an eye for the appropriate; John Brannigan – best of colleagues, best of friends – was of immeasurable help, support and reassurance. Foolishly, he even volunteered to carry out all manner of thankless tasks (which he'd have been asked to do anyway). Thanks also to Richard Andrews, who generally puts up with a lot at the best of times and who is there also at the worst of times. And to all our colleagues at Luton, who attended the conference, chaired the sessions, shepherded the confused towards the coffee and the food, as well as making intellectual contributions, and who have helped in so many ways: thank you all.

James Kincaid talks, in his preface, of parties and partying. This metaphor catches the double moment of the conference and this volume. So, in the words of Bruce Willis-as-John McLane, 'Welcome to the party, pal.'

RUTH ROBBINS, JULIAN WOLFREYS
Bedford, Kew

Part I
En-Gendering Debates:
Masculinity, Femininity
and National Identity

1

Rhoda Broughton's *Not Wisely But Too Well* and the Art of Sensation

Helen Debenham

'Not wisely but too well': Othello's words are so familiar that the
title of Rhoda Broughton's first novel is easily overlooked. Yet, read
with its original context in mind, the title points to more than conventional borrowing from a pre-eminent master. Broughton's
unwise lover is Kate Chester, who plays Desdemona's role of en-
thralled victim to the dangerously attractive (literally murderous in
the first version) Dare Stamer. What happens when Desdemona
takes over Othello's words? When blackamoor becomes black-
guard? When a woman rewrites a male plot? The title in fact initiates an extensive series of allusions which raise questions like these
about gendering and narrative. Some of *Not Wisely But Too Well*'s
hundreds of quotations, allusions, references and echoes are undoubtedly, as Michael Sadleir complains, 'silly ostentatious
swagger' (Sadleir 1944, 102) but modern criticism which ignores
them and reads Broughton's early novels simply as sensation
fiction, or rather through definitions of sensationism derived princi-
pally from the narrative practices of Wilkie Collins, Mary Braddon
and Ellen Wood, can often do little except praise the assertive sexuality and deplore the conventional moralising. Even Lyn Pykett,
whose 1992 study of the 'improper' feminine could provide a
strong argument for reading Broughton as sensationist, adds little
to Elaine Showalter's dismissive verdict in *A Literature of Their
Own*.[1] Reading the '*cordon sanitaire* of literary display' (Beer 1994,
26) through Bakhtinian ideas of heteroglossia, on the other hand,
can highlight Broughton's intense engagement with contemporary
ideas of literary genre and specifically the way in which *Not Wisely*

But Too Well addresses itself to mid-nineteenth-century debates (often fuelled by sensationism) over control of the literary high ground.

Not Wisely's polyglot dialogue is complicated by the novel's existence in two forms: the original serial published in the *Dublin University Magazine* in 1865–66, which ends with the already-married Dare killing Kate and himself after she for a third time refuses to run off with him, and the much milder three-volume work which reached the wider reading public in 1867.[2] A full comparison of the two would tell a great deal about the boundaries of the permissible, and hence about the reproduction and refashioning of culture, in mid-nineteenth-century fiction. Even in its bowdlerised form, however, Broughton's novel, with its gleeful mixing of discourses and genres, its appropriation and re-presentation of (often masculine) 'high' culture, offers useful insights into the young female writer as reader, responding to her culture's definitions of her as a woman, and negotiating her right of entry to and her difference from the literary establishment that shaped those definitions. No attempt to chart a novel's 'critical interanimation of languages' (Bakhtin 1981, 296) can hope to be complete; this essay focuses on a few aspects only of intertextuality in the light of Patricia Yaeger's contention that '[a]lthough words enact the repressions of the dominant culture, language can also deflect and begin to reconstruct the dominant culture's direction, especially in those moments when words themselves become the objects of representation' (Yaeger 1988, 111–12).

At the heart of Broughton's narrative strategy lies her development of the new kind of heroine she had found in Anne Thackeray's deceptively gentle *The Story of Elizabeth* (1863). Thackeray presented, for Margaret Oliphant,

> the most daring sketch of a troublesome girl which we remember to have seen; ... [Elly] is cross, she is disobedient, she is sullen and perverse; and even, perhaps the most unpardonable sin of all, she is untidy. (171)

Broughton found this a 'wonderful novelty' (Ritchie 1924, 118). Her Kate, in turn, schemes, sulks, mopes, fights with her family, fusses about her appearance, and flirts – for self-gratification and to spite her sister. These are ordinary girls, for all their beauty and charm, and their ordinariness clashes with and problematises the narrative context of romance-reform in which they are placed. Like the more obviously heroic Jane Eyre and Maggie Tulliver, Elly and Kate both love a man who has ties elsewhere, are chastened by suffering and illness, and have a morally worthy alternative suitor. Each girl's reform, her final feminine respectability, is confirmed by an appropriate fate: one marries, one dies. Thackeray's work perhaps showed Broughton the subversive potential of an early guarantee of ultimate moral orthodoxy when dwelling on feminine excess. Certainly, in both novels the 'emphasis added', in Nancy Miller's terms, to the foreshadowed end draws attention to the conventionality of the romance framework, creating conflict between the ordinary, the seemingly 'real', woman and the fictional and ideological constructions permitted her. Again in both novels, this contest is sharpened by 'the permanent corrective of laughter, ...the corrective of reality that is always richer, more fundamental and most importantly *too contradictory and too heteroglot*' (Bakhtin 1981, 55, his italics) to be contained within narrowly prescriptive rules.

Unlike Anne Thackeray, however, Broughton aspired (or so she claims in her late, self-deprecatory, autobiographical novels)[3] to replace the conventions she challenged with a 'new' truth about love, one derived from her promiscuous reading in poetry and drama as well as fiction. Ironically, her attempt to establish her own authoritative discourse requires the use of 'words that are already populated with the social intentions of others' and predictably discovers the contradictions as well as the possibilities of 'compel[ling] them to serve [her] own new intentions' (Bakhtin 1981, 299–300). Kate couples the naughtiness of the low mimetic world of social comedy with a 'wild, mad, reckless fervour of passion' (*NW*, 27) more appropriate to a heroine of high romance. The product of this interpenetration of modes – Cleopatra in suburbia with an entourage of nosy siblings – overtly dialogises female and male romance paradigms. Kate's story not only rewrites Jane Eyre's, it also rewrites male plots and interrogates male ideas of 'great' women, the mythic Helens and Cleopatras, and the poetic, especially Tennysonian, 'dream[s] of fair women'. And it does these explicitly, it seems, in reaction to sensationism and possibly as a direct response to W. H. Mansel's attack on sensation literature which appeared in the *Quarterly Review* in April 1863, at about the same time that Broughton must have read *The Story of Elizabeth*.[4]

Mansel's major fears were the commercialisation of literature and the blurring of class lines between 'kitchen' and 'drawing room'.

He begins his review with a reference to popular sermons and goes on to complain that sensation fiction:

> consists of nothing [but incident]. Deep knowledge of human nature, graphic delineations of individual character, vivid representations of aspects of Nature or the workings of the human soul – all the higher features of creative art – would be a hindrance rather than a help to a work of this kind. The unchanging principles of philosophy, the 'thing of beauty that is a joy forever,' would be out of place in a work whose aim is to produce temporary excitement. (486)

Broughton, who could have read similar comments in other periodicals in the early 1860s,[5] chooses the same quotation from Keats as the text for her opening 'sermon' about the workings of 'a tender "loving passionate human soul"' (*NW*, 1). Much of her 'literary display' purports to demonstrate 'knowledge of human nature', while the text as a whole avoids incidents and plot-devices of the type usually associated with sensation novels by contemporary (and modern) critics. In the book Kate is twice tempted and twice resists. There are some coincidences but no crime, unless one so defines an invitation to adultery, and no secrets, except Dare Stamer's early-revealed marriage and James Stanley's unspoken love. The serial version certainly appears more overtly sensational, culminating as it does in murder and suicide, but this crime forms the conclusion, not, as so often in Braddon and Wood, the mainspring of the plot and it patently derives from Elizabethan drama. Broughton rejects sensation fiction's lower-class connotations of melodrama while at the same time she wholeheartedly endorses its most profoundly transgressive feature, the detailed 'representation of physical sensation and sexual feeling' (Pykett 1992, 27). Whether or not she was consciously answering Mansel and other critics, her text debates and challenges their assumptions that the intensity of feeling associated with female sexuality has no place in ordinary middle-class life and is not a proper object of 'creative art'. Her argument comes from the literary tradition itself.

Jane Eyre is, as already suggested, a canonical model of passionate Victorian heroines to be both invoked and revised. Similarities of plotting are underlined by clear verbal reminders, such as Margaret's response when asked if she sings (34–5), Dare's questions about how friends bid each other farewell (102), his Luciferian determination (117), and his description of his unfortunate wife (125).[6] Jane's narrative authenticates and validates Kate's story, but Brontë's subordination of female assertion to feminine virtue is in turn problematised both by Kate's character and by parallels and contrasts, some direct, some inferred, with other passionate loves and other choices between love and duty with which Broughton expects her readers to be equally familiar. Intertextuality is emphasised from the start. '"What absurdly false pictures novels do give one of love"', Kate muses after weeping over the end of G. J. Whyte-Melville's *The Interpreter* in Chapter II (12). This judgement is deliberately premature, for her train of thought leads her to contemplate '"Juliet, and Imogene, and Francesca da Rimini, and Fatima"' and hence to conclude that to reject male representations of love is to reject the truth that supposedly lies in great poetry. As an attempt to pre-empt objections to Broughton's own picture of love this was not wholly successful – Geraldine Jewsbury almost hysterically begged Bentley not to publish the novel;[7] nonetheless it sets a pattern. By the time the *Jane Eyre* echoes become overt the reader has been reminded, in varying ways, not only of Whyte-Melville's unfortunate trio and the women they brought to Kate's mind but of Guy Livingstone and Tannhäuser, recent heroes respectively of a novel and a long poem, both torn between good and evil loves; of Helen, Cleopatra and Enid; possibly of Lucy Snowe and even of Brontë herself, conflated with her heroines; of Samson; of Maud and her lover-narrator; of Rose, 'the gardener's daughter'.[8] The list, which selects only from allusions to other treatments of love, could go on.

It is against this background of competing narratives that Broughton's Chapter XIV replays and partially conflates Jane's parting from Rochester before her return to Gateshead and the proposal scene. The setting has shifted from Brontë's deceptively Edenic garden to a conservatory seething with displaced sensuality, where:

> [g]orgeous, stately flowers, that had hitherto revealed their passionate hearts, fold after fold, to the fainting air of some cloudless, rainless, tropic sky, now poured forth all their sweets, put on all their brilliant apparel.... There great dark leaves, moss-green, rose-veined, drooped heavy with their own weight. (98)

Brontë's cool night-time gardens temporarily suspend social hierarchies to facilitate Jane's claim of equality with Rochester. The con-

servatory, an 'ambiguous threshold location' which, as Michael
Waters notes, often serves in Victorian literature to 'raise the emotional temperature and suspend the operation of public codes of
behaviour' (Waters 1988, 270), keeps the emphasis more single-
mindedly on the sexual basis of the encounter. The availability of
the 'language of flowers' as an acceptable discourse of sensuality
allowed this scene to survive censorship virtually uncut and so to
remain a surprisingly graphic account of Kate's emotions. Indeed,
the displacement of erotic feeling on to nature enables the narrator
accurately to reflect both the intensity of Kate's response and her
maidenly ignorance of all its causes and effects:

> And when there stands in this temple, among these gorgeous
> flowers, a lovely woman – lovely with the ripe womanly devel-
> opment of one of Titian's Venuses, ... – the subjugation of the
> senses may be supposed to be complete. Kate was in ecstasies.
> She ran hither and thither, smelling first one, and then another.
>   'Delicious!' she cried, 'wonderful! I wish I was gardener here.
> Flowers are one of the very few weak points in my character. Oh,
> oh!' (98)

The wealth of enjoyment in that last 'Oh!' beggars description. Sally
Mitchell cites the one significant cut to this chapter, two lines describing Kate's physical response to Dare's embrace, when arguing that
'[r]emoving the physiological detail forces Broughton to deny her
heroine's sensual experience and keeps the reader from realising that
Kate was physically attracted to Dare' (Mitchell 1981, 89). Certainly
the revisions mute Kate's response but only an extremely naive
reader could remain unaware of her physical reaction to Dare's presence.[9] In the conservatory's wild zone between house and garden,
temperate and tropical climes, her sexual excitement is both naturalised as ordinary and assimilated, through association with the
exotic, into the realm of myth and poetry. Kate, the ordinary girl, the
'sulky female martyr' to social propriety (26), joins forces with heroes
and heroines of alternative narratives to interrogate the heroically
victimised Jane Eyre about the probable motivation and outcome of
the scene. Jane's fierce integrity may be more noble (and vital to the
later development of Broughton's plot) but Kate's half-swooning surrender to sexual arousal is undeniably plausible.

Dare's part in stripping the moral gloss from Brontë's narrative is
even less equivocal. Rochester's appeal, especially to the female

reader, lies more in his transgressions, his implied sexual knowledge, than in his reform; his reform, as many readers and critics
have noted, is associated with images of castration and disempow-
erment. More crudely, Guy Livingstone's reform from 'muscular
blackguardism' (cit. Terry 1983, 25) leads directly to paralysis after
a fall on the hunting field. If the typical feminine path to reform is
through illness – or in-validation – male reform leads *to* lives of feminine restrictions and inactivity. Dare, in contrast with his prede-
cessors, is all transgression, by possible inference, therefore, all
male. Where Rochester's teasing enables Jane to prove her worth,
Dare's near-sadistic taunting of Kate explicitly increases his own
arousal; his Luciferian ambitions to create his own rules are
stripped of Rochester's tormented good intentions about atone-
ment; the eventual proposal is a sexual not a spiritual claiming.
Wherever the *Jane Eyre* parallels appear, Broughton's text chips
away Brontë's justifications and providential framework. Kate's
love serves no teleological purpose; it is the occasion not the cause
of her salvation. Dare is resolutely unworthy in everything but
physical attraction; his despised wife is loving and sane; he dies unrepentant, denying Kate the consolation of reunion after death
which the text tries to assert. Kate's death (in the book) is less a vin-
dication than an escape, and morality brings few rewards. Nothing,
least of all Broughton's own attempt at a countervailing moral
message through James Stanley, finally competes with passion for
centre-stage. Jewsbury's panic about *Not Wisely*, in the context of
contemporary disputes about truth and realism, was not without
cause.

In invoking the literary tradition as authority for its more 'sensational' emphases – its dwelling on the female form, its evocation of
woman not only as object but as subject of desire – Broughton's
novel inescapably reflects what Margaret Homans has called 'the
special ambiguity of women's simultaneous participation in and exclusion from a hegemonic group' (Homans 1983, 205) but with few
signs of the anxiety twentieth-century feminist criticism often wants
to detect. Its carnivalesque heteroglossia of allusion and interpolated
quotation is first a claim to ownership of the tradition and then a
challenge to it, questioning artistic representations of women and
conventional assumptions about women's right to represent themselves. Poetry, especially Tennyson's, in the first instance supplies a
discourse for female sexuality: 'the light did seem to fall lovingly, as
in the case of the "Gardener's Daughter," on "the bounteous curve

of such a breast as pencil never drew"' (10), a breast later conspicu-
ously '"gowned in pure white, that fitted to the shape"' (31). Enid's
sexual tension explains Kate's insomnia (65). Fatima speaks the
passion of her first kiss (102), Elaine her brief subsequent sense of
peace (109). 'Love and Duty' war in her parting embrace (128). A
deliberately provocative pose recalls Cleopatra in 'A Dream of Fair
Women' (199).[10] Tennysonian preoccupations and motivations are
persistently evoked. Kate's love, in particular, has the unwilled fa-
talism of the Idylls rather than the psychological plausibility of
realist fiction – a youthful version, perhaps, of the narrator's vision
in 'A Dream of Fair Women' of 'Beauty and anguish walking hand
in hand/ The downward slope to death' (ll. 15–16).

Other poets and a few prose writers, of course, are also called as
witness, reinforcing depictions of male as well as female sexuality
and bolstering Broughton's claims to authority. Generally, quotation and allusion are most dense and interesting in the passages
dealing with sexuality, more conventional and less frequent during
Kate's spiritual struggles – a citation of the seventeenth-century
Archbishop Leighton seems pure posturing by the Reverend
Broughton's daughter (98). Many of the sources are still canonical,
among them Shakespeare, Herbert, Milton, Dryden, Wordsworth,
Byron, Keats, Shelley and Longfellow. Christina Rossetti and
Elizabeth Barrett Browning make token appearances alongside
hymns and popular rhymes. Other sources, now less familiar, were
equally important for Broughton in defining the culture she wished
to claim, a salutary reminder for the modern reader of the dangers
of generalising about cultural matters from too narrow a range of
reading. Owen Meredith (Robert Bulwer Lytton), though unnamed
in the text, almost rivals Tennyson in her apparent esteem. His long
poem, *Tannhäuser* (co-written with Julian Fane and pseudony-
mously published in 1861), vies with *Jane Eyre* for control of the
plot through a similar mixture of quotation, allusion and structural
echoes, and underpins her arguments about Greek mythology
(most notably at the beginning of Chapter IX). James Stanley is
Tannhäuser's friend and rival in love, Wolfram, as well as Milton's
good shepherd, Lycidas, in his care for Kate.[11] Like Tennyson, from
whom he is often derivative, Meredith inspires mood and preoccu-
pation as well as direct quotation. *Tannhäuser*, subtitled *The Battle of
the Bards*, focuses on the singing contest, hymning the competing
merits of pure and fleshly love. As in Broughton's 'prose paeon'
(Fryckstedt 1986, 87), fleshly love, officially condemned, wins both

fair lady and tacit narrative endorsement by its greater energy even while that energy proves destructive. The twice-quoted 'Last Words' (*NW*, 43, 167), in which a dying poet reflects on 'the confident spirit, once mine, to dare and to do', is more pervasively echoed in the moments of gloomy exaltation, the narratorial pose of world-weary knowledge justifying a new sense of mission. The full contribution of Meredith's combination of Tennysonian lushness and ostentatiously cynical modernity (not to mention his George Sandisms) to Broughton's style and content can only be guessed at.

Compared with Meredith, Richard Monckton Milnes, with only one direct reference and one unacknowledged misquotation (65),[12] is insignificant, except that the misquotation comes from the most explicitly erotic part of 'The Northern Knight in Italy', another variant on the Tannhäuser theme, in which the knight first enthusiastically succumbs to the fairy lady's charms, then decapitates her in a fit of post-coital moralising, goes home, marries, and lives happily ever after. When Broughton immediately afterwards labels her direct quotation (from 'The Brookside') 'Monckton Milnes's rather pretty conceit' (65), it seems a pointed rejection of the prurient sentimentalism his poems affect. While still appropriating his language for her own purposes she signals her discrimination among poetic discourses, aligning her own writing with the more open celebration of sexuality. At the same time, here as elsewhere, Broughton's text blurs the boundaries between poetry and prose and challenges the hierarchisation of genres, the special status granted poetry which is typified in the Shirreff sisters' solemn assertion that poetry moves and ennobles readers because its 'ideal beauty' cannot be mistaken for real life whereas fiction has merely 'the semblance of reality, without truth' (Grey and Shirreff 1850, II, 224). By the late 1860s, when such confident illogic was already faltering, *Not Wisely* perhaps achieved its effect less by presenting the new message about love and the defence of fiction its young author envisaged than by affording further evidence for those who feared a decline in recent poetry towards corruption and 'effeminacy'. Alfred Austin names it and Broughton's second novel, *Cometh Up as a Flower*, among other evidence that 'the "improper" feminine' was 'unrestrainedly rioting in any and every arena of life' (Austin 1869, 469), not least in Tennyson, Robert Lytton (Meredith) and, Austin's chief *bête noire*, Swinburne.

Intertextuality for Broughton extends beyond the printed word. Her text also exploits and opposes special privileges accorded the fine arts. Whyte-Melville had perhaps pointed the way in *The Interpreter*:

> Ah! those Rubenses, I can see them now! the glorious athletic proportions of the men, heroes and champions every one, the soft, sensuous beauty of the women, – none of your angels, or goddesses, or idealities, but, better still, warm, breathing, loving, palpable women, the energy of action, the majesty of repose, the drawing, the colouring, but above all the *honest manly* sentiment that pervades every picture. (221, emphasis added)

Not Wisely shares, or adopts, similar criteria for beauty (Jewsbury particularly objected to the repeated descriptions of Kate as 'soft') and is quick to take advantage of artistic parallels to circumvent other taboos on graphic description but, as a female-authored text, it inevitably questions that all-permitting 'honest manly sentiment'. Family portraits, classical paintings, Greek sculptures, are all scrutinised as cultural texts for their part in the discourse of sexuality. The respectable Lely ladies on the walls of the Stamers' 'sham' castle wear 'such easy flowing robes that one wonders by what matchless ingenuity they got them to stick on at all' (25). 'Women, saints, Magdalens, virgins' glance with interchangeable demure provocation from paintings by the great favourite, Guido Reni (55). Naked Venuses and Apollos, the Laocoon, on display at the Crystal Palace, excite general admiration (Chapter XXVII). Repeated references to paintings drive home the hypocritical discrepancy between the licence permitted to the plastic arts by so-called polite society and the constraints on the written word. The complaint resurfaces strongly in Broughton's third novel, *Red as a Rose is She*,[13] which in fact ran concurrently with Austin's three articles on poetry in *Temple Bar* in 1869 (forcing some circumspection in his references to her work). Again, his distinction, with reference to painting, of the modern 'undressed' figure, sign of rampant disorder, from the somehow acceptable 'nude' (468) underlines her topicality.

Various devices, frequently exploiting the carnival potential of laughter, show *Not Wisely*'s dialogical relationship to 'high' culture to have been as self-conscious as its intertextuality. In the opening pages, for example, Keats and the ancient Greeks are cited only to be rejected in favour of a supposedly higher morality, which in turn is subverted by reference to the feminine authority of copybooks (1–2). 'Big men did big things' interrupts a pseudo-learned disquisition on history (3). Throughout, tone and register change constantly: slang (modified but still conspicuous in the book) jostles with poetry, jokes with pompous maxims. Like the recurrent bathos, they prevent a too-easy acquiescence in any single discourse. Kate jumps into Dare's dogcart 'pretty agilely; tearing, however, a vast rent in her cotton frock' (57). The conservatory scene notoriously ends, 'I've done. I'm tired of writing about lovemaking' (103). The effect is a persistent destabilising of genre and a questioning of gender-based assumptions. The early ostentatious disclaimer, 'I am not Tennyson' (4), assumes a less modest meaning when the narrator immediately sets her own 'real' woman against his 'dreams' (4–5), demanding a reading as difference, not deference. The dialogue of 'real' with 'dream', of prose with poetry, in fact epitomises the novel's argument with the conventions of representation it is so quick to appropriate. That gown of 'pure white, that fitted to the shape' is more suitable for the dinner party to which Kate wears it than for gardening as Tennyson's Rose does. Broughton accepts poetic images and symbolism but questions the displacements by which poetry so often justifies its material, the medieval or exotic settings, the quasi-pastoral that establishes Rose's innocence, the lower class that authorises her sexuality. Kate may be a lily or a blushing peony, a Cleopatra, Fatima or Maud, but she is also a city-girl of the 1860s with siblings and cousins, an ordinary girl who gossips and flirts, who has the right to have her story told and told from a woman's point of view, a point of view in itself, as Wayne Booth imagines Bakhtin admitting, 'as important as carnival laughter' (Booth 1983, 77).

Rose is the silent and acquiescent object of the male gaze. Always picturesquely disposed for the male eye, the gardener's daughter speaks only to disclaim independent existence: 'I am thine' (l.230). The 'fair women' of 'A Dream' speak in the context of the male vision; their voices re-enact their sacrifice to male interests. Even Fatima is framed, her emotion specularised by male authorship. Broughton's text does not reject or resist specularisation of the female so much as draw attention to it. Kate is introduced as a portrait in a gallery and is frequently exhibited by the text as a picture, but she is also granted the capacity to break out of the frame. She is an agent as well as an object. She constructs herself for Dare's gaze, choosing a single '"heavy-folded rose"' (31) for his taste,[14] and both know, and know that the other knows, why she has done it. Even surrounded by tracts and attempting virtue Kate cares for her appearance. 'Only in books', the narrator comments, do 'pretty women neglect their toilette when crossed in love' (133). The degree of agency is not exaggerated – the self-styled Little Red Ridinghood goes district visiting and meets a real wolf in the bargeman who teases her because she is a female out of her 'proper' frame (Ch. XXI) – but it creates a perspective in which women's self-construction through appearance can serve more purposes than male delectation, as the sewing scene in Chapter XIX indicates.

When the text tries to claim for women the same rights of the gaze as men, it moves on to more dangerous ground. George Chester, primping in the mirror, watched and laughed at by Kate's sister, Margaret, in a scene which effectively confirms her 'ownership' of him (Chapter XXX), might be acceptable. Much more problematic is the implicit demand to allow a female sexual fantasy the same status as male ones. Dare, despite male-authored forebears like Guy Livingstone and Samson and male admiration from Kate's brother, is constructed almost entirely by and for the female eye: 'a big, powerful figure; …deep-chested, clean-limbed, thin-flanked', with 'luminous dark eyes' and 'harsh swart features' and 'a great, soft, black-brown moustache, drooping silkily' (28), he approaches 'in physical conformation to Achilles or Telemonian Ajax' (241). His is an entirely physical presence, strikingly prefiguring the later pulp-fiction heroes his name evokes. The changes between serial and book suggest that Dare's overt sexuality was of greater concern than Kate's, and perhaps for deeper reasons than the unwelcome evidence he affords of female sexual fantasising. Writing, according to Yaeger, 'gives women an unprecedented power of dialogue with the dominant tradition, a power, above all, of interrupting that tradition and revealing its violence' (156) and, interestingly, what is consistently played down by the revisions is precisely Dare's violence. The serial's murder and suicide are the logical if explosive outcome of his steadily mounting threats against Kate should she not submit to him. In the book's tame echo of *Guy Livingstone*, Dare is conveniently and fatally injured, allowing Kate to attend his unrepentant deathbed before herself retiring to a convent. Sally Mitchell sees the issue here as female autonomy: 'For the publisher, heroic martyrdom [Kate's putting her own soul first] was not permissible but compassionate sacrifice was' (83). Other Victorian heroines, Callista and Hypatia among them,[15] might demur, as would, of course, Jane Eyre, whose 'I care for myself' is Kate's obvious model. While much of the novel's dialogue with culture can be ignored, at least on a conscious level, by the reader, Dare, in the serial, rather too explicitly enacts the repressions of the culture that formed him in Broughton's fancy. 'O dead woman!' the narrator apostrophises Kate in Chapter 1. 'You have caught his speechlessness from your grim bridegroom, Death' (5). Dare silences Kate just as patriarchal culture silences Rose and sacrifices the 'fair women', and even the rewritten book does not wholly obliterate the close connection between his proprietorial jealousy (so like Othello's) and the punishment patriarchal society demands for female transgression.

The scenario is not a simple one of male oppression and female victimisation, for writing permits 'dialogue with the dominant tradition' not escape from it and the plot could be said to celebrate female silencing. Kate and the text collude in her fate. Both embrace the *idea* of romantic love in all its literary fatality. A tiny mise-enabyme in the serial foretells Kate's moral (and possibly physical)[16] fate if she becomes Dare's mistress: the poppy which he begs from her in Chapter X withers with the ferocity of his kisses once he gains possession. Yet the plot requires her, once emotionally possessed by Dare, to be as effectively dead to other men as when murdered, cloistered or indeed 'properly' married. (The dead poppy reappears as a sentimental cliché at the book's end.) As Kate flirts without serious intent with her cousin George, so the text debates other options of love, through Margaret, through the Chester cousins, and especially through James Stanley – it even mocks Kate's singlemindedness – but still Kate's status as heroine depends not so much on her resistance of Dare as on her and her creator's acquiescence in a construction of femininity that allows a woman to love once only. Romance, narrowly interpreted according to strict patriarchal imperatives of female monogamy, is presented as the only worthwhile narrative of female life.

Dialogue, of course, precludes this closure also. Rose's voice asserts the subjectivity her words deny and, even while Broughton's plot rewards Kate's self-silencing with the status of heroine, her text proclaims women's right to feel and to speak in ways previously granted only to men. Simply by incorporating male voices into a female text, Broughton interrogates their gendering of roles. Kate, as desiring subject, becomes both Tannhäuser and his Elizabeth, both transgressive male and responsive but virtuous female. She can identify with the tormented hero, Victor, in *The Interpreter*, and with his good wife and bad lover. She plays

Rochester as well as Jane Eyre. In this version of *Othello* Desdemona gets centre-stage.

If ambition far outstrips accomplishment in *Not Wisely*, this is un-surprising given the youth of the author and her later claim that it was written in six weeks. In some respects the muddles, the naivetés, the brash self-confidence with which Broughton's text takes on the literary world make it more interesting than a more polished performance might be. It openly taps a 'vein of long-standing and well-developed fantasy', which Sally Mitchell finds typical of many first novels, but rather than being therefore 'more of a personal document and less a reflection of society's own stand-ards' (Mitchell 1981, 66), *Not Wisely But Too Well* is both intensely personal and intensely revealing of the extent to which that person, the fantasising subject, is constructed by and through the literary discourses she has absorbed. The 'vein' of 'fantasy' exists neither prior to, as Mitchell seems to assume, nor apart from the influence of society; nor need it derive, as Sadleir supposes, from personal experience of an unhappy romance (Sadleir 1944, 87). Broughton's undeniable early love affair, as this essay has suggested, is with lit-erature, with reflections in poetry, drama and fiction of the culture that controls her capacity to conceive of love. *Not Wisely But Too Well* clearly demonstrates the extent to which, in Wayne Booth's words, '[w]e speak *with* our ideology – our collection of languages, of words-laden-with-values.... We are *constituted* in polyphony' (57, his italics). At the same time, consciously and unconsciously, by its exuberant exploitation of polyphony, the text reveals the in-consistencies of the dominant culture and disputes its authority. Particularly by finding in already-existing literature means and justification for the unashamed articulation of female desire Broughton's novel finds a voice for the silenced that slightly but in-evitably changes the literary tradition. This does not make it a great work of art but it does make it a significant part of the work of culture.

Notes

1. Showalter in fact conflates *Not Wisely But Too Well* with *Cometh Up as a Flower* (173–5). For Pykett, see *The 'Improper' Feminine* (34–5) and *The*

Sensation Novel (47–8). Broughton is not mentioned by either Winifred Hughes in *The Maniac in the Cellar* or Thomas Boyle in *Black Swine in the Sewers of Hampstead*. Other studies of sensation writing often do little more than list her among 'fast' women writers of the 1860s (Rance 1991, 74; Taylor 1988, 2–3). Sally Mitchell and Kate Flint both make useful reference to her in their studies of women's reading in the nineteenth century. Mitchell's *The Fallen Angel*, with which I disagree about details of interpretation, is one of few recent works to pay serious attention to Broughton. Flint in *The Woman Reader, 1837–1914*, like Taylor, notes the difficulty of categorising Broughton's early works as sensationist (282, n.26) and comments briefly on the metatextual implications of the title and some allusions in *Not Wisely* (283–4). Flint's work is the most comprehensive account currently available of the context of literary debate within which this chapter sets the novel. The best general introduction to Broughton's work remains the chapter on her in R. C. Terry's *Victorian Popular Fiction*. Marilyn Wood's recent biography contains useful information about Broughton's life but is limited in its grasp of the literary context and wrong in asserting that the version of *Not Wisely* published by Tinsley Brothers in 1867 was significantly extended to reach three-volume length.

2. The serial appeared in twelve instalments from August 1865 to July 1866. Where it is necessary to distinguish this from the three-volume version in this essay the terms 'serial' and 'book' are used.

3. *A Beginner* (1894) and *A Fool in Her Folly* (1920, published posthumously).

4. *Not Wisely But Too Well* was written about two years before its serial publication, probably, that is, in 1863.

5. For example in 'Article VII', *Christian Remembrancer* NS46 (1863): 209–36. (Reprinted as 'Our Female Sensation Novelists', *Littell's Living Age* 3rdS XXII (1863); 352–69.) Even in *Temple Bar*, alongside Braddon's *Aurora Floyd* in 1862, Robert Buchanan, in 'Society's Looking Glass,' was criticising sensation fiction for being 'intensely impersonal. It merges the individual in the incident. Its object is an intensely commercial one. It appeals not to the sympathies of the educated few, but, to those of the general public; and the purpose of its followers is to make money . . . . It entails no originality' (136–7). 'Not a New Sensation,' (*All the Year Round* 9 (1863): 517–20) ostensibly defends sensationism but denies its status as art.

6. Compare *Jane Eyre*, 151, 283, 169 and 366, and 375 (in the serial's equivalent passage to *NW*, 125 Dare uses Rochester's word, 'strapper,' to describe his wife). Compare also *NW*, 243 and *JE*, 554–5; and *NW*, 248 and *JE*, 246. Occasional apparent echoes of *Wuthering Heights* can also be found (Kate is, after all, *Catherine* Chester) but these lack the specificity of the allusions to *Jane Eyre*.

7. As a reader for Bentley's in the 1860s, Jewsbury apparently forgot her own notorious novel, *Zoë*, (1845), which certainly contributed to *Not Wisely*'s 'indecency', if only indirectly through the Brontës.

8. The novel denies (28), where the serial claims, Dare's likeness to Samson and Guy Livingstone. Intertextually, the effect is the same.

See *Tannhäuser*, 52, 49 and *NW*, 29; *Tannhäuser*, 17 and *NW*, 72. For Helen and Cleopatra see *NW*, 3. For Enid see *NW*, 65 and Tennyson's 'The Marriage of Geraint,' l.531. The Brontë echoes may be fortuitous. Kate's determination to 'bury [her idol] in this dark wood, under one of these branching trees' (50) resembles Lucy Snowe's burying of her letters in *Villette*. Kate's seeing 'all things through the medium of one feeling' (46) recalls Harriet Martineau's criticism of *Villette*, printed in the third edition of Elizabeth Gaskell's *Life of Charlotte Brontë* in 1857 (401). For Maud, see *NW*, 52 and *Maud*, II, i, 3. For Rose, see *NW*, 10, 25, 31, 56, 60 and 'The Gardener's Daughter,' ll.139–40, 75, 125, 140–41, and 110 (but see note 12 below).

9. See also *NW*, 65 and 80.
10. See 'The Gardener's Daughter,' l.531; 'Fatima,' ll.19–21; 'Lancelot and Elaine,' l.833; 'Love and Duty,' ll.65–6; 'A Dream of Fair Women,' l.128.
11. See *NW*, 253 and *Tannhäuser* 10; *NW*, 146 and 'Lycidas' ll.116–17.
12. Broughton's phrase, 'warm gusts "oppressed with perfume"', conflates Monckton Milnes's 'the air/ Oppressed with odours' with Tennyson's 'one warm gust full-fed with perfume' ('The Gardener's Daughter:' l.110).
13. For example: 'in the middle of this lawn, exactly opposite Esther's eyes, as she sits at breakfast, is an unique and chaste piece of statuary, entitled "The Rape of the Sabines." The space afforded by the stone pediment is necessarily limited, and consequently Roman and Sabines, gentlemen and lady, are all piled one a-top of another in such inextricable confusion as to demand a good quarter of an hour's close observation to determine which of the muscular writhing legs belong to the Roman ravisher and which to the injured Sabine husband. As the sculptor has given none of his *protégés* any clothing, the snow has been kind enough to throw a modest white mantle over them' (*Rose*, III 4–5).
14. The quotation here is from *In Memoriam*, XCV, l.59.
15. Martyred heroines respectively of eponymous novels by J. H. Newman (1856) and Charles Kingsley (1853).
16. *Guy Livingstone* contains the cautionary tale of a runaway wife who falls into a decline and dies despite excellent reasons for leaving her husband and impeccable treatment by her lover. Similar accounts, of course, occur in many Victorian novels.

2

Labours of a Modern Storyteller: George Eliot and the Cultural Project of 'Nationhood' in *Daniel Deronda*

Carolyn Lesjak

If one were momentarily to suspend disbelief as to the wisdom of appealing to an artist for an interpretation of her own work, a particularly rife place for doing so would be with George Eliot and *Daniel Deronda*. Writing to Barbara Bodichon in October 1876, Eliot claims of her last novel that she 'meant everything in the book to be related to everything else there' (Haight 1955, 290). The history of criticism on *Daniel Deronda* seems for the most part to take us in quite the opposite direction, following the lead, as it does, of F. R. Leavis's pronouncement on the well-nigh ungodly split between the Gwendolen/Grandcourt plot and the Deronda/Mordecai plot (1949, 79–125). This latter, often referred to simply as the 'Jewish portion' of the novel, is, in Leavis's view, nothing more than a blight upon the rest of the book – there simply to be done away with; in his words, literally to be cut away. When, *pace* Leavis, the two parts of the novel *are* read together, the Jewish portion is often interpreted as a corrective to the dehumanised personal relations defining the Gwendolen plot.[1] In other words, the Mordecai/Deronda story finds itself in the unusual position of being deemed either completely superfluous or utterly indispensable to the novel as a whole. In whichever case, the two plot-lines are in some sense treated as separable from one another.

Added to this critical bugbear is the difficulty of situating *Daniel Deronda* within Eliot's *oeuvre* itself, given its especially weighty place as the last novel and also the only contemporary, urban novel. Should it be read as a strange and final aberration or as the culmination of Eliot's life-long concerns, or perhaps as something else altogether? In the following reading, I will articulate the structure of 'relationality' in *Daniel Deronda*, and show how Eliot's attempt to imaginatively reconstitute some form of *community* free from the ravages of industrialisation dovetails with emergent national discourse in Britain's 'Age of Empire'. As such, *Daniel Deronda* offers a representative moment in which to investigate the ambivalent and contradictory negotiations over the frontiers of 'nation', both in terms of how the novel connects to England's larger cultural project of 'nationhood' and, more specifically, in terms of how the novel negotiates the very mechanics of its own narratability.

Important critical legwork has already been done on the ways in which the Gwendolen plot functions as a microcosm of the larger system of imperialism, a system which Eliot implicitly criticises through the trope of empire she uses to describe Gwendolen's relationship with Grandcourt.[2] 'Empire' repeatedly defines their relationship: Gwendolen is the 'princess in exile' lording over her 'domestic empire' with 'her power of inspiring fear' (71); whenever she might lose her confidence – as when she is shocked by the sudden appearance of the Spanish death mask during her dramatic debut at Offendene – she as quickly would recover and regain 'the possibility of winning empire' (95); after she receives Grandcourt's note upon her return from Leubronn, she 'feels some triumph in a tribute to her power...as she again seemed to be getting a sort of empire over her own life' (337), while Grandcourt, conversely, wishes 'to be completely master of this creature' (346). Grandcourt's desire is multiplied by the anticipatory pleasure he receives from the challenge of mastery – with his pleasure, fittingly, all the more heightened by Gwendolen's resistance: 'He meant to be master of a woman who would have liked to master him, and who perhaps would have been capable of mastering another man' (365).

Like the colonial subject, rendered by dominant English culture as subservient and powerless, Gwendolen will be brutally quashed by the powers that be. Should we happen to miss this parallel, the narrative draws it for us, in its hypothesising of Grandcourt as coloniser:

if this white-handed man with the perpendicular profile had been sent to govern a difficult colony, he might have won reputation among his contemporaries. He had certainly ability, would have understood that it was safer to exterminate than to cajole superseded proprietors, and would not have flinched from making things safe in that way. (655)

The eerie foreshadowing of Marlow's 'Exterminate the brutes!' aside, this passage highlights the interrelatedness, if not interchangeability, of Grandcourt's domestic and imperial mentalities. Insofar as it is Grandcourt's unflinching treatment of Gwendolen throughout the novel which fosters this hypothesis, Eliot's feminism here becomes a powerful instrument in her critique of imperialism.

Nevertheless, instantiations of Eliot's feminism in the novel are at least as complex as (and thoroughly related to) her representations of imperial Britain. On the one hand, *Daniel Deronda's* narrative works to persuade us of the double standard operating by way of gendered social limitations. Initially, we are meant to read Gwendolen's mistaken perceptions and desires *vis-à-vis* men in general and Grandcourt specifically as a misrecognition; as a marker that within the social world in which she exists she is already asking for the impossible: to be happy, to have control over her own body; in short, to be a master of sorts over her situation. On the other hand, Gwendolen ultimately loses, Eliot seems to be saying, in part because a woman should not want what is innately a man's. At once there is a recognition of gender disparity and the upholding of that disparity by recourse to a reinforcement of sexual difference.

Eliot's vision of empire, contained as it is within the Gwendolen plot, tells us something significant as well about the increasingly alienated relationship between private life and the public sphere in England's cultural representation of itself. What Gwendolen's fate as Grandcourt's wife so effectively illustrates is a generalisable state of dissociation between public and private realities: a state amounting to, in Lukács' words, a kind of 'transcendental homelessness', which defines not only the particular fate of Gwendolen under Grandcourt's imperial thumb but the fate of the individual modern subject under monopoly capitalism, the economic stage of imperialism (1985, passim).

Gambling typifies this state for Eliot. Our first encounter with Gwendolen finds her in search of passion, playing the roulette table, while around her numerous other bourgeois Europeans mill about the gaming tables, all seemingly as displaced as Gwendolen, all driven by the desire to win – and most importantly, to win at someone else's expense. Despite the fact that they all appear superficially to be quite different, the narrative is quick to reduce these mere differences to the far more profound similarities that exist among these players: 'But while every single player differed markedly from every other, there was a certain uniform negativeness of expression which had the effect of a mask – as if they had all eaten of some root that for the time compelled the brains of each to the same monotony of action' (37). What we are given, then, is a vision of levelling sameness, of a mind-numbing and automaton-like monotony; a taylorisation of the psyche that throughout the novel is connected with the dominant English culture, and with the culture of the educated, metropolitan upper middle classes. This is, in the full Benjaminian sense, the disenchanted object world of the commodity system.[3] And, as with Benjamin, this disenchanted world radically redefines the position of the 'modern' storyteller attempting to communicate with her 'public,' a point to which I will shortly return.

Within Eliot's novelistic universe, the moral paucity of this reified existence is underscored by the fact that Grandcourt actually relishes this dissociation, seeing in it the means to his power: lips curled, he gloats over the knowledge that 'everybody must do what was expected of them whatever might be their private protest – the protest (kept strictly private) adding to the piquancy of despotism' (736). But while Grandcourt might strike us as an extreme example, the 'condition' he embodies is by no means a limited one; we are clearly meant to read him allegorically as a representative product of an imperialist mentality, expressive of nothing less, as the 'foreigner' Herr Klesmer banefully notes, than a 'puerile state of culture...the passion and thought of people without any breadth of horizon' (79).

Such a fate, as Fredric Jameson argues, entails an increasing opposition between lived experience and the economic and social forms that govern that experience; that is, between lived experience and structure (1988, 349). Of particular interest in this contradiction are the problems of figuration it poses: if, as Jameson posits, the phenomenological experience of the individual subject rests within a limited corner of the social world but the structural coordinates of that experience lie elsewhere – bound up with the whole colonial system that comes to define the economic stage of imperialism –

how does the artist go about representing such a dilemma? It is precisely a version of this dilemma with which I see Eliot grappling in *Daniel Deronda*. And, given this problematic, what we can then read in the Gwendolen narrative is a double relationship to imperialism: at the level of lived experience (or content), imperialism is (metaphorically) critiqued, while at the level of structure, it is in a sense re-enacted, both in terms of the opposition between public and private that afflicts Gwendolen, Grandcourt and the others and in terms of its antagonistic relation to the Deronda narrative itself.

It is seemingly against this 'condition' of imperialism that we are given the 'Jewish portion' of the novel. For critics desirous of drawing a straight and uninterrupted line from the beginning of Eliot's fiction to the end, her choice of Judaism in this context becomes just one more application of her doctrine of sympathy – this time to yet another group in another time and place, namely Jews. Such a reading misses a significant component of *Daniel Deronda*, however, if it does not also acknowledge the specificity of Eliot's choice of Judaism. It is not simply a matter of substitution, even if George Lewes might have us believe so when he writes that just as Eliot 'formerly contrived to make one love Methodists, there was no reason why she should not conquer the prejudice against the Jews' (Haight 1955, 196).

Such a smooth equivalence of Jew with Methodist overlooks the particularity with which Mordecai and the Jews are defined. Certainly, within the novel, there are good and bad Jews: the former, represented by Mordecai, and eventually Deronda himself, are defined by their deep spirituality, and the social vision that would put this spirituality in the service of a concrete, realised form of *social action*, namely *nationalism*. One brief, early indication of this desired combination of intellect and action is foreshadowed when Daniel as a child opts for the heroic figures of Pericles and Washington, over and above the purely contemplative faculties of a Porson or Leibnitz. Within the context of Eliot's treatment of Judaism, it is no accident that the two figures to whom Daniel is attracted are both statesmen. In other words, it is not just that these men are not philosophers and are thus so-called 'men of the world', but that they also both founded national states. At some level then, as Christina Crosby has pointed out, Eliot's treatment of Judaism becomes inseparable from Zionism; that is, the thrust in the novel toward a materialisation of thought and belief *in statehood* ultimately collapses the one into the other (1991, 35).[4] Always, in *Daniel*

Deronda, the 'nation' is equated with the historical institution of the state; Judaism thus becomes one with the establishment of a Jewish state where a rootedness to place is now redefined in terms of an identification with a mythic 'national' narrative.

Zionism, within the context of nineteenth-century nationalist movements, itself represents an extreme example. The clearly 'borrowed nature' of its programme, to use Eric Hobsbawm's term, with respect to both language and territory, dramatises the acquired processes whereby a sense of national identity was created (1989, 147). Due to the exigencies of mass migration, most notably the lack of any claim to an exclusive territory, among the Jewish Diaspora (as well as in the Habsburg Empire), an alternative definition of nationality was developed:

> It was seen here as inherent, not in a particular piece of the map to which a body of inhabitants were attached, but in the members of such bodies of men and women as considered themselves to belong to a nationality, wherever they happened to live. As such members, they would enjoy 'cultural autonomy'. (Hobsbawm 1989, 148)

In contrast to a territorialist view of nationality (which established the identification of nations with an exclusive territory, modelled after the French Revolution), this severing of 'home territory' from 'nation', more accurately reflected the relation between a geography and a national identity. These non-territorialists recognised, in a way a territorialist view did not, the metaphorical, imagined nature of the 'nation', which, as Hobsbawm underscores, was no more akin to 'home territory' than the father in fatherland is to a real parent. Zionism thus represents the extreme example that proves the rule: it foregrounds the artificial, *constructed* nature of 'nation' operative in any consolidation – non-territorialist and territorialist alike – of national identity. Within the parameters of *Daniel Deronda* it will be this kind of national 'belongingness', or claim to cultural autonomy, which will carry applicability not only for the Jews themselves but for the English as well.

Offset against the icon of the actively spiritual Jew is the 'bad Jew', defined primarily through Eliot's representation of the spiritually empty, because materially 'filled', Cohen family, and secondarily through the anti-Semitic stereotyping lightly bantered about in the genteel (and not-so-genteel) world of English society.

Within its society, this latter category of Jews will simply comprise a litany of stereotypically ethno-religious characteristics, ranging from descriptions of Jews as dirty, large-nosed, money-grubbing, and so on and so forth. Hans Meyrick's hope, for instance, that Mordecai is not 'a fellow all smiles and jewellry – a Crystal Palace Assyrian with a hat on' (640) is but one offshoot of a bountiful crop of such stereotypic cataloguing.

For our purposes, what is important about the figure of the greedy, materialistic Jew is that even in its most heinously stereotypical form Eliot's representation of the Jew *always* ranks above the figure of the Easterner, who is apparently of so little substance and interest that one or two mere mentions of barbarity is all the novelistic treatment they are afforded. Representation of the East or Easterners is relegated to a purely marginal status, referenced only in order to reinforce through repetition an 'Oriental despotism' in stark contrast to Western freedom. In this context, it is important to reiterate two central points made by Edward Said. First, he underscores the view of the despotic 'orientalised' East upon which the Zionist project is premised and which is supported by the vision of Palestine as an unpopulated piece of land. Secondly, he points out the way in which such an attitude toward the East says less about the East than it does about the Occident's construction and representation of itself *vis-à-vis* the 'Orient' (1979, 56–114).

Mordecai, articulating the relationship of separation to nationality within Judaic history, assigns to Judaism the status of a national collective which carries 'the culture and the sympathies of every great nation in its bosom' as the transmitter of 'the brightness of Western freedom amid the despotisms of the East' (595). Unlike the Jew, then, whose stereotyping by others in the novel works for the most part to critique the narrowness of the English vision – and moreover is continually undercut and overturned by alternative representations which belie the stereotype – the Easterner is never represented as anything other than despotic; indeed, the Easterner is never really represented at all. The sheer invisibility of the East – as nothing more than a land without people, and most easily and summarily summed up with one word, 'despotic' – contributes ideologically all the more to a seamless fulfilment of the goals of Zionism. Once the map of the East has been rhetorically depopulated, erased even, there is no longer anything blocking its transformation into the Jewish homeland.

Also focusing on race, Sander Gilman provocatively notes that Eliot's treatment of racial difference within the novel slips dangerously within what may be termed a polygenetic view, a nineteenth-century pseudo-scientific theory which posited an *innate* genetic difference between the races (1985, 239). Basing his argument on the seemingly offhand comment made by Eliot's narrator that 'one man differs from another, as we all differ from the Bosjeman, in a sensibility of checks, that come from variety of needs, spiritual or other', (370) Gilman goes on to argue that this 'we' of Eliot's effectively establishes an absolute racial divide; a view of racial difference buttressed by genetics and the innate difference it implies. Not surprisingly, on such a chain of being, blacks occupied an antithetical position to whites, with the Hottentot woman on the extreme end of the scale as the essential Other. Within this kind of racial configuration, Jews, as Gilman concludes, fall just this side of human on the 'scale of humanity', yet still unequivocally on the right side, so to speak, of the racial divide. In other words, in some profound sense, they still occupy a position potentially on the 'inside', so long as, *Daniel Deronda* seems to say, they conduct themselves, for Eliot's purposes, in a suitably exemplary way, appropriate to the needs of her spiritually and culturally marooned Englishmen.[5] Hence the clear distinction between two kinds of Jews in the text – the Ezra Cohens versus the Ezra Mordecais – which seems to imply that the national state would be a sorry one indeed were our pawnbroker to be its model. Or, as Eliot pithily distinguishes within her own taxonomy, 'there are Ezras and there are Ezras' (628).

In this way, Eliot's own use of grossly stereotypical descriptions of Jews both undercuts and elevates simultaneously: the so-called vulgar Jew confirms the worst fears of the English about Jews, while the deep and historically durative spirituality of Mordecai and, ultimately, Daniel, only shines forth all the more brilliantly in contrast. The choice between the two versions is not a given, is not innate or genetic, as it is in the case of the African bushman or the Easterner; instead it is an active and chosen course, one which, therefore, is as available to the English as it is to the Jews.

It is to these latter Ezras that we need now turn, namely to Mordecai himself. Likened as he is at one point to Spinoza, Mordecai seemingly offers a strategy for reconciling the opposition between lived experience and structure with which we began. As a Spinozan figure, Mordecai stands, in some sense, as the embodiment of a kind of metaphysical rationality. His visions are 'the creators and feeders of the world'; as he will proclaim: 'I see, I measure the world as it is, which the vision will create anew' (555). Significantly, Mordecai as rational visionary opens up within Eliot's text the possibility of an *emotional* or *passionate intellect*, of a visionary eye which

> may have absorbed into its passionate vision of possibilities some truth of what will be – the more comprehensive massive life feeding theory with new material, as the sensibility of the artist seizes combinations which science explains and justifies. (572)

Through his imaginative sensibility, Mordecai transmits a whole series of unities, whose lost medium or imminent dissolution threatens the dominant English society of the novel: mind and body; the present, past and, most notably for Eliot, the future; the public and the private; lived experience and structure; practice and theory; culture and 'nation'. His is the voice of an alternate public sphere, one which would seemingly break down the divisions found elsewhere in the novel through its 'expression of a binding history'(417) and an alternative culture of non-exchange-based social relations.[6] To reshape the future out of the context of a 'second nature' over which human subjects are seemingly powerless: herein lie the Utopian longings of Eliot's narrative.

But ultimately the unification of each of these pairings is predicated not on a recognition of the semi-autonomy of each of the terms but on a colonisation of one term by the other. To take one example, in Mordecai's case, it is the fact of his consumptive body which fuels the intense energy and active commitment of his mind. It is thus the *lack* of a body, of a body literally being consumed, which feeds his great mental and visionary energy. There is a unification, but only in terms of an absence, an erasure. Again, lived experience proves itself problematic, blocked, as it were, by structure: like the vision of 'nation' which Mordecai upholds, an erasure of lived experience, of bodily presence, lies at the heart of its unity.

The shift to an international frame helps control this problematic desiring domestic body to a certain extent. *Because* of Eliot's treatment of the East throughout – her virtual erasure of the living, desiring bodies of its inhabitants – the specific vision of nationalism Mordecai espouses is separated from the kind of domination and

power which the narrative identifies – through Gwendolen and
Grandcourt – as imperialist. Whereas the social dynamic among the
Gwendolen/Grandcourt society is repeatedly identified with gambling – a 'sport' to which Deronda explicitly objects on the grounds
that it artificially sets up a situation in which one player gains at the
desired expense of another's loss – the expression of Jewish nationality through achieved 'nationhood' is presented as a situation in
which there are no losers. When Mordecai makes his appeal for nationality, he is able to claim that 'the world will gain as Israel gains'
(595). And finally, this *national* collective will of 'the people' will
constitute itself as an organically linked community by virtue of its
separateness from other races and nationalities. This vision of 'separateness with communication' seems to embody an attempt on
Eliot's part to counteract the kind of levelling, or creeping sameness and disintegration of experience which threatens English
society at large and is, by implication, associated with imperialism.
Race, separateness and nationality thus ally themselves against
money, uniformity and assimilation.

This is new terrain for Eliot. The so-called split or opposition here
is no longer between country and city as in her other fiction, but
rather is *international*. And indeed Eliot finds herself somewhat at a
loss when it comes to representing, or more literally *mapping*, a
vision of such an international community, given her attachment,
especially in the later novels, to an organic model of class and social
relations. Whereas in *Felix Holt*, for instance, Eliot's organicism
could be productively employed to quell the incipient violence of
what Eliot perceived as an all-too rapid (read as well all-too
working-class) movement for social change, literally by slowing it
down, in *Daniel Deronda* this kind of organicism no longer seems an
adequate blueprint for reconstituting a meaningful community of
some sort. While Eliot does attempt, rather feebly, to transport her
organic language into the novel – at one point likening the life of a
people to 'a power and an organ in the great body of the nations'
(585) – she wisely does not press the point. Moreover, organicism
per se no longer functions as the organising principle of *Daniel
Deronda*, unlike in *Felix Holt* or *Middlemarch*. Instead, the operative
model or metaphor replacing that of the body is 'nation' itself: in
place of biological functions, which by homology become social
duties, we have racial difference translated into separate nationalities which then coalesce (or not, as in the case of the Easterner or
Kalahari bushman) as an international community under the

shared sign of Western culture. Whereas the former model of organicism by its very nature denies individual organs/domestic
subjects autonomy, the latter national model operates precisely by
carving out regions of difference premised on national and cultural
autonomy.

As we have seen, the ground for such a model of national identity has been prepared by the implicit construction of a racial chain
of being – of white vs. African, Westerner vs. Easterner – within
Daniel Deronda. Despite this preparation, however, Daniel's own
figuration testifies to the hybridity underlying any construction of
racial or national purity that the narrative attempts to create. It is
even emphasised that Daniel *cannot* lose his English upbringing entirely, that he could in no way abandon his very English education
(724). Of course, this claim can be countered with a view that maintaining a sense of English culture alone hardly qualifies as a big
step over the racial divide, especially since, as Christina Crosby
points out, this equation of Daniel with English culture to a large
extent accounts for the comfort with which Eliot can deal with Jews
at all. That is, because the project of a Jewish state is so closely modelled on that of the English state, it can be more properly viewed
not as a recognition of cultural difference so much as a collapsing of
cultural difference altogether, thereby leaving the British imperial
attitude essentially unchanged and solidly intact.[7] Additionally,
given the numerous ways in which even some slim notion of hybridity is challenged, it is doubtful whether it can be said that any
sustained vision of racial, national or cultural mixing is proffered.
Throughout the novel, long before it is revealed to Daniel that he is
a Jew, he is repeatedly either (directly) interpellated by other Jews
as a Jew or (indirectly) viewed as somehow different, the latter
occurrences most often stemming from some differentiation posed
in terms of physical appearance.

But these counterclaims themselves work two ways: the insistence, on one level, of a racial purity is counteracted, on another
level, by the mere fact that Daniel is nonetheless figured as both a
Jew *and* an Englishman. In this sense, then, despite the narrative's
thrust toward a history of pure nationality, Deronda is symptomatic of a hybrid national reality, of an expression of 'Englishness'
which undermines that of his uncle, Hugo Mallinger, precisely
because it marks the presence of difference *within* it. As both insider
and outsider, Deronda, heading off to Palestine at the end of the
novel, thus bears the traces of hybridity underlying any construc-

tion of national identity. The historically specific boundaries of late-nineteenth-century British 'nationalism' are here being constructed and renegotiated, with the East now figuring as the 'negative' space upon which a properly English, that is, civilised as opposed to un-civilised, identity can be projected; a national identity that can through negation constitute itself as a coherent internal unity.

Shifting registers for a moment, if we return once more to the do-mestic shores which *Daniel Deronda* ultimately attempts to circum-navigate, this process of negation and its implied assumption of a domestic sameness over and against a foreign otherness itself is un-moored. Significantly, when Daniel transports his national message abroad, he leaves Gwendolen behind. As the narrator understates, 'the distance between them was too great' (767). But while the nar-rative, like Deronda, may be unable to bridge this distance, it does circumvent the obstacle preventing this joining – even as it flees the domestic sphere of the 'national' in order to establish an 'organic' community no longer possible within those national borders. Notably, *Daniel Deronda* is not able to incorporate or absorb Gwendolen seamlessly into its denouement. She remains as a glimpse of another possibility, of the existence of chaotic desires, of a *dis*continuous sense of self, of the *internal* splits and ruptures that disrupt or refuse the production of a coherent, cohesive national identification. With her 'play of various, nay, contrary tendencies' she operates as a force of excess and decentred exchange. She is subject to and a subject of a 'new gambling in which the losing was not simply a *minus*, but a terrible plus that had never entered into her reckoning' (659). Consumed by 'world-nausea', yet immune to the redemptive cures of nationalism prescribed by Deronda, Gwendolen is left, literally and figuratively, 'crushed on the floor', her grief displaced but not entirely eclipsed, as the narrator con-cludes that 'such grief seemed natural in a poor lady whose husband had been drowned in her presence'(767). Thus Gwendolen too is implicitly a critique of British nationalism (specifically) and of the system of representation (generally) which defines the nation-state; a system from which she is not only provisionally excluded but in whose exclusion, given her allegorical positioning as figure of domestic (and domesticated) experience, rests the very precondi-tions for such a nationalism.

The changed 'national' world of *Daniel Deronda*, its world-nausea coupled with nationalist awakening, is reflected in Eliot's changed role as storyteller, itself symptomatic of the increasing commodification and reification of daily life, of the widening gap between lived experience and structure. The aesthetic distance Adorno ascribes to the position of the traditional realist narrator becomes unfixed and questionable in the face of the newly emerging experience of modern everyday life (1991, 31). This is marked in the text on a number of different levels. First, *Daniel Deronda* is Eliot's only contemporary, urban novel. As such, it is the closest she comes to properly 'modernist' preoccupations. The opening scene at Leubronn, for instance, is one which is unimaginable within the provincial compass of Middlemarch. Secondly, the narrator's role is abstracted and dispersed, for the most part, into the epigraphs. Working almost singularly through irony, the epigraphs reflect an altered sense of narrative distance in that they 'communicate' not so much through their representation of lived experience but by an undercutting of that experience.[8] This kind of distance calls into question the very conditions of *narratability*; the ground of narration itself is fundamentally shaken by what Benjamin terms the diminishing 'communicability of experience' (1969, 86). Exemplary of this narrative instability is the epigraph to Chapter 26: framing the chapter in which Gwendolen succumbs to Grandcourt's marriage proposal after vowing *not* to, it consists of a poem outlining the virtues and pleasures of maintaining a firm resolve in the face of temptation and 'Enticement' (332). The literal contradiction between the structural frame which the epigraph erects and the actual narration of Gwendolen's experience with Grandcourt upsets any notion of either a coherent internal identity or a continuity between structure and experience. As Adorno phrases it, 'the identity of experience in the form of a life that is articulated and has internal continuity – and that life was the only one thing that made the narrator's stance possible – has disintegrated' (1991, 31).

In search precisely of such 'internal continuity,' *Daniel Deronda*'s narrative grounds itself in an *innate* sense of race, attempting, as it does, to carve out a space of resistance to the ravages of an imperialist economy. For it is this vision of a racial purity, realised through the cultural project of 'nationhood', that not only solidifies the self *qua* self but also the self in relation to a collective national vision. In terms of the individual, we have only to think of the different characterisations of Gwendolen and Mirah: whereas Gwendolen is all excess and decentred exchange, Mirah is neatly contained, almost incapable, the narrative would have us believe, of any sort of internal/external incoherence or psycho-social overflow, simply because she 'has no notion of being anybody but herself' (253). As Mirah abjures in response to Hans's conjectures otherwise, 'I am not pretending anything. I shall never be anything else...I always feel myself a Jewess' (546). She is, in short, never masked, never appearing to be something other than what she *essentially* is. Mirah is, moreover, conveniently willing and, even more to the point, 'made to submit', (as in 'made to order', not forced) suggesting yet another way in which Eliot is wont to fall back upon *innate difference* – in this case, sexual difference – to ground her social vision. If one were to ask hypothetically what would happen if Mirah in fact refused to submit, the answer would be fittingly close at hand: we would need only turn our attention to Daniel's mother, Alchirisi, suggesting just how tenuous and ambivalent even this articulation of unity between Daniel and Mirah is within the 'imagined community' of the novel.[9] Hence, the benign vision of nationalism meant to find its embodiment in the coupling of Mirah and Deronda is itself built upon the very structure of domination – of conqueror and conquered, albeit with the difference that Mirah willingly *accepts* her place as conquered – that Eliot is critiquing in Grandcourt and Gwendolen's relationship.

This contradiction is to Eliot's credit. Indeed, it is in keeping with her alimentary brand of materialism which would have it that 'it is hard for us to live up to our own eloquence, and keep pace with our winged words, while we are treading the solid earth and are liable to heavy dining' (288).

In terms of the collective, the separateness which defines Eliot's sense of nationality carries with it the possibility for a revitalised 'organic' community, embodying both an historical continuity with the past as well as a present relationship with the future, unified in the naturalised image of 'resolved memory'. Deronda, as the spokesperson for such a nationalism, essentially recovers what he has always been when he discovers his Jewish paternity. And a crucial aspect of that recovery is the apparent uniting of past and present, of lived experience and structure that such a recuperation signifies, underscored by Deronda's rhetorical question: 'Unless nationality is a feeling, what force can it have as an idea?' (583) Paradoxically, then, the 'threat' of imperialism is resisted by a domestic nationalism. Eliot's narrative thus enacts the contradictory stance of critiquing imperialism from the perspective of British nationalism as if imperialism and nationalism did not, at this particular historical juncture, in fact work in concert with one another.

Indeed, it is precisely these two impulses that can be read as the defining coordinates of *modernity*. On the one hand, the European nation-state and its concomitant development of national cultures served as the motor of capitalist expansion. On the other hand, this process of expansion – of the increasing globalisation of capital, labour, and goods – moved across and thus broke down those self-same national boundaries. As Stuart Hall has observed, 'the so-called 'logic of capital' has operated as much *through* difference – preserving and transforming difference (including sexual difference) – not by undermining it' (1993, 353).

From this perspective, the tension between the two plots in *Daniel Deronda* can be viewed as symptomatic of the tension between, on the one hand, the tendency of capitalism to develop the nation-state and national cultures and, on the other hand, its transnational imperatives: whereas the historical development of a *national* culture is 'invented' through Eliot's representation of the Zionist project (that is, through the so-called Jewish portion of the novel), the detrimental effects of the *transnational* imperatives of capital are delineated through the Grandcourt/Gwendolen plot. These two tendencies are inseparable from one another; each is a figure of the other.

A direct homology is drawn between the English and the Zionist project, as Daniel claims of his mission: 'The idea that I am possessed with is that of restoring a political existence to my people, making them a nation again, giving them a national centre, such as the English have, though they are scattered over the face of the globe' (875). It is in this context that Eliot's own 'scattered' comments about Britain's colonial possessions take on a deeper and more sustained relevance within the text of *Daniel Deronda* as a whole. For it is as a result of imperialism – itself a product of capitalist development – that the English are covering the map with their now scattered national population. The fear for Eliot in such a scattering is all too clear, involving, as it does, the feeling of loss of an organic centre and with that loss an encroaching corruption of lived experience. Urban cosmopolitanism figures as that which supplants 'organic' community; its aesthetic instrumentalises all social relationships, reducing them to the reified 'sport' of gambling. Given this recognition, the equivalence which Eliot's text draws between British nationalism and Zionism is an odd one. Zionism, taking English nationalism as its model, is to somehow answer to the national and cultural impasse which England itself has reached. But as *Daniel Deronda's* text so convincingly relates, nationalism is part of the problematic, not a solution to that problematic. In other words, Eliot's critique of imperialism, with its resultant vision of an alternative nationalism via Zionism, bears within it the very structure of the object of its critique.

A partial explanation for this contradictory stance is the fact that for the most part Eliot's critique of imperialism remains aimed at home: that is, she locates the horrors of empire on the domestic shores of England, not abroad, in the actual sites of British colonial rule, sites which, as noted above, only enter the novel as asides, be it in the reference to Gwendolen's family fortune coming from West Indian plantations, or in the scattered remarks about the Jamaica Uprising in 1865.[10]

Yet the inclusion of these references at all does register a changed state of affairs – of the increasing interpenetration of the foreign and the domestic, of the move toward a more global economy that imperialism represents – if only in the limited terms of its effect on England. But while Eliot's neat lining up of paternity, race and nationality in the final coupling of Mirah and Deronda promises to master the excess that is imperialism, the nationalism she invokes to do so is already only the marker for a loss, the loss of an organic community that is itself a product of the permanent structural imbalance that is capitalism and its means of expansion, imperialism.

In this respect it may be most useful to think of *Daniel Deronda* in a Brechtian sense, reading its antagonistic plots and its only provisionally resolved tensions – Gwendolen, after all, is never absorbed completely within the narrative unlike Dorothea in *Middlemarch* – as its most radical content. Perhaps then it is this structural antagonism itself, the very antagonism that Leavis would cut away, that is the novel's strength. For as Slavoj Žižek warns in his discussion of resurgent nationalism in Eastern Europe, the danger at this historical juncture is not one of feeling too alienated but rather of not feeling alienated enough (1990, 62).

Notes

1. One version of this kind of reading is Irving Howe's. In contradistinction to the extended 'play' of systematic debasement in the Gwendolen/Grandcourt plot, he sees the Deronda plot as the search

for a locus for moral standards and obligations, for the 'ideals' which Eliot 'finds increasingly difficult to authenticate in her own world.' See 'George Eliot and the Jews', *Partisan Review* 46 (1979), 374.

2. See, for example, Katherine Bailey Linehan, 'Mixed Politics: The Critique of Imperialism in *Daniel Deronda*', *Texas Studies in Literature and Language* 34:3 (Fall 1992), 323–46.

3. Benjamin himself directly addresses the figure of the gambler, drawing an analogy between the worker under capitalism and the gambler in terms of the way in which each have been cheated out of experience, their lives mechanistically reduced to those of automatons. See Walter Benjamin, 'On Some Motifs in Baudelaire', *Illuminations* (New York: Schocken Books, 1977), pp. 155–200. For a more Foucauldian reading of the relations of power in the gambling scene, and of the workings of what he terms the 'body-machine complex' in the culture of realism see Mark Seltzer, 'Statistical Persons', *Diacritics* 17:3 (Fall 1987): 82–98.

4. Interestingly enough, when contemporary reviews of *Daniel Deronda* dealt with the so-called Jewish portion of the novel at all, or specifically with its Zionist project, they did so, for the most part, only in terms of focusing on its indefiniteness, improbability, or impracticability, concluding that such 'idealism' was simply futile. Often it was even conjectured that Eliot must be being satirical, or just not serious in the Zionist aspects of the plot. See Carol A. Martin, 'Contemporary Critics and Judaism in *Daniel Deronda*', *Victorian Periodicals Review* 21:3 (Fall 1988). In a recent article, Susan Meyer, focusing on what she labels the 'proto-Zionism' of the novel, argues that Eliot applies the idea of Jewish return opportunistically, primarily in the service of British interests both at home in England and abroad *vis-à-vis* the 'Syrian Question'. In my view, however, such a reading does not adequately account for the interconnectedness (and urgency) of Eliot's representation of Zionism to the fate of the English in the novel. See '"Safely to their Own Borders": Proto-Zionism, Feminism, and Nationalism', *ELH* 60 (1993), 773–58.

5. See, for example, Christina Crosby, *The Ends of History: Victorians and 'The Woman Question'* (New York and London: Routledge, 1991), pp. 12–43.

6. Interestingly, *Daniel Deronda* has been discussed in terms of its similarities to the science-fiction sub-genre of the alternate history. See, for example, Kathleen McCormack, 'George Eliot and Victorian Science Fiction: *Daniel Deronda* as Alternate History', *Extrapolation* 27:3 (1986), 185–96.

7. Ultimately Crosby sees *Daniel Deronda* shoring up the limits of humanism by 'displaying the workings of a humanism which will do whatever is necessary to consolidate one norm, one standard, one reality, the humanity of western white bourgeois man' (1991, 42).

8. Jameson too speaks of the formal practice of irony as a response to this historical situation: 'what we begin to see is the sense that each consciousness is a closed world, so that a representation of the social totality now must take the (impossible) form of a coexistence of those

sealed subjective worlds and their peculiar interaction, which is in reality a passage of ships in the night, a centrifugal movement of lines and planes that can never intersect' (1988, 350).

9. Benedict Anderson uses the term 'imagined community' to reflect the invented nature of nationalisms. Following Anderson, I am using the term not as an indicator of falsity as opposed to genuineness but with a focus on the style in which *Daniel Deronda's* community is being imagined. See *Imagined Communities: Reflections on the Origin and Spread of Nationalism* (London: Verso, 1983).

10. At once, this is both a traditional novelistic trope inherited from Austen and the Brontës and a more significant indication of a radically altered state of affairs which, as discussed above, signals the dispersion of the meaning of one's everyday reality throughout the vast colonial network. For more on this trope in Austen and Brontë, as well as other Victorian writers, see Edward W. Said, *Culture and Imperialism* (New York: Alfred A. Knopf, 1993). In the context of the form and development of the *Bildungsroman*, Franco Moretti reads this shift as well in terms of the transition to a new historical phase, the 'age of the masses'. For Moretti, then, Eliot, by attempting to tell her tale of the masses (in both *Daniel Deronda* and *Felix Holt*), yet with only the worn-out, historically outdated narrative form of the *Bildungsroman* at her disposal has set herself an impossible task: to capture this new 'collective' subject through the lens of a symbolic form centred on the biography of an individual. See *The Way of the World: The Bildungsroman in European Culture* (London: Verso, 1987), pp. 181–228.

3

An Anatomy of the British Polity: *Alton Locke* and Christian Manliness

David Alderson

There is no definitive document of Christian manliness. It was never given formal theoretical expression, and what we can say about it must be gleaned from the various novels and sermons which were written or preached in its favour. This in itself is a significant fact, since a hostility to theories and an appeal to intuition and commonsense principles were partly definitive of the phenomenon. Necessarily, then, the conceptualisation of manliness which Kingsley (especially) promoted synthesised dominant ideologies and definitions to produce a version of ideal masculinity which was both conservative yet apparently innovative. Centrally, it has been interpreted as an attempt to resolve the tensions between corporeal existence and spiritual aspiration,[1] but questions about the historical conditions of its emergence have been largely neglected.

Christian manliness was nascent within the thought and activities of the Christian socialists, who were committed both to rejecting the ambitious political demands of the Chartists and to achieving the reform of a British polity increasingly committed to the principles of political economy; a route, they believed, to social entropy. Kingsley's novel about Chartism derives from this, but also lays bare most clearly the anxieties and ideological commitments which produced his influential conceptualisation of the relationship between the masculine body and social order. Of course, the body–state analogy has an ancient provenance, but this does not render the relationship ahistorical, and my concern here is with the imperatives of a counter-revolutionary and Protestant culture which enabled the Kingsleyan sense of the ideal male body to become so central to the masculine self-definition of Britain's rulers.

ALTON LOCKE: THE BODY IN BRITISH HISTORY

Alton Locke is a significant text in the representation of the demise of Chartism as being a result of the movement's own ineptitude, petering out in the April rain, never to be revived. John Saville comprehensively revises this long-standing view and meticulously details the repressive measures and ideological panic with which the British state responded to the Chartist threat (Saville 1987). By 1848 the state had massively expanded its repressive apparatus – police constables, militia and volunteer groups (state forces available for action in London at the 10 April demonstration were nearly 100 000 strong [Saville 1987, 109]); it had initiated a range of legislation to deal with political threat – frequently in response to insurrectionary possibilities in Ireland – including, most significantly, the Crown and Security Act (passed in April 1848) which created a new offence of treasonable speaking; and, with the issue of a warrant for the arrest of Ernest Jones on 2 June, the intimidatory political trials of the leaders of the movement began: 'Chartism was finally broken by the physical force of the British State, and having once been broken it was submerged, in the national consciousness, beneath layers of false understanding and denigration' (Saville 1987, 202). Equally important, then, was the triumphalist press coverage in the wake of Chartism's defeat, emphasising three central aspects of counter-revolutionary ideology: the association of revolution with the foreign, the stupidity of egalitarian ideas and claims for the right to work, and,

> the most important and pervasive, the belief, which amounted to an article of faith, that in England the liberty of the subject had been assured by centuries of growth and development and that nowhere else in Europe were the practices of free speech and the possibilities of political change so self-evident as in Britain. (Saville 1987, 164)

It is important to acknowledge this in an account of *Alton Locke*, not simply because of the way this novel misrepresents the actual circumstances of Chartism's demise, but precisely because of the centrality of the idea of English historical continuity – of the kind Saville outlines – and of racial unity to Kingsley's sense of national community: he presents the emergence of a politically conscious working class and the *laissez-faire* state policies which contributed to this emergence as related historical aberrations. If Kingsley was ever mistaken for a radical it is because he was really a paternalist, and his analysis of Chartism is deeply indebted to Carlyle's in which the 'dumb' masses present themselves in need of being governed.[2] Kingsley's denunciations of political economy were based on the sense of their betrayal of the moral economy, declaring as late as 1871 that he believed the feudal system – ideally, if not in practice – to be the most noble form of social organisation (Kingsley 1890a, 311). In 1852, he wrote to Thomas Hughes that

> I have never swerved from my one idea of the last seven years, that the real battle of the time is – if England is to be saved from anarchy and unbelief, and utter exhaustion caused by the competitive enslavement of the masses – not Radical or Whig against Peelite or Tory (let the dead bury their dead), but the Church, the gentleman, and the workman against the shopkeepers and the Manchester school…. A true democracy, such as you and I should wish to see, is impossible without a Church and a Queen, and, as I believe, without a gentry. (Kingsley 1890a, 130)

In this, then, Kingsley was consistent. Democracy, to him, meant simply the opposite of the social disintegration which was implicit in the individualist philosophy of the political economists. The spectres of anarchy, unbelief and national exhaustion represent a kind of diabolical trinity for him, all three being inextricably linked in his sense of the dangers to British nation-state formation.

Appropriately enough, one of the first scenes of *Alton Locke* to be written was Locke's final conversion (Chitty 1974, 133). The narrative is written from the perspective of the converted tailor, and Locke retrospectively laments his failings, usually failings of conscience or of perception. The telos of the novel is the message of the Christian socialists: the necessary moral reform of all British citizens, the promotion of a Christian brotherhood (*sic*) across class divisions, and the recognition of the central role of the clergy – a kind of Coleridgean clerisy – in the realisation of these ends. This is what Kingsley referred to as 'true democracy', and Eleanor – who preaches this message to Locke – exemplifies all of this when she speaks of Christ:

> as the great Reformer; and yet as the true conservative ... the justifier of His own dealings with man from the beginning. She spoke of Him as the true demagogue – the champion of the poor; and yet as the true King, above and below all earthly rank; on whose will alone all the real superiority of man to man, all the time-justified and time-honoured usages of the family, the society, the nation, stand and shall stand for ever.[3]

The institutions and historical development of British society are sanctified and vindicated. The basis of this understanding of history is Providence, but this passage only appears at the end of a book which outlines the contemporary precariousness of that order which it claims to be coterminous with Providence.

The threat in the novel is dual, and the component parts are causally related: revolutionary action is precipitated by a lack of national fraternity on the part of the ruling class. Revolution itself is consistently identified with malign foreign influences – with France and the Irish. Examples of this are obvious in the novel. The main Chartist leader – who at one point inflates the anti-Establishment rhetoric of an article written by Locke – is O'Flynn (a reference to Feargus O'Connor), and, in the lead-up to the April demonstration of 1848, Locke claims his friend Crossthwaite 'was always quoting French in those days' (Kingsley 1850, 305). When Locke and Crossthwaite arrive at the house of the Irishman Mike Kelly to find out about a claim – actually made by a government spy – that there are hundreds of men in government offices ready to support any insurrection, there is 'a hubbub inside Kelly's room of English, French, and Irish, all talking at once' – clearly symbolic of a chaotic confusion of national characteristics (Kingsley, 307). Kelly himself becomes symbolic of the ineptitude of the foreign-led movement, pre-empting the disaster of 10 April, and by this time Locke is already disenchanted with the mendacity and lack of patriotism – to *Britain*, that is – of the Irish.

There are obvious historical reasons for all of this, but there is also great significance in the religious affiliations of these other countries, since the alien character of the revolutionary forces is bound up with one of the central components of British identity.[4] It is related, in part, to the constitutionalism of British political culture, a widely-held conviction that the settlement of 1688 guaranteed the British citizen freedom from arbitrary power under the nation's constitution.[5] The religious significance of this constitutional settlement is itself important, as Linda Colley has pointed out: the Protestant monarchy underwrote this constitution at the same time as repeated wars with Catholic France throughout the eighteenth century and into the nineteenth were instrumental in forging a British identity.[6] The rhetoric of freedom was not simply the result of official versions of it under the Protestant constitution, though: it was also reinforced by the main doctrinal distinctions between the Protestantism and Catholicism which characterised these opposing nations. Protestantism's central defining difference from Catholicism lies in its solifidianism – justification by faith – an assertion of the independent and immediate relationship between the individual and God which rejects Catholicism's mediations.[7] Catholicism has been seen by Protestants historically as a system – almost a conspiracy – inimical to this immediate relationship and one which kept the laity excluded and in ignorance, thereby resulting in a lack of conscientious virtue. Hence, the repeated emphasis in British anti–French writings on the French people's slavery to the material world. Colley cites the following example, which – though it doesn't mention Catholicism directly – I agree is indicative of the general relationship:

> Let France grow proud, beneath the tyrant's lust,
> While the rack'd people crawl, and lick the dust:
> The manly genius of this isle disdains
> All tinsel slavery, or golden chains.
>
> (Colley 1992, 34)

The sense of freedom posited here in opposition to the physical oppression of the poor and in disdain of the spiritual corruption of the rich emphasises both gender and independence ('genius') at the same time as it promotes the sense of a truly national Protestant community. *Manly* freedom, then, denotes both individual autonomy and virtue, the two being inseparable in the Protestant experience. Moreover, this virtuous independence is not only characteristic of individuals, but definitive of social maturity: 'manly genius' slips undecidably between reference to the individual and to the nation. The importance of this should not be underestimated, since it is a part of that process of perceiving in the characteristics of the individual the stage of development of the nation, and in the early part of the nineteenth century this took on an important pedagogic value. David Newsome has argued for the synonymity of 'manly' with 'mature' in the Coleridgean ideal which was influential on Thomas Arnold among others,[8] and Arnold himself makes this equation of individual with national development in his famous aim to 'form Christian men, for Christian boys I can scarcely hope to make ... they are not susceptible of Christian principles in their full development upon their practice, and I suspect that a low standard of morality in many respects must be tolerated amongst them, as it was on a larger scale in what I consider the boyhood of the human race' (Stanley 1881, 75). The Protestant earnestness which was Arnold's legacy – partly through the myth which others created of him – promoted a sense of the advanced state of the nation and of its consequent improving purpose in the world. His inaugural lecture set the urgent tone of his message: 'if there be any signs, however uncertain, that we are living in the latest period of the world's history, that no other races remain behind us to perform what we have neglected, or to restore what we have ruined, then indeed the interest of modern history does become intense, and the importance of not wasting time still left to us may well be called incalculable' (Arnold, cit. Newsome 1961, 19).

Arnold also demonstrates here, though, the fallacy that conscience could simply be allowed free reign – actually, it must first be internalised – and this was a more compelling problem in the policing of the governed. Henry Newman was an astute, conservative critic of Protestant culture, and his commitment to social order – precisely to external authority – was explicitly one of the reasons for his commitment to Catholicism: speaking of private judgement, Newman challenged Protestants to 'Take your First Principles, of which you are so proud, into the crowded streets of our cities, into the formidable classes which make up the bulk of the population; try to work society by them. You think you can; I say you cannot' (Newman 1892, 295). The resolution of this problem for Anglicans like Kingsley lay in erastianism, and the relationship between Church and State was reaffirmed by key conservative intellectuals in the aftermath of the French Revolution. For Burke, the alliance of Church and State was a means of sanctifying national development: the Established Church 'hath solemnly and for ever consecrated the commonwealth, and all that officiate in it' (Burke 1986, 18). Coleridge – a more significant thinker for Christian socialists –

went further. One of the major functions proposed for 'cultivating' national clerisy was that of teaching individual subjection to national development. Coleridge's idealism was capable of bellicosity: the final cause of his proposed office of the clerisy is

> to form and train up the people of the country to obedient, free, useful, organizable subjects, citizens, and patriots, living to the benefit of the state, and prepared to die for its defence. The proper *object* and end of the National Church is civilization with freedom; and the duty of its ministers ... would be fulfilled in the communication of that degree and kind of knowledge to all, the possession of which is necessary for all in order to their CIVILITY. (Coleridge 1976, 54)

Coleridge not only perceives no conflict between social control and freedom, but actually recognises in the imperative of State continuity the very condition of citizens' freedom as a consequence of precisely the uninterrupted, pristine sovereignty of the Church and State whose idea he is defending. The clerisy would be the means of securing individual subjection to the exigencies of a State whose organic development is proof of its divine justification. By this means, true inner conviction based on divine promptings is reconcilable with the interests of the nation.

This process of thought in Coleridge reflects an alignment between Protestant appeals to interiority – and against authoritarian dogma – in the dominant British response to the French Revolution. Edmund Burke's central argument is an anti-enlightenment hatred of 'systems': 'All our sophisters cannot produce any thing better adopted to preserve a rational and manly freedom than the course that we have pursued, who have chosen our nature rather than our speculations, our breasts rather than our inventions, for the great conservatories and magazines of our rights and privileges' (Burke 1986, 121). Burke's sense of nation-state development is unquestionably idealist, but the substance of his argument rests on a pragmatic realism. The opposition is ultimately between being guided by 'our breasts' – an *interior* guiding principle – and accepting the impositions of systems. He explicitly argues that the revolutionaries 'are so taken up with their theories about the rights of man, that they have totally forgot his nature.... They have perverted in themselves, and in those that attend to them, all the well-placed sympathies of the human breast' (Burke 1986, 156). In this way, the appeal to 'rational and manly' freedom connects Burke's argument with the discourse of anti-French Protestantism already outlined. Indeed, in his discussion of the treatment of the French monasteries by the new regime, he considers the superstitions of the old religion and the new philosophers as almost equivalent (though he favours the established order on moral grounds [Burke 1986, 267–70]). The repudiation of systems here, then, equates individual duty with the protection of the current order, and the organic metaphor which sustains Burke's argument confers on this gradualist opposition to systems an orderly naturalism. Again, the principle of interiority is reconciled with conformity.

Arguments dependent ultimately on Burke are deployed in Carlyle's 'Chartism' pamphlet which argued that Chartism's origins lay in the renunciation of paternal responsibility by Britain's rulers, and the consequent sense of injustice – of abandonment to economic chance – provoked in the governed. Significantly, injustice for Carlyle was

A deeper law than any parliament-law whatsoever, a law written direct by the hand of God in the inmost being of man, incessantly protests against it. What is injustice? Another name for disorder, for unveracity, unreality; a thing which veracious created Nature, even because it is not Chaos and a waste-whirling baseless Phantasm, rejects and disowns. (Carlyle 1986, 177)

Again, there is the appeal to interiority to validate order and this internal sense of injustice is in touch with the natural abhorrence of disorder; it is itself part of the organic process.

Christian socialism continued this tradition of hostility to the systematic nature of social theories. The leading intellectual of the group, Frederick Maurice, was motivated primarily by such a hostility: according to Edward Norman, he believed systems were 'a "miserable, partial, human substitute" for the divine order. They were particularly inappropriate to the English, for whom "system-building" was "not natural"' (Norman 1987, 21). Kingsley followed Maurice in this, but was also quite explicit about the analogy between the oppressive systems of Catholicism and the systems of the political thinkers of the French Revolution. Indeed, one provoked the other: the prime responsibility for the Revolution, Kingsley told one potential convert to Catholicism, fell on the Jesuits who caused the Revolution. Madam, the horrors of 1793 were the natural fruit of the teaching of the very men who not only would have died sooner than bring about these horrors, but died of them, alas! by them. And how was this? By trying to set up a system of society and morals of their own, they uprooted in the French every element of faith in, and reverence for, the daily duties and relations of human life, without knowing it – without meaning it. May God keep you from the same snare, of fancying, as all 'Orders,' Societies and Sects do, that they invent a better system of society than the old one, wherein God created man in His own image, viz., of father and son, husband and wife, brother and sister, master and servant, king and subject. (Kingsley 1890a, 160)

The obliteration of organic ties – which are 'uprooted' – destabilises the proper processes of history, and just as surely bears its own 'fruit' (another organic reference certainly, but one which also has obvious tragic connotations). Similarly, in *Alton Locke* Eleanor asserts that if the people turn their attentions from God,

there will be no lack of priestcraft, of veils to hide Him from them, tyrants to keep them from Him, idols to ape His likeness. A sinful people will always be a priest-ridden people; in reality, though not in name; by journalists and demagogues, if not by class-leaders and popes; and of the two, I confess I should prefer a Hildebrand to an O'Flynn. (Kingsley 1983, 377)

We are reminded here of O'Flynn's alterations to Locke's article on Cambridge, inflating its charges. The moderate truth spoken by Locke becomes lost in the rhetorical excess of O'Flynn. Indeed, Locke's sense of self – as Catherine Gallagher has noted – is constantly undermined (Gallagher 1985, 88–110), but this is not the result of an irresolvable contradiction between a free will mysteriously reconcilable with Providence and material determinism. Nor is it a product of writing's capacity to demonstrate 'the fictional nature of the singular identity' (Gallagher 1985, 107): throughout the novel Kingsley is deliberately suggesting Locke has an intuitive sense of the falseness of his own thoughts and actions, an intuition which makes his final conversion inevitable and confirms Eleanor's conclusions about the nature of his compromise in the service of religious truth.

A case in point – demonstrating the Protestant alignment of truth with interior conviction – is the key moment of Locke's 'fall' when he agrees to 'emasculate' (Kingsley 1983, 183) his poetry, to censor its truths in complicity with the demands of his 'aristocratic' admirers. This is performed largely out of a desire to please Lillian: 'Could I not, just once in a way, serve God and Mammon at once? – or rather, not Mammon, but Venus: a worship which looked to me, and really was in my case, purer than all the Mariolatry in Popedom' (Kingsley 1983, 182). The reference to Mariolatry again insists on the falseness of mediated relations with God, and Locke's love for Lillian is a form of idol-worship (as the appeal to paganism demonstrates), a form of enslavement. Lillian herself proves unworthy – as her marriage to Locke's Tractarian cousin demonstrates – and it is her sister, Eleanor – whose *external* conduct leads Locke to consider her his enemy – who actually proves to be his guardian and the true democrat (in the Kingsleyan sense). Indeed, once Locke has become disabused of Lillian's character, Eleanor asks the rhetorical question 'What was it that you adored? a soul, or a face? The inward reality, or the outward symbol, which is only valuable as a sacrament of the loveliness within?' (Kingsley 1983, 358)

Lillian does not maintain her beauty, though, and the means by which form and interior condition are made to correspond is of more than passing significance in the context of the book's overall fascination with organisms. Lillian contracts typhus, but recovers in a degenerate form. Her husband – Locke's cousin – dies of the disease, as do one of his servants and the shopman who sells him the coat which harbours the disease. The coat itself was the product of sweated labour, made by a former workmate of Locke, Jemmy Downes. Prior to its sale, it was used to cover the bodies of Downes's dead family, as Locke himself witnesses (Downes's family die of the effects of drinking the water which they also defecate in). Locke comments that his cousin's death 'was the consistent Nemesis of all poor George's thrift and cunning, of his determination to carry the buy-cheap-and-sell-dear commercialism, in which he had been brought up, into every act of life!' (Kingsley 1983, 372). The contamination of the fabric of the coat is both the means of contaminating the rest of society and a metaphor for that contamination – a reference to the *social* fabric, of course – and therefore an insistence on the impossibility of denying social ties. Kingsley is prone to mixing the metaphors which govern his thoughts, and the disease which traces the tortuous route from Jemmy Downes's house to Lillian inevitably returns us to a consideration of the social as organism. Inner value and physical form finally correspond in Lillian, and she is made to stand for the degenerate body politic, a condition precipitated by the systematic application of political doctrines.

Other organisms feature prominently in Kingsley's narrative as victims of the system–building of humanity. Consequently, they are rarely healthy. As a young boy, Locke reveals an interest in natural forms of life which contradicts the severity of his mother's Calvinist dogma – 'God's love shines out in every tree and flower and hedge-side bird' (Kingsley 1983, 12) – but the contemporary city perverts nature. At one point, Locke imaginatively pictures the natural world of the tropical islands described to him in missionary tracts, and contrasts this with his own Cockney environment:

> one day, I recollect it well, in the little dingy, foul, reeking, twelve-foot square back-yard, where huge smoky party-walls shut out every breath of air and almost all the light of heaven, I had climbed up between the water-butt and the angle of the wall for the purpose of fishing out of the dirty fluid which lay there, crusted with soot and alive with insects, to be renewed only three times in seven days, some of the great larvae and kicking monsters which made up a large item in my list of wonders: all of a sudden the horror of the place came over me; those grim prison-walls above, with their canopy of lurid smoke; the dreary, sloppy, broken pavement; the horrible stench of the stagnant cesspools; the utter want of form, colour, life, in the whole place, crushed me down, without being able to analyse my feelings as I can now; and then came over me that dream of Pacific Islands, and the free, open sea. (Kingsley 1983, 14)

The constraining environment of the city produces its own aberrant organisms and also a consequent intuitive desire for freedom in Locke in the form of a desire for an unspoilt natural environment. This is a demand to be able to develop naturally, physically as a man, in a way which is coterminous with divinely-sanctioned growth (inevitably towards light). Freedom is not only freedom from the physical environment, though, since there is a constant slippage between physical and moral description: Locke's desire for natural physical development is necessarily a desire to be able to develop morally.

At the same time as natural development is equated with moral freedom, the city's imposition of forms on organisms precipitates their inner degeneration, most pronounced in the conditions of the workers: the production of aberrant forms of the body results in corresponding aberrant convictions. On being told he is to become a tailor, Locke considers his compatibility with his environment:

A pale, consumptive, ricketty, weakly boy, all forehead and no muscle – have not clothes and shoes been from time immemorial the appointed work of such? The fact that the weakly frame is generally compensated by a proportionally increased activity of the brain, is too unimportant to enter into the calculations of the great King Laissez-faire. Well, my dear Society, it is you that suffer for the mistake, after all, more than we. If you do tether your cleverest artisans to tailors' shop-boards and cobblers' benches, and they – as sedentary folk will – fall a-thinking, and come to strange conclusions thereby, they really ought to be much more thankful to you than you are to them. (Kingsley 1983, 22)

Political dogma solidifies into physical restraint, and this provokes unnatural mental stimulation. This displays both an anti-intellectualism and an alignment of the healthy body with social order which is more than simply a repetition of the ancient body–state analogy: health of body and mind become one with the practice of sublimating energies to nation-state development (there is also the same sense that over-intellectualism produces ungrounded abstractions that is demonstrated in Burke's characterisation of rational systems as 'inventions' or Carlyle's sense that nature abhors 'baseless Phantasm').

This association of sedentary occupation with revolutionary intellectualism is further reinforced in Crosthwaite, who

might have been five-and-twenty; but his looks, like those of too many a working man, were rather those of a man of forty. Wild grey eyes gleamed out from under huge knitted brows, and a perpendicular wall of brain, too large for his puny body. He was not only, I soon discovered, a water-drinker, but a strict 'vegetarian' also; to which, perhaps, he owed a great deal of the almost preternatural clearness, volubility, and sensitiveness of mind.... the marks of ill-health were on him.... (Kingsley 1983, 29)

In fact, Crossthwaite shares certain characteristics with Kingsley's portrait of Shelley – including his vegetarianism – who is compared unfavourably with the manly, intelligible Byron who adhered to classical (natural) forms. In his sensitivity, Shelley was 'Tender and pitiful as a woman; and yet, when angry, shrieking, railing and hysterical as a woman' (Kingsley 1890b, 47). The effeminacy of Shelley is dictated, for Kingsley, by his physical and nervous condition, his lack of control and of an ability to express himself with discipline. Like a child, he is 'inarticulate, peevish, irrational'. This essentially aesthetic disorder in Shelley – of both poetry and body – is also aligned with his political convictions, and, of course, this is the key to his similarity to Crossthwaite: over-sensitivity, weakness and disrespect for political order.

In terms of contemporary thought, this reflects the relationship between body and mind established in what Bruce Haley has described as Victorian 'psychophysiology', one of whose classificatory types was that of the nervous temperament: those in whom the cerebro-neural system predominates over the rest of the body. Sir James Beale – physician-in-ordinary to the Queen – described the nervous temperament as 'characterized by a highly developed nervous system; there is extreme sensitiveness to all impressions; the passions when evolved are impetuous, and the countenance animated and expressive; in such persons all is excitement and mobility'.[9] Though this psychological type was the basis of Kingsley's characterisation of the 'effeminate' man, Kingsley was also convinced that the body's state was expressive of an explicitly Christian condition: 'Body is that which expresses the spirit to which it is joined; therefore, the more perfectly spiritual the body, the better it will express the spirit joined to it' (Kingsley 1890a, 232). The spiritual condition which Crossthwaite's body expresses, though, is a deranged radicalism. Spiritual condition, reason and bodily health, then, are complexly related, but in their ideal alignment, they should express the metaphysics of nationhood. Perversions of organic forms are therefore symptomatic of a departure from conformity with the reasonable British polity.

Among all the fears of national degeneration precipitated by class conflict, there is one moment of transcendence in the novel, a moment which simultaneously symbolises most clearly the assimilation of divine order to national supremacy. Locke witnesses his cousin in a Cambridge boat race:

It was a noble sport – a sight as could only be seen in England – some hundred of young men, who might, if they had chosen, been lounging effeminately about the streets, subjecting themselves voluntarily to that intense exertion, for the mere pleasure of toil. The true English stuff came out there; I felt that, in spite of all my prejudices – the stuff which has held Gibraltar and conquered at Waterloo – which has created a Birmingham and a Manchester, and colonised every quarter of the globe – that grim, earnest, stubborn energy, which, since the days of the old Romans, the English possess of all the nations of the earth. I was as proud of the gallant young fellows as if they had been my brothers – of their courage and endurance (for one could see that it was no child's-play, from the pale faces, and panting lips), their strength and activity, so fierce and yet so cultivated, smooth, harmonious, as oar kept time with oar, and every back rose and fell in concert – and felt my soul stirred up to a sort of sweet madness.... My blood boiled over, and fierce tears swelled into my eyes; for I too was a man, and an Englishman; and when I caught sight of my cousin, pulling stroke to the second boat in the long line, with set teeth and flashing eyes, the great muscles on his bare arms springing up into knots at every rapid stroke, I ran and shouted among the maddest and foremost. (Kingsley 1983, 131–2)

Here, the ideal masculine body becomes the symbol in which all classes can recognise themselves as part of a superior racial group whose achievement of an empire which surpassed the Romans' is their Providential reward. Aspects of the literal body depicted here become the principles of the unity of the nation: work, discipline, purpose, all manifest in the body's own lineaments and all functioning – at least potentially – in the service of nation. At the same time as this body is distinctly masculine, though, its self-control mitigates the potential of male energy to spill over into barbarism (it is 'so fierce yet so cultivated'). Just as it demonstrably shows signs of its own self-rule, then, it also conveys its ability to rule others – in particular, other, 'immature' races. Where Paley would have seen in the body's musculature evidence only of a benevolent design (an aspect of the body's constitutional orderliness [Paley 1844, 461–7]), Kingsley sees the natural expression of a divine and national purposiveness. It is this myth of national – indeed, racial – unity which Kingsley was able to forge from the State's defeat of Chartism and from the dual ideologies of freedom and continuity.

THE RULE OF CHRISTIAN MEN

The fact is that all breaches of the laws of health are *physical* sins.
Herbert Spencer (1861, 190)

Within a few years of Chartism's defeat, Christian socialism lost its impetus. Kingsley himself became increasingly unmotivated in its cause, and from 1859 – when he preached at Buckingham Palace for the first time – embarked on a career as Establishment figure. In 1862 he censored his criticisms of Cambridge in *Alton Locke* – though he increased his attacks on the Tractarians – and, in a new preface he wrote for the fourth edition of his novel *Yeast*, he even praised the effects of the Poor Law Amendment Act – for making labourers more independent, and of free trade – for improving the diet of the workers (Kingsley 1879, iii–iv). This may seem to mark him out as a political renegade, but in fact only draws attention to his main and consistent concern: the moral condition of the workers and the symbolic importance in this respect of physical health. Even after his desertion of Christian socialism, his obsession with sanitary reform was maintained. After the early fifties, indeed, the innovative aspect of Kingsley's writing ended; there was nothing more to add to his message, only clarification and defence.

His – and Thomas Hughes's – ideal of the body did succeed in becoming influential, though, through its passage into the games ethic as the public schools processed greater numbers of bodies from aspiring middle-class backgrounds and themselves grew in number in a culture still dominated by the ideal of the gentleman. By the early 1900s the number of public schools reached '– depending on the degree of exclusiveness or snobbery – anything between 64 and some 160 more or less expensive schools ... deliberately training their pupils as members of a ruling class' (Hobsbawm 1987, 178). Games became increasingly central to the curriculum; their institutionalisation was 'extended and perfected' by 1900 (Mangan 1981, 86). Time after time, the exaltation of games in sermons, doggerel, stories and novels by enthusiastic masters celebrates the subordination of self to *esprit de corps* and the development of bodies whose physiognomies and musculatures were an index of the capacity of the individual to perform virtuous work. As Hobsbawm's comment suggests, this was a training for what was expected of the individual after his graduation from school: team became nation, and work the practical business of spreading the interests of that nation. The contempt for both luxury *and* ascetic bodily denial, and the imperative of a discipline which was also natural, remained the central moral features of this institutionalisation.

It should also be emphasised that Kingsley and Hughes *did* also promote an aggressive masculinity, albeit one ideally subordinated to what they considered to be Christian action. Developing an apology for Hughes's defence of the necessity of pugilism on the grounds that the concept of 'fighting' is as much morally defined as it is physically defined[10] may be a corrective to former accounts of 'muscular Christianity', but it misses the central aspect of that crucial passage – the striking elision between self and nation, and the further elision developed between national service and the service of higher ends through a Pauline rhetoric which itself has a long tradition in British Protestant thought and which took on a renewed zeal in the militaristic atmosphere of the later nineteenth century:

> From the cradle to the grave, fighting, rightly understood, is the business, the real, highest, honestest business of every son of man. Every one who is worth his salt has his enemies, who must be beaten, be they evil thoughts and habits in himself or spiritual wickednesses in high places, or Russians, or Border-ruffians, or Bill, Tom, or Harry, who will not let him live his life in quiet till he has thrashed them. (Hughes 1989, 282)

It is precisely this physically active loss of self in the struggle to promote divine and national law that distinguishes the authentic message of Christian manliness, and it was this which was fully preserved in the ideology of athleticism in the later nineteenth century.

Enthusiasm for games was variable, but agreement on its benefits was general. They didn't come much more enthusiastic than Hely Hutchinson Almond – headmaster of Loretto School from 1862 – who demanded in one sermon, 'a holy alliance between the athlete and the Christian', in which the egotism of the athlete and the disciplines of religion would find common cause against their joint enemies: 'intemperance, and indolence, and dissipation, and effeminacy, and aesthetic voluptuousness, and heartless cynicism, and all the unnatural and demoralising elements in our social life'. Examples of the ideal 'consecration of the body' included carrying 'the banner of the Cross to distant lands' and winning Christian victories 'among ignorant natives or coarse British traders', even 'protecting some rough colony from the inroads of civilised effeminacy and vice' (Almond 1886, 173–5; a common biblical justification for the moralising work of colonisation lauded here was that of 'subduing the wild earth', a phrase which expresses the physical practice of bringing to other countries and their natives the order of British rule).

Edward Bowden, though not sure about the desirability of the compulsory status of games, still placed an almost ineffable value on the practice of playing football:

> when you have a lot of human beings, in highest social union, and perfect organic action, developing the law of their race and falling in unconsciously with its best inherited traditions of brotherhood and of common action, I think you are not far from getting a glimpse of one side of the highest good. There lives more soul in honest play, believe me, than in half the hymnbooks. (Bowden 1902, 331)

The body becomes a living expression of the ideal purposiveness of the 'race', rising above the potentially dead letter of the hymn, and that metaphysical appeal to the 'the law of their race' conflates the natural, national and divine.

Through the adoption of Christian manliness by the pedagogical institutions of Britain's ruling class, it became the established form of masculinity up to the First World War – contributing to the attitudes of Britain's officer class – and somewhat beyond. It was a major ideological factor in the legitimation of imperialism,[11] and at home contributed to – as it arose from – anxieties about national degeneration. Except in the public schools – where it was ubiquitous – its literary career was limited as a consequence of its didacticism,[12] but this itself helped to reinforce the isolation of 'culture' from (moral, upright) society to the extent that art could become as self-absorbed and self-valorising (and consequently suspicious) as it did among the aesthetes. As with any dominant ideology, Christian manliness was modified, resisted and challenged, but what is remarkable is the consistency of the writings of the schoolmasters who promoted it and the duration of the period in which it maintained – even increased – its ascendancy among the rulers of Empire. Built on the myth of the natural integrity and durability of the British polity,

Christian manliness became symbolically central to that nation's claims to a uniquely blessed supremacy – and the proof was at work in the active bodies of its agents.

Notes

1. Norman Vance, *The Sinews of the Spirit: The Ideal of Christian Manliness in Victorian Literature and Religious Thought* (Cambridge: Cambridge University Press, 1985) is the best general account along these lines.
2. See Thomas Carlyle, 'Chartism', in *Selected Writings*, ed. Alan Shelston (Harmondsworth: Penguin, 1986), especially pp. 187–200.
3. Charles Kingsley, *Alton Locke* (Harmondsworth: Penguin, 1983), p. 356. All further references are incorporated in the text.
4. I am aware that it is impossible to talk of a British identity without recognising the divisions within that polity. I use the term to signify a dominant identity – one that is at least partly 'official' and centred on England – and I intend it to carry connotations of (often violent) subordination.
5. See E. P. Thompson, *The Making of the English Working Class* (Harmondsworth: Penguin, 1968), Chapter 4, pp. 84–110.
6. See Linda Colley, *Britons: Forging the Nation 1707–1837* (New Haven: Yale University Press, 1992), especially Chapter 1, pp. 11–54.
7. On this definitive distinction, see Christopher Hill's 'Protestantism and the Rise of Capitalism' in *Change and Continuity in 17th Century England* (London: Weidenfeld, 1974), pp. 81–102. Hill argues for the liberating, individuating tendency of Protestantism in relation to Catholicism, and shows that its contemporary relationship with emergent capitalism was a mutually reinforcing one in this respect. Clearly the Protestant/Catholic distinction he draws, though, has a more than local historical significance.
8. David Newsome, *Godliness and Good Learning: Four Studies on a Victorian Ideal* (London: Murray, 1961), pp. 196–7. It follows from the rest of my argument that I think Newsome wrong to make an essential distinction between the manliness of Arnold and that of Kingsley and Hughes. Apart from anything else, the narrative structure of *Tom Brown* clearly emphasises his development from childhood to manliness, and this structure contains an implicit sense of national development from the simple robustness of the rural community to the moral manliness of Brown's late youth.
9. Sir James Beale, *The Laws of Health in Relation to the Mind and Body* (London: John Churchill, 1851), p. 152; quoted in Bruce Haley, *The Healthy Body and Victorian Culture* (Cambridge, Mass.: Harvard University Press, 1978), p. 32.
10. See George M. Worth, 'Of Muscles and Manliness: Some Reflections on Thomas Hughes', *Victorian Literature and Society: Essays presented to*

Richard D. Altick, ed. James Kincaid and Albert J. Kuhn (Ohio: Ohio University Press, 1984), pp. 206–7.

11. See J. A. Mangan 1981, especially pp. 191–6; also, his book, *The Games Ethic and Imperialism: Aspects of the Diffusion of an Ideal* (Harmondsworth: Viking, 1986), covers much the same ground but also describes the extent to which that ethic permeated the Empire.

12. See John C. Hawley, 'Charles Kingsley and the Literary Theory of the 1850s', *Victorian Literature and Culture*, 19, (1991): 167–88.

Part II
Against the Grain

4

Ante-Anti-Semitism: George Eliot's *Impressions of Theophrastus Such*

Nancy Henry

For some time now, literary critics have addressed *Daniel Deronda* and the eighteenth chapter of *Impressions of Theophrastus Such* – 'The Modern Hep! Hep! Hep!' – as important treatments of anti-Semitism in Victorian culture.[1] But should it matter to us that George Eliot never used the term anti-Semitism? Does it make a difference to our description of these works that her attempt to identify and articulate the historical manifestations of Jew-hating came before their conceptual synthesis within a single category? The case of 'The Modern Hep!' suggests that the use of the now-current term 'anti-Semitism' is an obstacle to our interpretation of Eliot's writing about Jews in late nineteenth-century England, over-simplifying and distorting her historical understanding of how in-herited texts and habits combined to shape the national character of England, a character she thought was troubled by a history of irrational hatred.

When anti-Semitism made its appearance in 1879, the year before Eliot's death, it was as the self-designating term of German political agitator Wilhelm Marr's *Antisemiten-Liga*. Without doubt, Marr was capitalising on increasing hostility toward Jews in Germany, but his new term borrowed from a discourse of nineteenth-century ethno-logical theories, themselves evolved from philological inquiries into the origins of language. This new term only made sense within a framework of assumptions about differences between peoples whose ancestors spoke languages which were irreducible to one another. Such assumptions were bolstered by the philological and racial theories of Joseph Arthur Gobineau and Ernest Renan. The context within which Marr added 'anti' to the accepted category of Semite, transformed the philological sense of the word, making it clear that Jews only, not other Semitic peoples, were implicated in his political platform.

Anti-Semites in 1880 were not old-fashioned Jew-haters. They sought to isolate Jews from all other peoples according to differences that could not be baptised away. Marr's popular pamphlet, 'The Victory of Judaism over Germandom, Considered from a Non-Religious Point of View', which ran through numerous printings before he established his Anti-Semitic League, emphasised the secular and essential characteristics of the Jews he opposed. Followers of Marr called themselves 'anti-Semites' as an antiseptic replacement for the morally unthinkable identity 'Jew-hater'. My point is that in 1878, Eliot was not addressing the people who would become the anti-Semites of the early 1880s, the Jew-haters Hannah Arendt called 'crackpots in general and the lunatic fringe in particular' (Arendt 1951, x). *Impressions* was written one year before the accepted point of origination for the term anti-Semite in Germany and three years before its translation into the English language.[2] Eliot is investigating forms of behaviour that are culturally located and which have nothing to do with genetics and language groups. Her meaning is closer to the use of anti-Semitism given by the *Encyclopedia Judaica* (1978) as the accepted one today – 'all forms of hostility manifested toward the Jews throughout history'. But at the same time, her potential to conceive of the identity 'anti-Semite' was crucially different from what it would have been after the term began to change the forms and the language old-fashioned Jew-hating could take.

It is my contention, with conceptual historians such as Ian Hacking, that 'all intentional acts are acts under a description. Hence if new modes of description come into being, new possibilities for action come into being in consequence.'[3] This does not mean merely that once the term was printed, the concept we now call 'anti-Semitism' came into being. Rather, once the term existed, it came to describe something its invention helped to create. Hacking calls this interaction between word and concept 'dynamic nominalism' and from this principle he argues that 'numerous kinds of human beings and human acts come into being hand in hand with the invention of the categories labeling them' (Hacking 1986, 236). Eliot was not describing anti-Semites because people who identified with the set of beliefs implied by that term did not yet exist. However, her writing in 'The Modern Hep!' about the English legacy of ignorance, intolerance, and hatred of Jews, was preparatory to the eventual emergence of the current category anti-Semitism – part of what made such a concept possible. Still, it is crucial to remember that Eliot herself was not writing about anti-Semitism with the attendant pseudo-scientific baggage of the late 1870s, nor about the morally indicting, trans-historical anti-Semitism which lumps all hostility toward Jews into a single category. How then did she go about examining the relationship between past and present forms of Jew-hating, while insisting on the specificity of various historical moments? By what mechanism does she describe more than the contemporary political climate in Germany but less than all hostility manifested toward Jews throughout time?

The interplay of past and present is crucial to *Impressions*. Eliot's Theophrastus, narrator of 'The Modern Hep!', is a Victorian instantiation of his namesake, descended from but not reducible to the classical philosopher Theophrastus. The book as a whole requires readers to think about both continuity and discontinuity between classical Greek and Victorian culture, as well as between generations within England. The 'modern' Hep! Hep! Hep! suggests a similar comparison between the Crusades and contemporary England.[4] 'Anti-Semitism' imposes a late twentieth-century concept of Jew-hating as a pathology, or as a continuous evil, on to Eliot's balanced historical parallels. Current assumptions about anti-Semitism are evident in the *Encyclopedia Judaica*'s interpretation of the late-nineteenth-century political scene in Germany when 'anti-Semitism became an acceptable element in German political life to be manipulated at opportune moments by political leaders seeking popular lower-middle-class support'. In this view, anti-Semitism is something which exists and endures, waiting to be manipulated. To understand 'The Modern Hep!', we have to see how Eliot explored its imaginative force as an empowering image for nineteenth-century Jews.

The significance of 'The Modern Hep!' is complicated by its presumed meaning: 'Hierosolyma est perdita' – a cry to take back the Christian city from the 'infidels'. Eliot's 'Modern Hep!' is a specific historical example which resonates in the present because Eliot has chosen to revive it in order to lay the groundwork for Theophrastus's argument that the Jews should 'take back' Jerusalem, 'return' to the land, revive the ancient nation, and transform it into a modern nation-state. Theophrastus, like Eliot's character Mordecai, is aware that such a revival draws equally on the rhetoric and vision of ancient Jewish tradition and current nationalist movements. At this particular moment in time, the Jews deserve to reconjure their heroic past as other de-nationalised people – Greeks, Italians and Germans, for example – have done for the purpose of inspiring the present generation to strive for a national future.

In 'The Modern Hep!', Theophrastus announces his topic in the following way: 'To take only the subject of the Jews: it would be difficult to find a form of bad reasoning about them which has not been heard in conversation or been admitted to the dignity of print' (Eliot 1994, 134). This appeal to reason is followed by an attempt to describe various points of view which together constitute anti-Jewish thought: 'but the neglect of resemblances is a common property of dullness which unites all the various points of view – the prejudiced, the puerile, the spiteful, and the abysmally ignorant' (143). Theophrastus uses a multiplicity of terms to describe various ways of behaving which are distinct from each other. The rubric he suggests to name what we would today call 'anti-Semitism' is 'the neglect of resemblances'. The largeness of the category is important because 'the subject of the Jews' is one example, one impression of 'that grosser mental sloth which makes people dull to the most ordinary prompting of comparison …'. Once Theophrastus gets down to his subject, his examples are many and specific. Still, his contemporary readers had difficulty defining exactly what Eliot's subject was.

For example, the Jewish critic and scholar Joseph Jacobs, reviewing *Impressions* in *The Athenaeum* in 1879, is unable to evaluate 'The Modern Hep!' because of the inevitable comparison with *Daniel Deronda*. Remarking that the novel is 'more effective' than the essay, Jacobs writes:

> Ignorance of, and want of sympathy with, modern Judaism may blind the reader to the extraordinary power of Mordecai's orations, perhaps the greatest *tour de force* of their author; but any one can see how much more effective, even from an argumentative point of view, are the passionate utterances of the latest prophet than the calm reasoning of his creator. (Jacobs 1879, 720)

Jacobs assumes that *Deronda* fails because non-Jewish readers are unable to sympathise with Jewish characters. He also assumes a common project in *Deronda* and 'The Modern Hep!', approving the former as the right way to make the argument. But what is this argument? Is it against prejudice? For Jewish nationalism? In what sense can the novel be said to make an argument? Jacobs's language when he talks about the Jews is much less explicit and more euphemistic than the text he is reviewing. When he alludes to 'ignorance of and lack of sympathy with modern Judaism', he does not broach the hostility – the history of violence against Jews – which is the primary subject matter of 'The Modern Hep!'

It is understandable that Jacobs does not bring up anti-Jewish feelings when he speaks of *Deronda*. Mordecai's (not Eliot's) arguments aim to rationalise his desire for a Jewish national homeland; they are not based on his fear of persecution within England. It is crucial to the novel that its Anglo-Jewish hero, Daniel Deronda, should never be the object of ridicule or hatred, nor ever suffer restrictions on his life or career because of his Jewish parentage. His reasons for embarking on a Jewish nationalist mission are more noble than any need to escape prejudice or persecution: leaving England is something Daniel chooses to do, not something he is forced to do. In this respect, Jacobs is wrong to equate the 'arguments' of *Deronda* and *Impressions* and his conflation of the goals of the two works betrays the conceptual difficulty contemporary readers had with 'The Modern Hep!'. Its subject matter – acts against different communities of Jews at different times in different ways and in different places – had no single concept and no name.

The emphasis of 'The Modern Hep!' is different from that of *Deronda*. While frequently echoing the words of Mordecai and ultimately asserting the value of modern nationhood, Theophrastus lays out for his English audience a series of historical abuses against Jews which every Christian must acknowledge as part of the history and inheritance of Christianity. Anti-Jewish attitudes cannot be dismissed as 'ignorance' or mere 'lack of sympathy with' Jewish culture. The relationship between Jew-hatred over the centuries and the modern revival of a national centre is played out in a dynamic of similarities and differences between English Christians and Jews. The English bear responsibility for the actions of their nation and for the identity it has assumed: 'We do not call ourselves a dispersed and a punished people: we are a colonising people, and it is we who have punished others' (146). When Theophrastus confronts English readers with their own historical role as oppressors, he too occupies that position, identifying as part of the English 'we', admitting himself to be a perpetrator of 'the scourge' rather than one of its victims. His ideal is that English Christians at the very least learn to understand through their own exalted virtues of reason and fairness that other peoples, in many ways similar to them, do suffer as they never have.

When Jacobs complains about the ineffectiveness of calm reasoning in 'The Modern Hep!', he does not mention that it is the superstitious irrationality of Jew-hating which motivates Theophrastus to focus on 'forms of bad reasoning'. Jacobs does, however, make an important distinction between past and present that illuminates a characteristic way of thinking about Jews and Jew-haters in Victorian England. His opposition does not admit of a continuity between different forms of Judaism over time, nor of a continuity between variously expressed anti-Jewish attitudes in different historical epochs. When Eliot was writing *Impressions*, the medieval Crusades, the expulsion of Jews from Spain in 1492, the 1819 'Hep! Hep!' riots in Germany were easily viewed as events unrelated to general anti-Jewish sentiment in late Victorian England, and had not yet been linked in the ahistorical, trans-national category of anti-Semitism. It was impossible to be an anti-Semite, although it was possible to misunderstand, hate, and enact laws against Jews.

I mention Jacobs's 1879 *Athenaeum* review of *Impressions* partly because he was so involved in writing about Anglo-Jewish history and partly because the first instance of the word 'anti-Semite' in English occurs in the *Athenaeum* two years later. Its appearance is revealing of the way the moral weight of the concept evolved once the term was in place. Originating in German, translated into English, the word could be used by an English reviewer in a way that inevitably sounds odd to modern readers. In his article on the making and moulding of the category of child-abuse, Ian Hacking writes: 'A mere description, it is said, never implies by itself an evaluation. But it is not possible, in our times, to describe someone as a child abuser without thereby making a moral condemnation' (Hacking 1991, 259). The same can be said of 'anti-Semite'; it is used to accuse and condemn; it cannot be used neutrally. In 1881, the 'Library Table' section of the *Athenaeum*, mentions a German book on modern Jews:

But we are glad to mention that at last a serious book has appeared on the present condition of the Jews and their statistics by Herr Richard Andree, with the title *Zur Volkskunde der Juden* (Leipzig, Velhagen, und Klasing). The author, apparently an anti-

Semite, has honestly collected second-hand information concerning the Jews in all countries, which may be usefully consulted since the sources are indicated in the foot-notes. (Anon. 'Our Library Table', 305/2)

Crucially, in 1882, anti-Semitism had not yet acquired its tone of accusation and disapproval. This casual and seemingly uncritical reference in *The Athenaeum* to the author who is an anti-Semite appears in the context of a lament over the lack of scholarship on contemporary Judaism. The book by the anti-Semite is called 'serious', 'honest' and 'useful', qualities which today would not be attributed to something produced by someone condemned as an anti-Semite.

In the nineteenth century many terms were racialised on the authority of 'scientific' research. Like 'Aryan', the word 'Semitic' was coined by philologists to designate a language group sharing a common ancestor; but when Marr appropriated the term racialised by philologists such as such as Renan, Max Müller and Franz Bopp (mentioned by Theophrastus in Chapter XI of *Impressions*), its associations with language and the study of ancient cultures, as well as with other peoples who spoke the so-designated Semitic languages, gradually disappeared: 'What was originally a merely linguistic term soon became a ethnical designation based on the results of comparative philology' (Deutsch, *JE*, 1901). With the coining of anti-Semitism, the inferiority of racial groups within the Semitic language group was redeployed as an identity for those who blamed the Jews for the problems of German society in particular and European culture generally. With a pretence to scientific objectivity, the word continues to hold the ugly notion of Jew-hating at the distance its inventors intended. At the time of its invention, anti-Semitism served exclusively to describe how some contemporary Gentiles felt about contemporary Jews, rather than how Christians through the ages inherited and perpetrated a set of myths and distortions about Jews and Judaism. Anti-Semitism provided a scientific overlay to those 'points of view' Eliot's Theophrastus itemises in multiple and morally charged words – 'prejudiced', 'puerile', spiteful', 'abysmally ignorant'.

The first occurrence of the term 'anti-Semitism' (rather than 'anti-Semite') in English listed by the *OED* is again in *The Athenaeum*. A review of Volume 13 of the Ninth Edition of the *Encyclopaedia*

Britannica criticises the article on 'Israel' in light of the relationship between ignorance and racial prejudice:

> It is to be regretted that no special article has been devoted to the post-Biblical history of the Jews, a subject which attracts considerable interest in these days of anti-Semitism. A couple of contemptuous pages at the end of Prof. Wellhausen's article 'Jews, Modern,' can scarcely be said to be sufficient.[5]

Significantly, anti-Semitism appears here in an evaluation of how knowledge is organised and categorised – in this case into the rubrics 'Israel' and 'Jews, Modern' – within the framework of what the review calls 'this national work'. The *Encyclopaedia Britannica* is a useful indication of how the organisation of knowledge changed over time, of how new and influential categories were invented to account for emergent concepts. By the Eleventh Edition, the information contained under the heading 'Israel' had moved to the heading 'Jews', and a long new entry on 'Anti-Semitism' was introduced. In 1882, the reviewer of the Ninth Edition of the *Encyclopaedia Britannica* judged 'Jews, Modern' to be an insufficient category relative to the interests of the time. By the Eleventh Edition in 1910, an historicised concept of anti-Semitism had been accepted as the appropriate term within which to accommodate the reaction to nineteenth-century European changes affecting the state of European Jews.

This establishment of anti-Semitism in the British national catalogue of what is known acknowledged its existence and defined its parameters. This article 'Anti-Semitism' in the Eleventh Edition is written by the Jewish historian Lucien Wolf, who is careful to limit the concept in the following way:

> Anti-Semitism is then exclusively a question of European politics, and its origin is to be found, not in the long struggle between Europe and Asia, or between the Church and the Synagogue, which filled so much of ancient and medieval history, but in the social conditions resulting from the emancipation of the Jews in the middle of the nineteenth century.[6]

It is important to Wolf, himself a historian of Jewish culture, to insist on the historical specificity of the term. For Wolf and subsequent readers of the Eleventh Edition, 'Anti-Semitism' names a

contemporary political phenomenon. It helps to explain the consequences of emancipation; it is not a continuation of historic religious conflicts.[7] This particular circumscription of anti-Semitism to
modern European politics, not long after the invention of the word,
highlights the importance of distinguishing between what it was
possible to describe before and after its invention. While reference
books and more specialised histories can assign a date and place
for the coining of the term, most assume that the modern word is
naming a phenomenon that already existed.

Take, for example the 1994 *Encyclopedia Americana* entry on 'Anti-
Semitism,' in which the first sentence traces the term to Marr in
1879, but the next sentence reads: 'Anti-Semitism may be said to
have begun in the Diaspora, when the Jews were forced to leave
their homeland'. The author, Raphael Patai, leaps from the historical specificity of the term, to the historical sweep of the concept,
highlighting the disjunction between the initial and current use of
the term and also the impossibility of linguistically separating term
and concept. In his conceptual history of the concept of 'sexuality',
Arnold Davidson writes: 'It is this automatic and immediate application of concepts, as though concepts have no temporality, that
allows, and often requires, us to draw misleading analogies and inferences that derive from a historically inappropriate and conceptually untenable perspective' (Davidson 1987, 27). In the case of my
example, what is the significance of Marr and 1879? Why is it noted
at all? Is the invention of the word merely incidental to the history
of the phenomenon? The assumption seems to be that Marr simply
named something that already existed, and afterwards, everyone
realised the appropriateness of the name to what had hitherto been
known but unnamed. Clearly, the establishment of the word had its
own reflexive effect, did more than name, but actually shaped the
potential for performing acts against Jews and identifying as one
who does them. My question now becomes, if we accept that anti-
Semitism is an inappropriate and anachronistic term to describe
what George Eliot was writing about, how can our awareness of
the history of the term – its contemporaneous emergence alongside
Eliot's last work – help us to understand this pre-historical moment
in the attempt to address and evaluate a related cluster of anti-
Jewish practices and attitudes which we would now call 'anti-
Semitism'?

Like Wolf's definition of anti-Semitism, Jacobs's comments about
'The Modern Hep!' in his review of *Impressions* do not provide a

causal explanation, nor offer a common description of past and present persecution of Jews. If he sees a connection, he wishes to de-emphasise it in order to focus on the material conditions of the current problem, rather than displacing the responsibility for the present on to an ongoing, monolithic and mysterious historical force. I think it is safe to say that the leap, facilitated today by the concept anti-Semitism, was not possible through the use of that term at the time of its invention. What I am interested in is how Eliot faced the challenge of making connections without the benefit of a totalising concept. How did she go about tracking the historical manifestations of Jew-hating from the 'Hep! Hep! Hep!' of the Crusades to the contemptuousness, even of prominent Victorian scholars of Semitic languages and biblical history, like Professor Wellhausen or Renan? Eliot, in *Impressions*, follows the prejudice against Jews through history, and this trajectory culminates in 'The Modern Hep! Hep! Hep!', which itself traces anti-Jewish attitudes to a point well before the Crusades.

Recalling that the apostles Matthew and Paul were Jews and, after their conversions, concerned themselves with speaking to Jews, Theophrastus uses the origin of Christianity as a point from which to survey anti-Jewish attitudes from pre-Christian Rome to the present:

> Modern apostles, extolling Christianity, are found using a different tone: they prefer the mediæval cry translated into modern phrase. But the mediæval cry too was in substance very ancient – more ancient than the days of Augustus. Pagans in successive ages said, 'These people are unlike us, and refuse to be made like us: let us punish them'. (164)

The medieval cry is of course 'Hep! Hep! Hep!', and the title of Eliot's essay connects Hebrews, Israelites, and modern Jews, as do other intimations of modern reincarnations invoked in the essay, like 'some new Ezras, some modern Macabees' (163). 'These people are unlike us – and refuse to be made like us' is a formula which establishes the oppositions of insider and outsider, us and them, and assumes the absolute good of conversion and assimilation.[8] Theophrastus views himself as the 'ugly unready man in the corner, outside the current of conversation', and what he attempts to achieve is the simultaneous views of the insider looking out and an outsider looking in. His ability to change, to make a different impression or cut a different figure according to his situation, is one of the characteristics which associates Theophrastus with modern Jews, whose ability to assimilate (that is, 'become like us') was both desirable and threatening to nineteenth-century English Christians. Jews were assimilated all over Europe, many so thoroughly accul-turated to the nation in which they lived, as to be indistinguishable from the 'real' nationals. This type of mixing and invisibility pro-duced suspicions which are well-documented in literature, for example in Trollope's *The Prime Minister* and *The Way We Live Now*, or in Eliot's presentation of local gossip about the suspected Jewishness of Will Ladislaw or Julius Klesmer.

Impressions has always been read as a disjointed set of unrelated essays, and the suspicion that an essay on the Jews does not belong in a book of essays-about English society has contributed to this misperception. For example, an 1879 *Saturday Review* article was one of the earliest evaluations which set the pattern for future read-ings of *Theophrastus*:

> The concluding paper, 'the Modern Hep Hep Hep,' asking why the Jews are not more popular than they are, opens a very wide speculation, taking the reader at unawares, and making a very sudden demand on his attention. The Jews, their history, their character, their standing in the world, their intellectual power, suggest no doubt questions of great interest and importance; but we are not prepared to answer these questions at the fag-end of a book avowedly devoted to other things, with which they bear no possible relation. The reader cannot at a moment's notice get up an interest in the Jews, and only wonders why the author takes them up, and why he has to read about them in connexion with such very alien matter. (Anon., *The Saturday Review*, 806)

Again, we see the difficulty another modern reader had with saying what 'The Modern Hep!' is about. In this case, 'why the Jews are not more popular than they are', is a particularly weak and unsym-pathetic attempt to name it. But the most important misreading here is in the perceived disjunction, disconnectedness of Eliot's book. The previous 17 chapters of *Impressions* are not devoted to 'other things' which bear no possible relation to the Jews, nor is the history of the Jews 'alien matter' to the rest of the book. The dynamic between insider and outsider, epitomised in the socially marginal English Gentile Theophrastus, is the book's primary unifying force. 'The Modern Hep!' is not an isolated essay on the Jews. Its direct confrontation of the parallels and intersections of English and Jewish histories functions as the finale to the leitmotif of Jews and other outsiders – like Merman or Mixtus – within English culture which links the previous 17 chapters.

In considering the persistence of the anti-Jewish 'Hep! Hep!' mentality, I want to note that in the first chapter of *Impressions* Eliot's Theophrastus presents himself as a kind of time-traveller whose simultaneous existence in Ancient Athens and Victorian London and whose encounters with literary and historical characters from various centuries, like Glycera, Laura, Clarissa, Ganymede, Pepin, to name a few, are never explained. Among these characters are names which ring unmistakably in a history of Jewish–Christian relationships in which Jews have been either abused or, through the process of conversion, erased. New Testament names like Barabbas and Apollos are included in those Theophrastus gives to his acquaintances. One of these encounters, early in the first chapter, called 'Looking Inward', places Theophrastus unambiguously, if obscurely, in the position of the Jews who, according to Church doctrine, have only themselves to blame for the miseries they suffer. Theophrastus says:

> Though continually in society, and caring about the joys and sorrows of my neighbors, I feel myself, so far as my personal lot is concerned, uncared for and alone. 'Your own fault, my dear fellow!' said Minutius Felix, one day that I had incautiously mentioned this uninteresting fact. (6)

There is no explanation in Eliot's text for this singular appearance by Minutius Felix, but for those who have read the Latin dialogue *Octavius* by the early Christian apologist and Church Father, Minutius Felix, the words carry only one meaning. 'The Jews have themselves to blame', is the refrain of the pro-Christian advocate Octavius and the summary of Christian attitudes toward Jews (falling in estimate even below superstitious pagans) in this once-influential text.[9] Minutius Felix is merely one illustration of how *Impressions* is coded with the textual history of Christian hatred of Jews. I say 'coded' because in order to see it, a reader must know intimately the texts with which Theophrastus has stocked his intellectual armoury.

But what is the point? Why is *Impressions* so allusive, so learned, so off-putting to readers? In struggling to understand Theophrastus, a reader is always uncertain whether allusions have been caught, whether he or she has been in on a joke, or is somehow the butt of one. Theophrastus is something of a border guard, checking for passports and thereby effecting the following reversal. An English 'anti-Judaic advocate', ignorant of his or her own culture, becomes potentially like a Jew in England – actively excluded from English culture. But in that awkward feeling of exclusion, a reader can also identify with Theophrastus, who feels himself an outsider to English society. In contrast, a 'really cultured man or woman' could feel welcomed into an elite community of those who have read Minutius Felix, Athenaeus, Sappho, Pliny, La Bruyère, Dr Johnson, Wordsworth, Bulwer Lytton, Darwin – the list goes on to encompass the works of George Henry Lewes and George Eliot. In other words, a reader might, as Theophrastus puts it in 'How We Encourage Research', 'laugh the laugh of the initiated' (33). This strategy of studding the text with intellectual shibboleths that work for and against inclusion, is one of the distinguishing characteristics of *Impressions*.

Enigmatic as some of these allusions may be without the history of anti-Jewish rhetoric in mind, what we do know of Theophrastus gives us reason to discern some similarities between him and those modern Jews whose cosmopolitanism or separateness provided the foundation for technically anti-Semitic objections. He is a middle-aged London bachelor – unloved, unpublished, unattractive, urbanised, exiled, bookish and clever. In addition to these modern characteristics which make him feel as much of an outsider in English society as if he were a Jew, he is also, through his name and the form of his book, the representative of a genre of writing – the Theophrastan character-sketch – which has itself undergone a series of transmutations and reformulations since the third century BC.[10] It is because of his role as the personification of a textual tradition that these meetings with figures from other texts makes sense.

The historical perspective of *Impressions* establishes a parallel between the transmission of a textual tradition and the transmission of negative stereotypes about Jews; both kinds of tradition combine in the mix of inheritances which make up English national culture. There is no single term, at least Eliot does not use one, for either of these forms of transmission. Although we are constantly aware of his presence, Theophrastus himself is not named in the text. What is he after all, but the diverse and contradictory impressions he makes on the characters he meets and on the readers who read him? Whether he is identifying as an insider or an outsider depends upon the character with whom he is interacting. Similarly, how are we to understand the current concept anti-Semitism, except as the particularised expression of an irrational hostility toward Jews, in conjunction with the traditions of the specific national culture, at a given historical moment?

It is likely that George Eliot never heard the word anti-Semitism and if she did, she would not have equated it with the social ill she wished to address. In 'The Modern Hep!', she is able to connect past and present hostility toward Jews without relying on a single, trans-historical concept that threatens to decontextualise atrocities grounded in particular historical conditions. What we call 'anti-Semitism' can only be recognised by its characteristic manifestations, and events which took place in the past are recorded in texts which become part of England's living present. Theophrastus carries with him all of the traces of his own translations from Ancient Athens to Victorian London. He is uniquely qualified to recognise the medieval cry, 'Hep! Hep! Hep!' translated into the modern phrase 'I never did like the Jews'.

Impressions anticipates the current usage of the term 'anti-Semitism'. But Eliot's text is characteristically ambivalent, and resists reduction to any single-term description. It is anachronistic and reductive to say that 'The Modern Hep!' is an essay about anti-Semitism. George Eliot, like her character Theophrastus, emerges through a multiplicity of textual impressions. One of these impressions is that of George Eliot, through Theophrastus, making the conceptual association between the violence of the Crusades and the narrow-mindedness of her contemporaries, even before an acceleration of violence in the 1880s marked a painful realisation of the new anti-Semitic rhetoric. George Eliot linked past and present, but preserved the historical specificity that enabled Victorians to recognise themselves as the criers of the modern 'Hep! Hep! Hep!'.

Notes

1. Recent examples include: Bernard Semmel, *George Eliot and the Politics of National Inheritance* (New York: Oxford University Press, 1994). Semmel calls 'The Modern Hep!' 'an essay attacking what she saw as

the persistence, in altered guise, of medieval anti-Semitism' (129). Susan Meyer, '"Safely to their own Borders": Proto-Zionism, Feminism, and Nationalism in *Daniel Deronda'. English Literary History* 60 (1993): 733–58. Meyer actually accuses Eliot herself of being an anti-Semite. Michael Ragussis, 'Representation, Conversion, and Literary Form: *Harrington* and the Novel of Jewish Identity'. *Critical Inquiry* 16 (Autumn 1989): 113–43.

2. Most of *Impressions* was written in the summer months of 1878, but owing to the death of George Henry Lewes, Eliot had its publication postponed until May 1879. The *Jewish Encyclopedia* (1902) calls the July 30th elections in Germany the 'birthday of anti-Semitism'. It also notes: 'So far as can be ascertained, the word was first printed in 1880', citing Marr's, *Zwanglose Antisemitische Hefte*, 1880. Other sources put the date at 1879.

3. See for example, Ian Hacking, 'Making Up People', in *Reconstructing Individualism*, eds. Thomas C. Heller, Morton Sosna, and David E. Wellbery (Stanford: Stanford University Press, 1986, 222–36), p. 231, and 'The Making and Molding of Child Abuse', *Critical Inquiry* 17 (Winter 1991), 253–88. See also Arnold I. Davidson, 'Sex and the Emergence of Sexuality', *Critical Inquiry* 14 (Autumn 1987), 16–48.

4. In a meditation on the workings of historical imagination, the narrator of *Daniel Deronda* conjures 'the scenery of St Mary Axe and Whitechapel imaginatively transported to the borders of the Rhine at the end of the eleventh century, when in the ears listening for the signals of the Messiah, the Hep! Hep! Hep! of the Crusaders came like the bay of bloodhounds ...'. George Eliot, *Daniel Deronda*, ed. Graham Handley (Oxford: Clarendon Press, 1984), p. 321. The passage asks how the ability to visualise the historic past of the Jews might change the way a visitor sees the 'dingy shops and unbeautiful faces' of the present.

5. In his review of *Impressions*, Jacobs never mistakes Mordecai's or Daniel's point of view for Eliot's, but when he refers to the voice of 'The Modern Hep', he refers to 'Mordecai's creator'. Like other contemporary reviewers, he fails to recognise that the voice is not exposing a spectrum of Anglo-Christian hypocrisies but rather that of her character Theophrastus (*The Athenaeum* [11 February, 1882]: 184/1).

6. See Lucian Wolf, *Encyclopaedia Britannica* (11th edn, 1910–11, Vol. 2).

7. It is worth noting that Wolf and Jacobs collaborated to write the catalogue for the 'Anglo-Jewish Historical Exhibition' in London (Royal Albert Hall, April–June, 1887).

8. The formula itself is probably a paraphrase of Haman's injunction in The Book of Esther: 'There is a certain people scattered abroad and dispersed among the people in all the provinces of thy kingdom; and their laws are diverse from all people; neither keep they the King's laws; therefore it is not for the King's profit to suffer them' (Esther 3:8). This, like the 'some new Ezras' connects 'The Modern Hep!' to *Daniel Deronda* by invoking the character Mordecai Ezra.

9. See *The Octavius of Marcus Minucius Felix*, trans. G. W. Clarke (New York: Newman Press, 1974), 33: 114.

10. The Theophrastan character-sketch describes 'types' observed by the author in contemporary society. Traditionally, following Theophrastus, each character is meant to illustrate a particular negative form of behaviour.

5

Tennyson and the Poetic Forms of Resistance

Claire M. Berardini

Throughout the nineteenth century, and thus throughout Tennyson's career, questions of individual agency governed the real daily lives of individual people and the social structure of England itself. Tennyson's poetic maturation after Hallam's death, his supposed anti-Romanticism and his laureateship have become tenets in the criticism of his poetry, and these in turn continue to uphold his reputation among contemporary readers as a pre-eminent arch-Victorian whose political conservatism surfaces in various forms of nationalistic sentiment and anti-individualism.[1] But it is not entirely clear that Tennyson abandons his interest in the individual in the ways that we have come to expect from England's state poet. Tennyson responds to the question of individualism by attempting to dispel the purely hierarchical relationship between society and the individual as it develops in the nineteenth century, developing poetic forms which express a more dynamic and thus more complex vision of the individual's social experience.[2] This is not to take a radical approach to Tennyson by relocating him on the side of militant individualism; many of Tennyson's poems situate the individual within broader social structures in ways which qualify or limit the individual's claim to anything like epistemological privilege. Rather, it is to take more fully into account the ways in which Tennyson's career intervenes with the increasingly problematic nature of individual agency in the nineteenth century.[3] The case can be made that what concerns Tennyson as 'the poet of his age' is the question of how individual subjectivities are formed and how individual subjects act upon the structures which form them.

Tennyson's poetry approaches the question of agency in ways that, in the wake of various poststructuralist theories of agency, are much more sophisticated than traditional readings of his career would allow. Structuralist theory in general, and specifically the antihumanist Marxism of Louis Althusser, subordinates the individual to the structural forces that surround it. When Althusser claims that human consciousness is embedded in social structure, he renders awareness and even self-awareness as illusory ideas created by ideology. As he claims that people exist in an 'imaginary relation to their real conditions of existence', Althusser forecloses on the possibility that individuals can possess agency by the fact of their singular, lived experiences (Adams and Searle 1986, 242). Given Althusser's argument that individuals are 'subjects' because they are never outside ideology, the problem for advancing a theory of human agency has become: how can we account for, or assert, agency without falling victim to charges of a naive humanism?[4] Often, the strategies for validating claims to agency have asserted the individual's lived, day-to-day experience or his or her ability to understand and be critical of his or her social circumstances, but these strategies are often criticised because they too little emphasise the reality and power of structure. Thus, a successful theory of human agency in the wake of Althusser, one that accounts for the lived experience of individual people, requires a new theory of structure. Poststructuralism, aided by Derrida's notion of the 'structuring of structure' – that is, the idea that structure is not a fixed or static entity but rather the site of internal play – has helped theorists in the project of theorising human agency. Notably, Anthony Giddens' theory of 'the duality of structure' employs the Derridean notion of play in the service of a theory which claims that structures, while they make up the conditions in which individuals live, are also acted upon by human agents (Giddens 1979, 61). This concept of play allows him to dehierarchise the opposition between individual and structure, and argue instead for a mutually constitutive relationship between structure and the singular lives of individuals.[5]

It is through his prolific experimentation with poetic form, and particularly in the evolution of the lyric into the dramatic monologue, that Tennyson imagines the capacity of individuals to act on the structures that otherwise seek to contain them as a paradigm for human agency. While Tennyson believes that external conditions or social structures determine subjects, his formal projects suggest that he does not accept the idea that individuals are utterly subjected by external structural forces. Tennyson's early lyric poems (1830–32) and the various states of imprisoned and introverted consciousness that they figure/investigate seem to be written against the dominant political desire to subordinate individual consciousness to social structure in order to preserve social cohesion. Although early poems such as 'Ode to Memory', 'Recollections of the Arabian Nights', 'Mariana', 'The Lady of Shalott', and 'The Lotos-Eaters' often extend the Romantic poets' interest in individual states of mind (an interest that led Tennyson's early reviewers to charge him with self-indulgent Romanticism), they also often situate individual consciousness in relation to some external presence. It is this admission of the individual's situatedness that allows Tennyson to investigate the possibility of human agency in the context of political and ideological structures. This agency is measured particularly in the degree to which the individual impacts upon the structure meant to confine or annihilate it, or in the recognisable ways in which the structure fails in its capacity to control.

Without exception, Tennyson's 1830 poem 'Mariana' has been classified as a lyric poem because it represents a single human consciousness and a single individual's pain and despair; because this pain and despair belong to Mariana, critical focus has remained almost exclusively on her. Consonant with the assumption that lyric represents a singular experience, that is, an experience not directly interfered with by social forces, is the notion that lyric poetry represents a kind of unmediated interiority. One problem with these assumptions is that they reduce the poem to an exercise in representing states of mind and/or emotion, an experiment that helps to perpetuate notions of Tennyson's immature, solipsistic Romanticism.[6] The problem, in turn, with this reading is that it obscures the relationship as Tennyson constructs it between the individual and the structures he or she inhabits. This second problem has led to a central misreading of the poem: the identification of Mariana as the poem's single concern and the subsequent dismissal of the poem's narrator.[7] Although this misreading is guided by the poem's intense interest in Mariana, it must be noted that the poem insists upon the presence of two distinct consciousnesses. This dual consciousness, or the admission of the poem's second external perspective in a poetic form which typically strives to represent only a single interiority, is not necessarily at home in a lyric poem as we conventionally understand the genre. In 'Mariana', lyric space is infiltrated by another presence, and this infiltration of traditional lyric space suggests Tennyson's awareness that the individual is always situated and thus never (as the conventional myth of lyric suggests) beyond social structure. In this way, Tennyson extends the boundaries of lyric, and this manipulation of conventional lyric modes of self-representation services his investigation of individual agency.

Undeniably, Mariana's presence in the poem is a compelling one. But her despair and psychic detachment are most intriguing and most helpful in scrutinising the broader binary opposition between structure and individual that Tennyson establishes and then dismantles. Tennyson constructs the relationship between Mariana and the narrator according to the practices of an organising external perspective, that is, according to the practices by which individuals are objectified within the operations of the structures they occupy:

> With blackest moss the flower-pots
>   Were thickly crusted, one and all:
> The rusted nails fell from the knots
>   That held the pear to the gable-wall.
> The broken sheds looked sad and strange:
>   Unlifted was the clinking latch:
> Weeded and worn the ancient thatch
>   Upon the lonely moated grange.
>   She only said, 'My life is dreary,
>   He cometh not,' she said;
>   She said, 'I am aweary, aweary,
>   I would that I were dead!'
>   (ll. 1–12)[8]

For most readers, the interest in this first passage typically extends no further than Tennyson's skill in transforming a landscape according to human emotion, in this case, Mariana's.[9] But this approach to the text remains unconvincing, for it does not take into account the unmistakable presence of the two consciousnesses at work here. Moreover, Mariana seems so little aware of the details of her immediate surroundings as to make this conclusion impossible.[10] The pathetic fallacy at l. 5 – 'the broken sheds looked sad and strange' – reveals the presence of an emotive and projective consciousness in the poem, but that consciousness belongs to the narrator rather than to Mariana. Tennyson is careful to establish a clear difference between the narrator's keen awareness of this neglected landscape and Mariana's detached misery. Moreover, the estimated measurement between the garden wall and the marsh in stanza four – 'about a stone cast from the wall' (l. 37) – is a crucial moment in the poem, for it is a moment in which the speaker identifies the presence of his own actively calculating imagination. For, just as the verb 'looked' in line 5 asks the reader to think of the person to whom the sheds appear sad and strange, the stone's throw, as a unit of measure, depends upon an agent, that is, the person who would throw the stone. The self-referential nature of the measurement forces the reader to consider the speaker's material reality, or the fact that the descriptive voice belongs to a material body and a consciousness that locates itself in the scene it observes.

The poem might better be described as a mediated lyric, a lyric whose emotional and psychic content belongs not to the person who is speaking, but to another. The narrator, who organises or mediates Mariana's consciousness, essentially identifies narrative position as the site of meaning. The narrator's function, which is primarily to objectify the consciousness with which he shares the poem, is accomplished through surveillance. In Foucault's analysis of social structure, the gaze is a function of power, for 'it is the fact of being constantly seen, of being always able to be seen, that maintains the disciplined individual in his subjection' (Rabinow 1984, 199). In this way, the grange becomes for the poem's narrator a 'domain of knowledge' (Rabinow 1984, 175). It is within this domain that Mariana as a separate, independent individual is transformed into an object. Thus, one way that the poem orders the relationship between individual and structure is to establish a visual hierarchy, to conduct, in other words, what Foucault refers to as 'a ceremony of objectification' (Rabinow 1984, 199). The poem's narrative process demonstrates the procedure of Althusser's structuralism generally; that is, the poem's narrative structure demonstrates the process by which the individual is given meaning, or objectified, by its structural reality.

Even though the intense emotional focus of the poem seems highly, if not hyper-personalised, given the way it situates Mariana in this field of surveillance, the poem suggests Tennyson's concerns about the reaches of a determining external authority and the ways in which poetic form may 1) represent that authority and 2) frustrate it. For the poem does insist that we also recognise Mariana's personal experience, that is, her abandonment and despair, despite the narrator's spectatorial intervention in that experience. At the same time, then, that we acknowledge Tennyson's formal display of the reaches of structure, we need to acknowledge his formal investigation of the individual's capacity to resist that structure. For Mariana's consciousness itself, her passive despair and her near-total silence, not only facilitate but mediate the speaker's steady visual intervention. In other words, at the same time that her reticence allows the narrator to dominate the poem visually and verbally, it also figures a form of non-engagement that signals a moment of resistance against his otherwise determining gaze. Totally available to the narrator's visual scrutiny, Mariana does nothing to suggest that the surveillance affects her at all. In other words, Tennyson's calculated representation of Mariana's total disengagement frustrates the narrative's desire to subordinate the individual to its own procedures. The gaze as Tennyson imagines it in 'Mariana' is not as seamless as the surveying gaze of Foucault's panopticism suggests. Mariana's sustained remoteness enacts the failure of the gaze to encompass its object, a failure that Tennyson dramatises by humanising and individualising the otherwise ubiquitous and anonymous panoptic gaze. Mariana does not submit to this external structure; she is so overcome by her own loss and in her own longing for her lover's presence – that is, by her own singular experience – that this experience neutralises the energy of the structure and holds it off as a simultaneous, but separate phenomenon rather than an encompassing or determining one. By implementing the refrain as part of its form, the poem plays out structurally the larger problem of positionality that Tennyson investigates through the relationship between the individual and external structure. Although the refrain is modified from stanza to stanza, the adverb 'only' is repeated throughout. As a modifier, 'only' simply quantifies Mariana's verbal reaction to her own experience. But, because the refrain itself is always positioned against the speaker's impressions of the grange and everything in it, 'only' also becomes positional, disconnecting the refrain and Mariana's sense of her own experience from the organising structure represented in the descriptive narrative of the lines before. Thus the narrative, which seems to behave to some degree as an uncontested source of meaning regarding the object of its narrator's gaze, is frustrated by its own reliance on the refrain, suggesting in turn that the structure is unable to account for Mariana's experience and is therefore inadequate, limited, disabled.

The poem's speaker seems to represent the kind of organising, external authority identified in contemporary theories of structure. Why, then, does Tennyson both shape and defy this noted authority? I think because he is attempting to represent an individual who is both subjected and not, who remains totally remote while in the presence of a determining gaze and who is thus both within and beyond its reach. Tennyson successfully equalises the status of both the individual and structure, and in doing so, deconstructs the hierarchy which in structuralism orders the binary relationship between self and society in favour of a determining structure. It is in this way that he puts structure into play, and that the lyric becomes an apparatus for deconstructing the opposition between structure and individual. One way finally to see how 'Mariana' deconstructs the binary is to see that the poem entertains a surplus of presence. To say this in formal terms, although the poem operates without a genuine admission of self, without the pronounced singular 'I' that generally inhabits lyric poems, the poem entertains two subjects, preserving the integrity of each so that what would be a hierarchy is transformed into a play of difference.

Although passive, Mariana's psychic remoteness acts as a kind of resistance against the determining force of the poem's narrative impulses. In his work in the field of education theory, Henry Giroux argues that resistance allows individuals to act upon the structures they inhabit; that resistance, in other words, is what prevents structure from completely foreclosing on the possibility of human agency (1983, 107). Giroux's theory of resistance stakes important ground for the possibility of agency. It is the idea of resistance which guides Giddens' more deconstructive analysis of power. Giddens argues that 'however wide the asymmetrical distribution of resources involved, all power relations manifest autonomy and dependence "in both directions".' He goes on to say that 'in all cases in which human agency is exercised within a relationship of any kind – power relations are two way' (1979, 149). Giddens identifies this reciprocity as the 'dialectic of control', and claims that 'an agent who does not participate in the dialectic of control, in a minimal fashion, ceases to be an agent' (1979, 149). Although Foucault is widely regarded as a structuralist, in an essay titled 'The Subject and Power', he, like Giddens, locates power in a mutually constitutive relation to human agency. I quote the following passage at some length to show the ways in which Foucault echoes and extends Giddens' theory of the dialectics of control:

power relations are rooted deep in the social nexus, not reconstituted 'above' society as a supplementary structure whose radical effacement one could perhaps dream of.... But most important is obviously the relationship between power relations and confrontation strategies. For, if it is true that at the heart of power relations and as a permanent condition of their existence there is an insubordination and a certain essential obstinacy on the part of the principles of freedom, then there is no relationship of power without the means of escape or possible flight. Every power relationship implies, at least *in potentia*, a strategy of struggle, in which the two forces are not superimposed, do not lose their specific nature, or do not finally become confused. Each constitutes for the other a kind of permanent limit, a point of possible reversal...it would not be possible for power relations to exist without points of insubordination which, by definition, are means of escape. Accordingly, every intensification, every extension of power relations to make the insubordinate submit can only result in the limits of power. The latter reaches its final term either in a type of action which reduces the other to total impotence (in which case the victory over the adversary replaces the exercise of power) or by a confrontation with those whom one governs and their transformation into adversaries. (1984, 431)

Foucault identifies resistance, or 'insubordination' as the locus of the dialectic between human agency and power. By arguing that power and resistance not only constitute the limits of each other, but also the potential point of the other's reversal, Foucault abandons the more strictly oppositional relationship between power and the individual that defines much of his earlier writing. It is the openness of structure to insubordination, as well as the notion of reversal, that Tennyson explores as he transforms the lyric's version of passive resistance into the dramatic monologue's more defined and forceful version of revolt.

Tennyson's interest in human agency proposes a denser field of inquiry for the dramatic monologue than do more traditional themes of anti-Romanticism and mature Victorian social-mindedness. Tennyson's careful development of an organising structure within the lyric space of 'Mariana' may be seen as a precursor of the dramatic monologue, one that helps the dramatic monologue to realise its formal potential to represent a more historically specific and socially recognisable structure, and thus a more openly militant version of resistance. Because its fiction of materially present bodies in direct verbal and visual encounter admits a more defined social interaction than the disengagement we witness in 'Mariana', the dramatic monologue is ideally suited for the staging of individual resistance. In the dramatic monologue, Tennyson can reformulate the psychic remoteness that in 'Mariana' holds the poem's supposed authority in check as a more active and aggressive resistance to an exteriority defined as overtly social. Speech and audition become the form's sites for investigating the relational nature of structure and individual agency, and it is the manipulation of these sites that provides Tennyson with the means of measuring both the individual's ability to resist and the vulnerability of structure to that resistance.

In his 1880 dramatic monologue 'Rizpah', Tennyson recontextualises the Biblical story of Rizpah in order to situate personal experience, in this case maternal grief, within a society structured by its various institutions: the law, ethics, Christianity, justice.[11] The two central aspects of Rizpah's experience prior to her encounter with the charity worker – her son Willy's public execution and her own subsequent incarceration in the insane asylum – provide a particularly dense backdrop for the encounter itself. These experiences, as well as the present experience of the encounter itself, situate Rizpah within an encompassing political/social structure that polices and disciplines its individual members. Moreover, on each of these three levels of experience, surveillance operates in some form as a central structural mechanism. In the case of her son's public execution, the criminal who is caught under the watchful eye of legal apparatus becomes the object of the public's compulsory gaze. The public execution demonstrates the workings of penal justice made available for scrutiny, and thus demonstrates coercion not only in the service of individual punishment, but in the service of subordinating other individuals to the structures they inhabit. Foucault suggests the latter of these when he asserts in *Discipline and Punish* that the execution of a criminal requires above all an audience; there is, he claims, no effect without an audience. The object of the execution, in other words, is not the body of the criminal, 'but the minds of those who watch' (Foucault 1977, 94–5).

Surveillance also services the maintenance of ideologically recognised and therefore licit forms of mental experience and behaviour. In the insane asylum, surveillance is linked to other forms of control, specifically the use of violence. Rizpah describes the violent practices of the madhouse:

> Then since I couldn't but hear that cry of my boy that
>   was dead,
> They seized me and shut me up: they fasten'd me down on
>   my bed,
> 'Mother, O mother!' – he called in the dark to me year
>   after year –
> They beat me for that, they beat me – you know that I
>   couldn't but hear;
> And then at the last they found that I had grown so stupid
>   and still
> They let me abroad again – but the creatures had worked
>   their will.
>
> (ll. 54–60)[12]

Although Rizpah's madness has been a dominant point of critical interest, it also serves Tennyson's purpose in dramatising the dominance of structure over individuals.[13] The voice of her dead son is socially unrecognisable and can only be eliminated by disciplining what the apparatuses of the social structure can reach: the body. Tennyson's representation of institutional violence anticipates, with great accuracy, Foucault's description of the ideological function of pre-modern incarceration, both for mental illness and for penal transgression. The body becomes the material locale for this institutional exercise of power, which works to make the body a 'subjected body' (Rabinow 1984, 172). While surveillance may be difficult to detect by those under scrutiny, physical discipline is a blatant form of coercion, one that results in increased domination (Rabinow 1984, 182). Rizpah remains under constant surveillance and continual physical restraint until she can be recognised by her silence as a sane, docile, subjected individual.

Her son's public execution and her own experience as the object of institutional surveillance and restraint display a clear disparity in power between the individual and social structure. Importantly, both of these versions of discipline implicate the form's own fiction of public spectacle – that is, its visual as well as auditory relationship between speaker and internal auditor – in the larger question of the individual's relationship to the structure it inhabits. Once the object of constant institutional watch, Rizpah, as the speaker of the monologue, now finds herself confronted with another audience. But Rizpah does not know initially that there is an auditor present. When the poem begins, Rizpah is talking to Willy, not the charity worker. Because the charity worker does not make her presence known immediately, the overtly disciplinary surveillance that Rizpah experiences in the madhouse is played out in the poem's fiction of unauthorised hearing/overhearing and visual scrutiny. In the case of 'Rizpah', the visual and sonic fields which normally help to constitute the speaker/auditor relationship in the dramatic monologue no longer supply a neutral verbal space, but a kind of microstructure supported by the mechanism of disciplinary surveillance. Specifically afraid that the charity worker has come 'to spy' on her, Rizpah associates the auditor, and Christian charity generally, with the larger disciplinary structures that effectively constitute her own experience prior to the interaction between the two women. Startled when she realises that the charity worker is present, Rizpah attempts to conceal what she has unwittingly and unwillingly disclosed in order to counteract the scrutiny to which her identity as the speaker of a dramatic monologue subjects her:

> Anything fallen again? nay – what was there left to
>   fall?
> I have taken them home, I have numbered the bones,
>   I have hidden them all.
> What am I saying? And what are you? do you come as
>   a spy?
> Falls? what falls? who knows? As the tree falls so
>   must it lie.
> Who let her in? how long has she been? you – what have
>   you heard?
> Why did you sit so quiet? you never have spoken a
>   word.
>
> (ll. 9–14)

The auditor's undisclosed entrance into the poem is a version of silent, or 'discreet' surveillance that Rizpah discovers only after she has begun speaking in what she believes is the privacy of her home.[14] The auditor's generic role as silent auditor, then, replicates to an uncanny degree the silent workings of social structure. Rizpah's suspicions about the charity worker position the poem's speaker and auditor in confrontation rather than in the more cooperative relationship between speech and audition that the dramatic monologue normally relies upon. In fact, this initial encounter between Rizpah and the auditor is a particularly antagonistic moment for any dramatic monologue. The poem's auditor, by virtue of her presence, violates its speaker, and this violation strongly challenges the dramatic monologue's own formal identity with the contradiction of an unwanted auditor.

Rizpah's initial mistrust of the charity worker reflects her fear and suspicion of the legal and moral ideologies which not only condemned her son to death, but which have constructed her own psychic and verbal responses to his death as illicit. But although her first impulse is to suspect the charity worker, Rizpah ultimately retains her, saying 'Nay, for it is kind of you madam to sit by an old dying wife'. Rizpah relinquishes the adversarial role which she initially assumes, and when she accepts the charity worker she essentially permits the surveillance, both visual and sonic, that the presence of an auditor will subject her to. Rizpah signals her choice to engage her auditor willingly with a rhetoric of self-correction, and her choice, then, reminds us of her more violent experience of enforced, institutionalised self-correction. But, and this ultimately is the point, this apologetic capitulation paradoxically offers her instead the possibility of actively resisting both her auditor and the disciplining and controlling structure that the auditor's presence replicates. It is the act of capitulation through which the form initiates what Giddens calls a 'dialectics of control', and which makes the point of reversal to which Foucault refers possible. The verbally one-sided nature of the form allows Rizpah to situate herself within the form's hierarchy of speech and audition in order to defy the auditory and visual scrutiny that makes her experience public rather than private and that makes the poem dramatic rather than lyric. In other words, by situating herself within the monologue rather than outside it, she can openly militate against both formal and institutional forms of control by asserting her own singular experience over other narratives that have been constructed to explain the events of Willy's crime and execution:

Heard have you? what? they have told you he never repented
    his sin.
How do they know it? are they his mother? are you of his
    kin?
Heard! have you ever heard, when the storm on the downs

began,
The wind that'll wail like a child and the sea that'll
   moan like a man?

(ll. 69–72)

For Rizpah, the dramatic monologue becomes a place from which
to contest other voices, voices which if not representative of law
and morality, are at least recognised as licit within the dominant
culture. She rejects the social narratives that reconstitute her own
individual lived experience as socially rather than personally meaningful, and subjects the charity worker to the similes which make
meaning of her own hallucinatory, and thus highly privatised auditory experience. In doing so, she claims the social encounter of the
dramatic monologue as personal space and positions this space
against the surrounding social structure within which the charity
worker hears rumours. As Rizpah inverts the domains of licit and
illicit, she reconstitutes her own prior experience of restriction and
domination as the present experience of her auditor; Rizpah rejects
anything heard outside the confines of her own experience. This inversion also initiates a reversal within the power relations first established by the auditor's presence, a presence that forced Rizpah
to accept a compulsory public status in the first place.

Turning her attention again to Willy at the end of the poem,
Rizpah reverses her initial impulse to disguise her verbal exchange
with her dead son. She now establishes him publicly as the poem's
primary auditor. Rizpah's second verbal encounter with Willy
becomes an aggressive resistance to the forces that have silenced
her in the past, a determined and militant speaking out in spite of
the various structural forces that work to repress this particular
verbal display. The dramatic monologue becomes the site from
which to dramatise the failure of social structure to dominate the
individual fully; it becomes a site of insubordination that suspends
the purely hierarchised relationship between structure and agency:

Madam, I beg your pardon! I think that you mean to be
   kind,
But I cannot hear what you say for my Willy's voice
   in the wind –
The snow and the sky so bright – he used to call in
   the dark,
And he calls to me now from the church and not from

the gibbet – for hark!
Nay–you can hear it yourself – it is coming – shaking
   the walls -
Willy – the moon's in a cloud – Good-night. I am going.
He calls.

                                              (ll. 81–6)

Tennyson dramatises madness here by making it the site of individual resistance. Rizpah's mental experience proves indomitable, and
the failure of the disciplinary function of the madhouse is measurable in the extent to which Rizpah exercises the agency it seeks to
curtail. Rizpah privileges an exclusively private and illicit system of
communication, and the charity worker is forced to witness an
apocalypse that is entirely personal. Moreover, Rizpah subjects her
auditor to a verbal exchange that is only partially audible. As
Tennyson manipulates it here, the speaker of the dramatic monologue disables her own auditor by speaking not to but in spite of
her. By compromising her auditor's generic identity, Rizpah reverses the pattern of compromise to which she is first subjected by
the auditor's unwelcome presence. Agency is finally measurable in
terms of Rizpah's ability to frustrate her audience, that is, in the
versions of resistance she directs against the various structures that
seek to contain her. This ability, realised and acted out within and
against the dramatic monologue itself, suspends the poem at the
very moment of actualising the possible reversal that Foucault
imagines.

Tennyson's contemporaries learned to perceive him as the voice
of Victorian England. This is a perception that may suggest far less
about Tennyson's poetry than about something that might charac-
terise the perceptual habits or temperaments of a Victorian reader-
ship. My sense, contrary to notions of Tennyson's 'representative'
Victorianism (a notion which persists and which derives in large
part from the modernist attacks of the early twentieth century), is
that Tennyson seems to have been interested in developing poetic
genres that not only test, but that imagine the limits of, the reaches
of political and social structures in the nineteenth century. I think as
Tennyson studies move away from more traditional narratives of
his career and open up instead to the possibilities of poststructuralism in general, the idea of Tennyson's Victorianism can change in
ways that can be profitable to the study of the both the topical range
and theoretical complexity of poetry in the nineteenth century.[15] To

reconsider the impulses that shape Tennyson's career is to reconsider Victorianism more generally. As the 'poet of his age', Tennyson's career bears the burdens and complexities of an age often urgently confronting questions of individual agency, questions which shaped themselves in a variety of ways: class mobility, the constant threat of organised social resistance and even anarchy, the 'woman's question', and gender and literary authority suggest only a few of these. As both the representative of Victorian authority and its site of rupture, Tennyson can put us more directly in contact with the dual impulses of Victorianism, that is, its insistence upon a stable centre and its equally stubborn drive to shatter it.

Notes

1. For various discussions of Tennyson's poetic maturation, see Jerome H. Buckley, *Tennyson: The Growth of a Poet* (Cambridge: Harvard University Press, 1960); Dwight A. Culler, *The Poetry of Tennyson* (New Haven: Yale University Press, 1977); Edgar Finley Shannon, Jr, *Tennyson and the Reviewers* (Cambridge: Harvard University Press, 1952); Joyce Green, 'Tennyson's Development', *PMLA* 66(1951): 662–97; E. D. H. Johnson, *The Alien Vision of Victorian Poetry* (Hamden: Archon Books, 1963); Christopher Ricks, *Tennyson* (New York: Macmillan, 1972). For a discussion of Tennyson's middle-class loyalties, see Alan Sinfield, *Alfred Lord Tennyson* (London: Basil Blackwell, 1986).

2. See, for example, Michael Timko, 'The Victorianism of Victorian Literature', *New Literary History* 6 (1974–5): 602–27.

3. For a discussion of poetry's function within the scope of Victorian economic and class anxieties, see Isobel Armstrong, *Victorian Scrutinies: Reviews of Poetry: 1830–1870* (London: The Athlone Press, 1972). For a discussion of the Victorians' spiritual and philosophic crises, see Michael Timko, 'The Victorianism of Victorian Literature', *New Literary History* 6 (1974–75): 602–27. Also see Walter E. Houghton, *The Victorian Frame of Mind: 1830–1870* (New Haven: Yale University Press, 1975). Also see Thomas Carlyle, 'Characteristics,', *A Carlyle Reader*, ed. G. B. Tennyson (Cambridge: Cambridge University Press, 1984).

4. For a discussion of various discursive fields that have insisted upon the possibility of agency, see Paul Smith, *Discerning the Subject* (Minneapolis: University of Minnesota Press, 1988). Smith also surveys recent theoretical attempts to free the otherwise 'cerned' subject of humanist discourse. See also Henry Giroux, *Theory and Resistance in Education: A Pedagogy for the Opposition* (Massachusetts: Bergin and Garvey, 1983). Giroux discusses the failure of the Frankfurt School to offer a successful theory of agency.

5. Smith criticises Giddens on the grounds that he does not account fully enough for Lacan's work on the unconscious in his theory of agency: 79–82.

6. Reviews of the poem by Tennyson's contemporaries, most notably those of Fox and Wilson, criticised its representation of an introverted, morbid state of mind. See Armstrong and Shannon for discussions of these reviews. See also Carol Christ, *The Finer Optic* (New Haven: Yale University Press, 1975); D. J. Palmer, 'Tennyson's Romantic Heritage', *Writers and Their Background*, ed. D. J. Palmer (Athens: Ohio University Press, 1975), pp. 23–51; Harold Bloom, *Poetry and Repression: Revisionism from Blake to Stevens* (New Haven: Yale University Press, 1976); Herbert F. Tucker, *Tennyson and the Doom of Romanticism* (Berkeley: University of California Press, 1988).

7. For exceptions, see John D. Boyd and Anne Williams, 'Tennyson's "Mariana" and Lyric Perspective', *Studies in English Literature* 23(1983): 575–93 and Timothy Peltason, 'The Embowered Self: "Mariana" and "Recollections of the Arabian Nights"', *Victorian Poetry* 21(1984): 335–50. Boyd and Williams come closest to my reading of the poem, claiming that there are two discernible consciousnesses in the poem. However, they underestimate the problematic shaped by these two consciousnesses, claiming that 'Tennyson makes no discernible effort to exploit' them.

8. All references to the poem are from Christopher Ricks, *Tennyson: A Selected Edition* (Berkeley: University of California Press, 1989).

9. See again Bloom, Palmer, and Tucker.

10. See Peltason, who makes this same observation.

11. See II Samuel 21: 8–11.

12. All references to the poem are from *The Norton Anthology of English Literature: Volume Two* (New York: W. W. Norton and Co., 1962).

13. For a thorough discussion of Rizpah's madness, see Roger Platizky, *A Blueprint of His Dissent: Madness and Method in Tennyson's Poetry* (Lewisburg: Bucknell University Press, 1989).

14. The term 'discreet' is Foucault's. See Rabinow: 192.

15. See Gerhard Joseph, *Tennyson and the Text: The Weaver's Shuttle* (London: Oxford University Press, 1992).

6

'Judas always writes the biography': The Many Lives of Oscar Wilde

Ruth Robbins

When I read the book, the biography famous,
And is this then (said I) what the author calls a man's life?
And so will someone when I am dead and gone write my life?
(As if any man really knew aught of my life,
When even I myself, I often think know little or nothing of my
  real life,
Only a few hints, a few diffused clews and indirections
I seek for my own use to trace out here.)
                    Walt Whitman, 'Inscriptions' from *Leaves of Grass*

Who wants to be consistent? The dullard and the doctrinaire, the tedious people who carry out their principles to the bitter end of action, to the *reductio ad absurdam* of practice. Not I. Like Emerson, I write over the door of my library the word 'Whim'.
                    Oscar Wilde, 'The Decay of Lying'

To give an accurate description of what has never occurred is not merely the proper occupation of the historian, but the inalienable right of any man of parts and culture.
                    Oscar Wilde, 'The Critic as Artist – Part One'

Three texts about Oscar Wilde.
First:
Between January and March, 1897, prisoner C.3.3. in H. M. Prison, Reading, one Oscar Wilde, was occupied in the task of writing a very long letter to one of his 'accomplices' in the 'crime' of which

he had been convicted: the addressee was his former lover and erst-while friend, Lord Alfred Douglas. In writing the letter, the prisoner C.3.3. was reasserting his identity as a man, not just a number, and as an artist rather than as a criminal. The letter was, of course, the document which we now call *De Profundis*.

De Profundis is many things. Wilde himself, in a letter to Robert Ross described it as:

> the only document that really gives any explanation of my extra-ordinary behaviour.... You will see the psychological explanation of a course of conduct that from the outside seems a combination of absolute idiocy and vulgar bravado. ... I am not prepared to sit in the grotesque pillory that [the Queensberrys] put me into, for all time. ... I don't defend my conduct. I explain it. (*Selected Letters*, 240)

Wilde saw his letter as an attempt both to explain himself, for and to himself, and to reinterpret himself for the benefit of posterity.

Other commentators have seen different motivations for its existence. Regenia Gagnier sees it as an exercise in self-therapy whose object is to 'pose a total imaginative world against the frozen time and alien space of imprisonment' (Gagnier 1987, 187) in order to resist the threatened loss of self represented by insanity. Jonathan Dollimore has described it as a 'conscious renunciation' of Wilde's pre-prison philosophies, and as a 'confessional narrative whose aim is a deepened self-awareness' (Dollimore 1991, 95). Both Norbert Kohl and Christopher Nassaar have commented on the letter's divided aim. Finally, for Wilde's most recent biographer, Richard Ellmann, the letter is not a confession but a dramatic monologue, and most importantly of all a love letter to Douglas, in which Wilde 'complains of neglect and arranges a reunion' (Ellmann 1988, 482, 483). It is an ambiguous text: a large document which, as Whitman might have said, 'contains multitudes'; it is contradictory in both conception and reception.

The structure of *De Profundis*, as Gagnier has demonstrated, alternates between the meticulous reconstruction of episodes from Wilde's shared past with Douglas and the attempt to create a philosophy which gives meaning to his current situation, since, as Wilde says, 'I could not bear [my sufferings] to be without meaning' (*Selected Letters*, 195). Now for Wilde:

Suffering ... is the means by which we exist, because it is the only means by which we become conscious of existing; and the remembrance of suffering in the past is necessary to us, as the warrant, the evidence of our continued identity. (*Selected Letters*, 164)

Dollimore is right to see Wilde as renouncing his previous philosophies. One phrase, repeated several times in the letter – 'The supreme vice is shallowness. Everything that is realised is right' – stands in direct opposition to his previous position that 'only the shallow know themselves' (*Writings*, 572).

The letter, however, is not consistent in its recantation of the past. As Gagnier has argued, two pairs of binary oppositions, Romance and Realism, and Romance and Finance, inform the structure of the letter, pulling it in different directions. The Romance of Wilde's earlier life as a 'man who stood in symbolic relations to the art and culture of [his] age' and who was favoured with 'genius, a distinguished name, high social position, brilliancy, intellectual daring' (*Selected Letters*, 194) is narrated in contrast both to Bosie's despicable behaviour, and to the prison cell in which Wilde now finds himself, as the logical consequence of Bosie's fatal influence over him. He begins by claiming to blame himself, and forcing himself – and by extension, Douglas – to realise his prison surroundings:

I blame myself terribly. As I sit here in this dark cell in convict clothes, a disgraced and ruined man, I blame myself. In the perturbed and fitful nights of anguish, in the long monotonous days of pain, it is myself I blame. (*Selected Letters*, 154)

In saying *mea culpa*, Wilde is also able to point to the difference in consequence between his own actions and Bosie's equally culpable ones.

In other words, whilst Wilde is clearly on a quest to understand and to give meaning to his own sufferings, he seeks also to make Bosie understand the extent of *his* responsibility for Wilde's downfall. *De Profundis* is not about developing self-knowledge alone (indeed, Wilde claims that prison has given him self-knowledge already). His aim is equally to explain Bosie to Bosie: 'The real fool ... is he who does not know himself. I *was* such a one too long. You *have been* such a one too long' (*Selected Letters*, 154, my emphasis). The letter is didactic. Wilde seeks to kill Bosie's vanity since self-realisation 'is the only thing that can save you' (*Selected Letters*, 153). Wilde had once written that 'All art is essentially useless', and inasmuch as it is didactic, *De Profundis* is not art, since it seeks to have an effect. Wilde wants to change his friend – to have, as it were, a moral or improving effect on him.

Wilde chronicles in detail the lifestyle into which, he argues, Bosie had led him. (The passive voice is often used in the letter; even when Wilde is blaming himself, it is for *having allowed himself* to be led astray.) He insists on the financial details of their extravagant expenditure together before the scandal broke, and he contrasts past luxury with his present misery. The money and the time which they wasted together represent a double failure in their friendship, which Wilde sees as an artistic failure. The time that they spent together meant that Wilde had neither the leisure nor the liberty to be a great artist; a typical day spent with Bosie left him less than two hours for writing. And the money that they spent on expensive hotels and meals has left Wilde debts which have led him to the Bankruptcy Courts. The fatal friendship has resulted in Wilde failing as an artist, as a man (in the worldly sense that he is now bankrupt), as a husband and father, and as a son.

Yet despite all the very good reasons for Wilde to reject Bosie's friendship, he seeks also in the letter to find ways of forgiving him. The medium through which forgiveness will come is the example of Christ. Alongside all the other facets of this text, Wilde also uses the letter to write an aesthetic biography of Christ, and he seeks a Christ through whom he too can be redeemed.

This Christ is very much a Christ of Wilde's own creation. As Ellmann has noted, the one aspect of Christ's life which has no influence on Wilde is his divinity (Ellmann 1988, 483). It is Christ's example, not his origin, which matters. The sufferings of the son of God are seen in the text as the paradigm for the suffering of the artist (Kohl 1989, 278), and for Wilde, the essential feature of Christ is his *personality*. He insists that Christ's value resides in the fact that he exemplified imaginative sympathy with suffering which makes his life into 'the most wonderful of poems' (*Selected Letters*, 205). Christ's miracles have nothing to do with the miracles narrated by the Gospels. For Wilde, Christ's story ends with 'the stone rolled over the door of the sepulchre' (*Selected Letters*, 205), not with the Resurrection. The other miracles are miracles dependent entirely on an extraordinary personality.

I see no difficulty at all in believing that such was the charm of his personality that those who touched his garments or his hand forgot their pain; ... and that to his friends who listened to him as he sat at meat the coarse food seemed delicate, and the water had the taste of good wine, and the whole house became full of the odour and sweetness of nard. (*Selected Letters*, 207)

That, of course, was the miracle of Wilde's own personality when he was at the height of his powers. His conversation, the stories he told to his associates, acted like a spell on those who listened to him. (Queensberry himself was charmed for a while. 'I don't wonder that you are so fond of him,' he said to Douglas. 'He is a wonderful man.' [Ellmann 1988, 393]) In Wilde's pantheon, Man is not made in the image of God; Christ is remade in the image of Wilde. 'Christ is the most supreme of Individualists,' he wrote in *De Profundis* (*Selected Letters*, 207); and again, 'There is something so unique about Christ' (215), remarks which could equally be applied to Wilde himself.

The letter, despite several instances of self-castigation, is certainly not an abject confession of past faults. Wilde describes himself as a 'born antinomian, ... one of those who are made for exceptions, not for laws' (*Selected Letters*, 196). And for Christ too, in Wilde's recreation of him, 'there were no laws: there were exceptions merely' (*Selected Letters*, 213). Like Wilde himself, this Christ is a disciple of Pater:

All that Christ says to us by way of a little warning is that *every* moment should be beautiful, that we should *always* be ready for the coming of the Bridegroom, *always* waiting for the voice of the lover. (*Selected Letters*, 214)

Which is not very far away from Pater's credo in *The Renaissance* that one should 'burn always with this hard, gemlike flame, ... maintain [the] ecstasy' (Pater [1873] 1961, 222).

And finally, Wilde rejects Christ's traditionally accepted abhorrence of sin. He claims that Christ regarded 'sin and suffering as being in themselves beautiful holy things, and modes of perfection' (*Selected Letters*, 215). In a characteristically heretical subversion of Christian doctrine, Wilde argues that sin is necessary; for without it there can be no repentance, and without repentance there can be no self-realisation. 'The moment of repentance is the moment of initiation. More than that. It is the means by which one alters one's past' (215). The alteration takes place because the teleology of sin is changed through the processes of confession and repentance. A sin which is not repented leads to hell; a sin which is forgiven brings rejoicing to heaven. The construction of a narrative of sin through confession, brings events to a comprehensible and moral ending, and thus alters not the facts of the past, but their meanings. This is the move which Wilde makes in the final paragraph of the letter, in which he suggests that the past is not irrevocable:

> Time and space, succession and extension, are merely accidental conditions of Thought. The Imagination can transcend them, and move in a free sphere of ideal existences. ... A thing *is*, according to the mode in which one looks at it. (*Selected Letters*, 239)

Wilde always mistrusted too factual an approach to history: it is not the facts which matter, but how they are interpreted.

A second text:

> I have become a problem in modern ethics, as Symonds would say, although it seemed to me at the time that I was the solution. Everyone is talking about my particular disposition now, for, as usual, I chose the proper dramatic moment to reveal my sexual infamy to the world. Even the Germans have become interested in the subject, and, of all the extraordinary things that have happened to me, the most extraordinary may be that I shall be remembered not as an artist but as a case history, a psychological study to be placed beside Onan and Herodias. I might even be mentioned by Edward Carpenter in one of his more suggestive passages. ...
> The problem, as always in modern thought is one of nomenclature. I am not inverted: I was diverted. (Ackroyd, 112)

These are not the words of Oscar Wilde, but the words of a fictional character who shares his name in Peter Ackroyd's 1983 novel, *The Last Testament of Oscar Wilde*. The novel chronicles the last months of the fictional Oscar Wilde in Paris in 1900.

These words mimic, in a very different tone, another letter which Wilde wrote in prison, this time to the Home Secretary. This second letter is humble, scientific and legalistic. Wilde asked for his sentence to be commuted on the grounds that he was not criminal, but a man suffering from sexual insanity. He borrows the register of contemporary sociology and criminology, and insists (as Ackroyd's Wilde does with satirical intent) that he is a case study, not an evil man. His crimes are 'diseases to be cured by a physician rather than crimes to be punished by a judge' (*Selected Letters*, 142). Depending on to whom is he is writing, Wilde is many things. He is a criminal, a madman, a martyr, a saint, an artist, a husband, a father, a man about town (a dandy or *flâneur*). As Ackroyd's Wilde puts it: 'I am positively Whitmanesque. I contain multitudes' (Ackroyd 1983, 8).

The Wilde in the novel, rather like the real historical personality, is a man who, through resisting stable interpretations and definitions of himself, also seeks to resist closure. It is not through suffering that this Wilde knows himself to be alive in the novel, but through the inscription and re-inscription of himself as a characterological palimpsest. He is unknowable, and finally unknown, even to himself. While he is anxious not to lose the thread of his narrative, to 'master the past by giving it the only meaning which it now possesses' (Ackroyd 1983, 75), he is also haunted by a fear that the multiplicity of significance which he has always embraced might simply collapse into meaninglessness:

Could it be that I, who have written so much about the powers of personality, do not – after everything which has happened to me – know what my own personality is? That would be the tragedy of my life, if tragedy is to be found anywhere within it. (Ackroyd 1983, 92)

The novel is cast in the form of a journal, always a double form of writing. The journal presumably helps the writer to remember and to make sense of his/her past, so its first intended audience is always the writer. But the journal also survives the writer, and is used as evidence for the interpretation of his/her life and (the 'death of the author' notwithstanding), his/her work. (It is significant that the 'real' Wilde wrote no such journal – that he sought to resist authoritative interpretation.) Facts are unimportant; far more important is how the facts are read. In *De Profundis*, the 'real' Wilde, described history as having a gothic element, and saw

Clio as 'the least serious of the muses' (*Selected Letters*, 159). In the novel, the fictional Wilde shows his journal to a fictional Frank Harris[1] and a fictional Bosie, and tells them that it is intended for publication. Harris responds with outrage: 'You cannot publish this, Oscar. It is nonsense – and most of it is quite untrue. ... It is invented. ... you have obviously changed the facts to suit your own purpose' (Ackroyd 1983, 160). Bosie's response is slightly different: 'It's full of lies, but of course you are. It is absurd and mean and foolish. But then you are. Of course you must publish it' (Ackroyd 1883, 161). In that exchange, Bosie's response is both crueller and more apt than Harris's. Earlier in the novel, a fictional version of Robert Sherard[2] drunkenly approaches Wilde with a project to write his biography in which he would 'explain [his] conduct to the world, and reveal [his] true character'. 'You will defend me at the cost of my reputation', the fictional Wilde retorts (Ackroyd, 1983, 69). 'If anyone were foolish enough to write my biography, then the fatefulness of my life would touch him also. There will, in any event, be no royalties' (15). A pun is intended here. Such a biography would not make any money; but equally it would be incapable of elevating Wilde's reputation. He cannot be redeemed through explanation.

Ackroyd's Wilde, looking back on his life, offers not one interpretation, but several. But while he is happy to resist narrative closure, he cannot resist the closure of death. As the novel progresses, the entries in the journal become shorter, and the narrative becomes increasingly disjointed. Towards the end of October 1900, the real Wilde had an operation for an ulcerated ear, probably the result of a fall he had suffered in Wandsworth in 1896. In real life, he never really recovered from the operation. Ackroyd's Wilde also has an operation, and its effect at first is that it makes him forget to write his journal, so that a significant chronological gap opens up in the journal – and for that fictional time, Wilde does not exist. A more important effect, however, is that the operation does not cure the ulcer or the pain, and the fictional Wilde is finally unable to write at all, so that the last few entries in the journal are not Wilde's own, but his words taken to dictation by his young friend and companion, Maurice Gilbert[3]. His sense of impending death produces a fundamental change in the fictional Wilde. It is not that he fears death; what he fears is the loss of control over his own personality – the possibility that another hand might 'write the end', and impose a final authoritarian significance on his life:

I feel curiously apart from my writing, as though it were another hand which moves, another imagination I draw upon. Soon I must ask Maurice to take dictation from me: no doubt he will invent my last hours, and the transition will be complete. (Ackroyd 1983, 180)

But while Ackroyd cannot, even in a fiction, prevent Wilde from dying, the final pages of the novel continue to resist the closure that would seem like such a betrayal. The last entries are headed: 'This is Oscar Wilde talking, taken down by Maurice Gilbert.' It may indeed be that Maurice sets out to fictionalise Wilde's ending, but his taking of dictation actually deconstructs the possibility that his version of Wilde's last days and hours is a final or authoritative one. As Wilde's words become increasingly incoherent, Maurice makes no attempt to tidy them up or to explain them.

30/11/1900
He is becoming delirious now but I will write it down for his words have always been wonderful to me It has been a hot summer has it not. I tried to get a cab this morning but he said it was too far out. You know when they found the body of Christ *I cannot follow what he is saying here* and then once more I shall be lord of language and lord of life, do you agree mother? *he is laughing* I knew I should create a great sensation *no more now*
Mr Wilde died at ten minutes to two p.m. on Friday, November 30 (185)

The last words may be significant: Wilde did indeed create a great sensation. But although they are the last words of the fictional Wilde, they do not have 'the last word'. Wilde is silenced by the only kind of historical fact which cannot be resisted – death.[4]

A third text:
In 1989, Terry Eagleton wrote a play entitled *Saint Oscar*, which deals with Wilde's Irishness, his relationship with his mother, and his friendship with the working-class renters whose testimony was an essential part of the evidence against him at his trials. The play received its premiere in the Guildhall, Derry on 25 September 1989, in a production by the Field Day Theatre Company. The published

version of the play includes a foreword by Eagleton in which he explains his motivation for having written such a piece. His first reason is that his Oxford students seldom realise that Wilde was Irish: 'Since Wilde himself realised this only fitfully, this is hardly a grievous crime, though it might be said to be evidence of one' (Eagleton 1989, vii). The crime he speaks of is that of British cultural imperialism which has long 'annexed ... gifted offshore islanders to its own literary canon' (vii). So, one of the origins of the play was the attempt to redress that cultural imbalance, and to rewrite Wilde's linguistic brilliance as an example of what is distinctively Irish about him.

The second point of origin is the way in which Wilde apparently prefigures so much of contemporary literary theory:

Language as self-referential, truth as convenient fiction, the human subject as contradictory and 'deconstructed', criticism as a form of 'creative' writing, the body and its pleasures pitted against a pharisiacal ideology: in these and several other ways, Oscar Wilde looms up for us more and more as the Irish Roland Barthes. (vii)

These two aspects, Wilde's nationality with its attendant history of colonial oppression, and his subversions of Victorian commonplaces, are, for Eagleton, connected, both to each other and to his own academic position. To each other since subversion is both the affirmation of one's own identity as a member of a colonised race, and at the same time, an attack on the very basis of the power which oppresses. To Eagleton himself because he is a man of 'Irish working-class provenance, now working in the belly of the beast at Oxford' (viii). A play about Wilde, he says, allows him to explore the connections between oppression and creativity, but the exploration takes place more 'for the sake of my own identity and allegiances than as a purely intellectual problem' (ix).

Eagleton seeks also, he says, to reinscribe Wilde as a political writer – following on from his indirect allegiance to Irish nationalism and his essay 'The Soul of Man under Socialism'. The area he does not seek to illuminate is Wilde's sexual politics: 'if I have tried to avoid writing a "gay" play about him, this is ... because it seems to me vital to put that particular ambiguity or doubleness back in the context of a much wider span of ambivalences' (xi). A gay approach would limit Wilde's potential multiple significance. His reading of Wilde is predicated on the assumption that 'nobody can write now of Britain and Ireland in Wilde's day without bringing to mind the tragic events that afflicted Ireland in the past two decades. Reflections on the past are always at some level meditations on the present' (xi).

In the play itself, therefore, the battle between Eagleton's Wilde and the English state is actually personified in the recreation of another historical figure, this time an Irish man (since 'if an Irishman is to be basted, you can always find another one to turn the spit'), Sir Edward Carson. The real Wilde had known Carson at Trinity College, Dublin in the 1870s. His fictionalised alter ego is in the play for two reasons; firstly Carson represented the Marquess of Queensberry when Wilde sued him for criminal libel in April 1895; secondly, Carson was later to become famous as a champion of the Unionist cause. One might assume, therefore, that when Carson and Wilde meet in the courtroom in the play, they are supposed to represent not only prosecution and defence, but also the two sides of the 'Irish question'. This turns out to be a false assumption.

Just like the 'real' Wilde, Eagleton's version is dismissive of facts and of the general artlessness of history:

> I find it impossible to take [history] at all seriously. Have you ever read a history of the human race? Don't bother, the plot is appallingly thin. I was reading one only the other day, and could hardly contain my incredulity. The author's imagination was ludicrously narrow; almost all of his French characters were called Louis. No narrative thrust: just a lot of sub-plots carelessly abandoned, themes left hanging in mid-air, a mishmash of sensational occurrences. Wars, famines, massacres, revolutions: I've never read anything more improbable in my life. (9)

This Wilde always rejects entrenched positions, and therefore, it is not he who represents Irish Nationalism in the play, but his mother, Lady Wilde. In real life, like her son, Francesca Wilde was prone to fictionalising her own life. She was famous in her own right in the nineteenth century, as the writer of ardent nationalist poetry under her pen-name, Speranza (Ellman 1987, 5–6). In the play, Wilde introduces her as the personification of the nation: 'Speaking of Ireland, here she comes' (9). Mother and son argue about what she sees as lack of political commitment to her cause. It is an argument which is repeated throughout the play, though the causes to which Wilde is asked to submit range from Socialism to Unionism; and Wilde consistently resists all attempts to shackle him to a cause. Lady Wilde wants her son to become a nationalist, as she is, and to devote his pen to the service of his country, to stir up the peasantry to revolt against the English. She asks him to adopt a more political attitude in his art, but he merely responds that 'Ireland is a third-rate melodrama in an infinite number of acts' (15). Similarly, Wilde's conversations with Richard Wallace emphasise his weak grasp on the actual political situation and his indifference to outrages in Trafalgar Square, to strikes and injustices. Just as he is incapable of acting in the political interests of other people, he is also unable to act in his own interests. He refuses to see that his affairs with Bosie, and with the renters, are bound to lead to the courtroom. Wilde is as indifferent to the Realist laws of cause and effect on his own person as he is to their operations on other people.

Eagleton's text operates on a different basis from Ackroyd's. Where Ackroyd is careful to get the 'facts' right, Eagleton's is a work about the interpretation of facts; not so much what actually happened, but what we believe to be the case. In the play, the trial is rendered farcical by the laying bare of its assumptions. All the things that one suspects might have been true about Wilde's treatment at the hands of English justice are openly presented to the court. Even the judge camps it up, making appointments to discuss the trial with the rent-boy witnesses, later, in his chambers, implying that the charge of which Wilde is accused is widespread among his accusers. Wilde's case is that he is the victim of conspiracy:

I am accused of homosexual relations by an Establishment for whom such practices are as habitual as high tea. Homosexual behaviour is as English as morris dancing, if somewhat less tedious. … [T]here is a conspiracy against me. When I lost a libel suit against the Marquess of Queensberry, the Judge who presided in the case sent a note of congratulation to the prosecuting counsel. Is that what is known as British justice? The young man with whom I am accused of buggery will never be brought to court because he is the son of an aristocrat. I am told that one of the rent boys with whom I am accused of consorting will not be called to bear witness at this trial because he is the nephew of the Solicitor General. Soliciting would seem to run in his family. (40)[5]

Carson's closing speech in the play trial equally lays bare some of the reasons for Wilde's prosecution – reasons which have nothing to do with his guilt or innocence under the 1885 Criminal Law Amendments Act. For Carson, an Irishman representing the English establishment, Wilde is a bad husband and father; he is immoral; he mocks the truths which the Establishment holds dear. 'He is vain, arrogant and self-deluded. ... He is a spoiled brat who has never done a decent day's work in his life, who at the ripe old age of forty presents the grotesque spectacle of one striving to perpetuate his undergraduate years' (45). It is time, Carson concludes, that Wilde grew up. Wilde's response to this, before he is led down to the cells, is that 'no Irishman can ever receive a fair hearing in an English court because the Irish are figments of the English imagination' (46). In that remark, Wilde refers, as it were *avant la lettre*, to the cases which are now always called the 'notorious miscarriages of justice' – the Birmingham Six, the Guildford Four, the Maguire Seven, and the case of Judith Ward. Eagleton's position is clearly that Wilde's trial for one kind of offence against the English state prefigures – predicts – the later injustices, and the basis for all these injustices is the same: the oppression of the Irish by the English.

The play ends with Wilde sitting alone and deserted after his prison sentence, outside a Paris restaurant. He sees his old friend Richard Wallace, who has, in the meantime, lost all his fiery left-wing ideals, and has become a cynical capitalist, demonstrating the defeat which is likely to attend all positions which are too firmly entrenched. When Richard leaves him in darkness, Carson appears, dressed in paramilitary uniform, surrounded by masked gunmen. And, in conversation with Wilde, he effectively repeats the arguments made by Lady Wilde in the first act, except that Carson's speech is in favour of loyalism, not Lady Wilde's nationalism. Now occupying an entrenched position himself, Carson can only reject Wilde's proffered hand of friendship; the lights go down on him and his paramilitary band, to the sound of a drum roll, and the words 'No surrender'.

Wilde's last words in the play repeat the theme of ambivalence, the refusal to be pinned down, which have been at the heart of Eagleton's interpretation of him. He muses over the words to be inscribed on his tombstone:

I want them to write on my tombstone: 'Here lies Oscar Wilde, poet and patriot'. No, that's a bit terse; not true either. How about: 'Here lies Oscar Wilde: socialite and sodomite, Thames and Liffey, Jekyll and Hyde, aristocrat and underdog.' I could have a double grave and double monument; friends could choose which one to mourn at, or alternate between the two. (64)

Like Ackroyd's Wilde, this Wilde too resists the closure of definitive interpretation. He says that he will have the last true word, and ends the play, slumped at the restaurant-table, speaking a nonsensical epigram: 'All men are natural Anabaptists; women remain true Presbyterians to the end.' The play closes with a song in which all contemporary injustices are reversed, and replaced with their exact opposites, an act of political 'inversion'.

The plot of *The Importance of Being Earnest* hinges on a life which has literally been mistaken for a text. Jack Worthing is swapped as a baby for a three-volume novel 'of more than usually revolting sentimentality'. His very existence is a fiction; and luckily for him, he belongs to Miss Prism's optimistic genre, in which the good end happily and the bad unhappily since that is what fiction means.

Like Jack Worthing, Wilde's life has also been mistaken for a text, not least by Wilde himself. He famously told André Gide that he had put his genius into his life and only his talent into his work; and his own interpretation of himself, *De Profundis*, the nearest thing in Wilde's *oeuvre* to autobiography, is dramatic in the extreme with few concessions to Realism. Wilde has not gone away. Despite the fact that he insisted himself that art should conceal the artist, the critic continues to seek him out. In one sense the reasons for this are easy to understand. It was indeed a spectacular life – a biography which demands the attention of the audience. From relatively humble beginnings with his early pretensions to poetry, he elevated himself to the top of the literary tree in six short years, from 1889 to 1895. At the time of his arrest, after the failure of the Queensberry prosecution, three of his plays were in production in the West End – he was at the height of his powers. When the crash came, it was absolute. In *De Profundis*, Wilde compares Christ's life to a poem: 'For "pity and terror" there is nothing in the entire cycle of Greek Tragedy to touch it' (*Selected Letters*, 205–6). The only difference between Christ and a Greek hero is that Christ had no tragic flaw, no hubris which brought him low. Wilde's own life also has the shape of Greek tragedy. It shares the trajectory of a meteoric rise followed by the most absolute fall. The fall is 'explained' in so many different ways that no explanation is adequate. Wilde himself saw that from the outside his conduct looked like 'a combination of absolute idiocy and vulgar bravado' (*Selected Letters*, 240), and he did not want to go down in history as a man renowned for a lack of intelligence, or for a lack of taste. Perhaps he found danger erotic, and took pleasure in going too close to the edge. Wilde's own assessment of himself partially supports such a reading: 'Tired of being on the heights, I deliberately went into the depths in the search for new sensations' (*Selected Letters*, 194). But no explanation can ever satisfy us; we want to know why, but we treasure Wilde's ambiguity. We try to trace out his motivations just as we trace the motives of characters in novels. We take the artistic shape of the life as an indication that the life had other artistic features, particularly the explicability and significance of action. Because we retell Wilde's life so often, we feel that it should mirror the features of textuality: we undertake a Wildean strategy, and make life follow art. 'As soon as we start to tell a story, we make connections where before there were none' (Josipovici 1994, 277).

In terms of Barthes's definition of the author, Wilde was not an author. What Barthes objected to was the tyrannical authority which the composite construction of the author imposed on textual criticism. And he distrusted the ways in which biographical information is used to explain the text (Barthes 1977, 143). But that 'authority' can only be derived when there is a general agreement about the meaning of the author. In a sense, Wilde took care to cover his tracks. We may all 'know' that he was convicted for homosexual offences, but we cannot know whether this represents a personal failure of his own moral code, or a failure of his mental health, whether it is the failure of the society which imprisoned him – or whether, indeed, it was not a failure at all, but a martyrdom which now signifies a form of triumph. The facts may not change, but their interpretation does with the passage of time and changing attitudes. Even at the moment of disgrace, in May 1895, we must beware of the re-creating a homogeneous audience all baying for Wilde's blood.[6] Interpretations in this case can only ever be partial and temporary – which is what helps to keep this author alive.

Wilde's own artistic philosophy, as well as seeking to conceal the artist, also (in typically contradictory fashion) virtually sanctions a biographical approach. For him, art is the expression of personality.

And it is in that word 'personality' that we must seek to understand Wilde. For despite the textuality of his life, the implied homology between his life and his art, Wilde was not a character in a three-volume novel or in a well-made play. Indeed, 'character' is a word he almost never uses, and the distinction between character and personality is essential.

The word character has its origin in the Greek word *kharakter*, meaning impress or stamp. The first dictionary definition is a printing term; the second defines character as a biological term, meaning the collective peculiarities of a species or race. The third definition originates from the idea of a written testimonial to a person's essential qualities, particularly his/her morality. Only with the fourth definition do we move overtly into the realm of literature. What comes out of this etymological investigation is that the word character implies stability, knowability. Character is stamped through the individual like the lettering in a stick of rock. It is a word better suited to fictions than to real people whose knowability must, after all, always be open to question.

Personality, on the other hand, comes from a Latin root – *persona* – meaning, in the first instance, 'actor's mask', or the face that one presents to the world. So personality refers not to the essential being but to a role which can be assumed and cast off at will. Consequently it is potentially inconsistent, knowable only in a conditional way, for the moments during which that particular mask is being worn. Wilde comments in *De Profundis*: 'Behind Joy and Laughter there may be a temperament, coarse, hard and callous. But behind Sorrow there is always Sorrow. Pain, unlike Pleasure, wears no mask' (*Selected Letters*, 201). One can only wear a mask which signifies pleasure, implying that pleasure is only to be found on the surface: pain cannot be acted. Wilde wore the mask of pleasure for so long that it was assumed that he could only be inconsistent, trivial and insincere. But beneath the mask there is always another possibility. Moreover, even the naked face may always reassume its disguise.

The admission of sincerity in sorrow was an extreme statement for Wilde. He is asking his addressee to see him unadorned, unprotected by his mask. In addressing Douglas like this – with a plea for acceptance despite his unadorned state – Wilde is taking a very large risk: Douglas had once commented that when Wilde was not on his pedestal, he was not interesting. Indeed, in *De Profundis*, Wilde refuses to occupy this lowly position for very long; he reassembles a personality which he then associates with Christ, thus replacing himself on the artistic pedestal from which the scandal had removed him. The maskless face of Sorrow is not a permanent condition; it does not reveal character – essence – but is in fact only an alternative personality which is soon rejected. If the letter is inconsistent in the sense that it is not just a humble confessional, or the letter of an injured lover, or a therapy, or an autobiographical explanation, it is at least consistent in its dramatisation of each of these roles in turn. It is a series of experimental artistic attitudes. It is not a resumé in which a life can be seen 'steadily' and 'whole' (Arnold 1980, 67):[7] it must be read sequentially.

Both Ackroyd and Eagleton have registered this multiplicity of readings. Their texts belong with the wealth of biographical materials about Wilde as well as with genre writings. As all biography is necessarily interpretation and in that sense is the fictive reconstruction of a life, so their works break down the distinction between fiction and historical fact. Wilde, by his own admission, lived more than one life, and the textuality of those lives resides in their multiple layers of signification. The biographer who seeks a single or simple explanation for Wilde is treacherous. Lives, even narrated lives, resist the closure of *the* authoritative interpretation. This is true of any life, but it is particularly true of Wilde's, who is fascinating precisely because he teeters always on the edge of contradiction.

In 'The Critic as Artist', Gilbert admits to a fascination with autobiography, which he says is irresistible. Every man must be his own Boswell, he says, since lives written by others are always betrayals. 'Every great man nowadays has his disciples, and it is always Judas who writes the biography' (*Writings*, 242). Biographers are 'the mere body-snatchers of literature' (*Writings*, 243). They are only outsiders who have no access to the really interesting secrets and indiscretions which make autobiography worthwhile. It is, for example, probably the desperation of *De Profundis* which makes it readable at all – the sense we get of a man not just writing his life, but writing *for* his life. But although the impulse of Ackroyd and Eagleton is partially biographical, and therefore – in Gilbert's eyes – a betrayal, the existence of these fictions among so many would perhaps have appealed to Wilde, especially as the interpretations of him in the present age mirror his own distrust of absolute answers. Their open-ended versions of his multiple personalities demonstrate an intimate connection between Wilde's Victorian literary life and our contemporary theories.

Notes

1. The real Frank Harris was a friend of Wilde's, even after his disgrace, and lent him money, and took him on trips abroad. He was a would-be writer and publisher, and speculated in any business venture he could, including a casino at Monte Carlo. In return for his kindness, Wilde gave him (or sold him) the scenario of a play he had thought of but could not write when he was released from prison, to be called *Mr and Mrs Daventry*. (The act was generous on Wilde's part, but unfortunately for Harris, Wilde was similarly generous with the same play scenario with several other friends.) The pay-off for this was that Harris wrote two outrageously inaccurate accounts of Wilde's life; but although the facts were often wrong, the spirit in which they were written was generous – unusual in accounts of Wilde in the early years of the century. By contrast, Bosie's accounts of his life with Wilde veered from the spiteful to the absurd to the nostalgic in turn. No one ever accused him of generosity.

2. Wilde first met Sherard, an Englishman (and great-grandson of Wordsworth) in Paris in 1883. Sherard apparently adored Wilde, and Wilde put up with his attentions, according to Ellmann because he was blond, handsome and idolatrous (202). Sherard also remained close to Wilde after the scandal, and even tried to effect some kind of reconciliation between Wilde and his wife. He wrote several accounts of Wilde's life including *The Story of an Unhappy Friendship, The Life of Oscar Wilde*, and, that most unlikely of stories, *The Real Oscar Wilde*. His tendency was constantly to romanticise his idol, and to make him more respectable.

3. Gilbert is also a fictionalised version of a real person. During Wilde's last months in Paris, he continued to pick up young men. Gilbert was a young soldier in the marine of whom Wilde made a special favourite; for example, he bought him a bicycle, and tried to educate him in the arts a little, taking him to visit Rodin's studio in the summer of 1900.

4. It is not clear whether Gilbert was actually at Wilde's deathbed, but in one sense, he did have the 'last word' on Wilde – or at least produced his last image. At the request of Robert Ross, he took photographs of Wilde's body laid out on the afternoon of his death.

5. These are all accusations for which there is some evidence. There is certainly a sense in which Wilde was not convicted only the basis of his sexual preferences, but because of the government's need to show its incorruptibility in the wake of a scandal, in 1894, in which Sholto Douglas (Bosie's elder brother, and private secretary to Lord Rosebery, the prime minister) had apparently shot himself to avoid exposure of his homosexuality. For more information on this see the Appendix to Regenia Gagnier's *Idylls of the Marketplace* (1987).

6. Yeats, for example, claimed that the whores danced in the streets when Wilde was convicted; but there were many, including Yeats himself and George Bernard Shaw who were deeply sympathetic to his plight.

7. The quotation comes from a lecture called 'On the Modern Element in Literature', delivered in 1869. Arnold is, in fact, quoting one of his own poems and relating his judgement to the claim of Sophocles to be an adequate writer which is based, he says, on the fact that 'he saw life steadily and he saw it whole'. This is contrasted in the lecture with the inability of modern writers to find any stable basis for their own world-view.

Part III
Cultural Formations and Modes of Production

7

Representing Illegitimacy in Victorian Culture

Jenny Bourne Taylor

This essay investigates some aspects of the complicated significance of illegitimacy in nineteenth-century narrative and culture,[1] looking at bastardy not as a set of fixed images, myths or stereotypes, but as a series of meanings based on a discursive and symbolic division between legitimacy and illegitimacy that, while seeming to be constant throughout Western culture (indeed, to be one of its foundational premises), is nonetheless composed of constantly fluctuating elements held in tenuous opposition, the boundaries of which are forever being redrawn, altering in accordance with shifts in forms of patriarchy and the law, changing conceptions of the family, heterosexuality, homosociality and marriage. Illegitimacy at one moment or in one culture might not mean the same as it does in another, though patterns may seem to reappear and repeat themselves across wide spans of time. Notions of bastardy emerge out of the convergence of distinctive material process, discursive practices and fantasies, each embodying different forms of authority: on law and religion; on reproduction and the social control of sexuality; on the state, citizenship and political power; on property-ownership and inheritance, genealogy, 'race' and kinship; on class and notions of social welfare. But these diverse processes converge around a common question of how to represent bastardy.

'Illegitimacy' may no longer exist in England as a set of specific legal disabilities and exclusions, but the term has recently resurfaced on the contemporary political stage with the Conservative government's attacks on single mothers in general and young working-class unmarried ones in particular.[2] The ill-fated 'Back to Basics' campaign of late 1993 drew heavily on the writings of the right-wing American sociologist Charles Murray, who saw illegitimacy as the hallmark of the 'underclass', a fast-growing margin of British society composed of work-shy, unmarriageable yobs and feckless, over-fertile hussies (Murray 1990). This attempt to reinvent bastardy, along with the furore around the Child Support Act, is one starting point; I want to excavate the history behind the Minister for Social Security Peter Lilley's comment in 1993 that 'inadvertently the State has nationalised fatherhood'.[3] The failure (on the whole) of the Right to implement Peter Green's exhortation to 'bring back stigma, all is forgiven!', or successfully to conjure up a much older image of the bastard as heir to vice and crime, forms part of a longer-term cluster of concerns around class, gender and the state control of pauperism to which I will be returning (Green, 'Preface', x). But first I want to explore the concept of illegitimacy itself, by briefly surveying various prototypes, who make their appearance at different historical moments, but whose stories weave in and out of each other through the nineteenth century.

There are the masculine malcontents of early modern drama who dwell not in a pauperised underworld but in the heartlands of power, the place where matters of sovereignty, state authority and gendered identity are most rigorously contested. At once natural and unnatural, either grotesquely ugly or exuding a powerful sexual allure, these figures often both subvert and reinforce the patrilineal forms of authority they so resent by replicating and mimicking them; they erode the distinction between margin and centre, become incarnations of the distinct kinds of crises of legitimation that these plays embody by embodying theatricality itself in their manipulativeness and self-conscious reflexivity. Edmund in *King Lear*, Don John in *Much Ado About Nothing*, Thersites in *Troilus and Cressida* are all creatures constructed out of the forces that exclude them, a 'core of envy', that emotion that so effectively undermines the hierarchies that it helps to keep in place.[4] There is the heroic bastard, the 'meta-legitimate' trope of classical and Judeo-Christian mythology, a crucial figure in national and religious origin stories: Theseus, Hercules and Ion, Romulus, Jesus, Arthur. These represent projections of an ideal or ambivalent relationship to a divine or semi-divine father, spreading his seed far and wide, and spring from distinct fantasies of maternal origin. There is the bastard as child of nature and 'natural' aristocrat, allied to the illegitimate liberal hero, who simultaneously embodies and interrogates modernist fantasies of autonomy, tracking the novel's own emergence as dominant cultural form out of unsanctioned origins. There are the 'love children' of both sexes who become crucial devices of melodrama and sources of narrative suspense, their problematic origins concealing secrets at the heart of the middle-class family. These children turn attention back to their mothers; they haunt nineteenth-century fiction and pervade twentieth-century popular culture in forms such as Hollywood melodrama, blockbuster family sagas, and soap opera. They return in pastiche form in much postmodern writing, for as a trope bastardy always teeters on the brink of the banal, the excessive, the clichéd. 'Romantic illegitimacy, always a seller', remarks Dora Chance, a natural daughter of the eminent 'Shakespearean' actor Melchior Hazard in Angela Carter's *Wise Children*, which parodies the concept of bastardy as metaphor for transgressive popular culture and makes use of it as kitsch and decadent music-hall joke (Carter 1991, 11). There is the bastard as ultimate hybrid, child of 'mixed' parentage in which metaphors of illegitimacy, racial ambiguity and miscegenation are inextricably entwined. The liminal, fluid figure of the bastard cuts across narrative and genre, and not only represents the best and the worst of the self, but also embodies ambivalence in all its forms.

'Illegitimate' and 'bastard' mingle various models of difference and transgression. 'Illegitimate' is defined through a binary opposition between the licit and the illicit, the proper and the improper, self and other, right and left, bent and straight; indeed in some ways it represents their fundamental form. 'Bastard' on the other hand is defined by the OED as 'born out of wedlock'; 'hybrid, adulterated'; 'counterfeit, imitative, spurious'.[5] In other words it suggests an identity constructed as an *aporia* – the indeterminate space in which an opposition breaks down and difference collapses into sameness – and as a simulacrum, a mimic, in which that sameness becomes strange, uncanny in the sense that Freud used the term. As 'hybrids' bastards can both embody exotic fantasies of originality and relate to the dominant forces that thus define them through reflection, mimicry and parody; they also raise the question: what exactly is hybridity?

The very instability of the illegitimacy/legitimacy divide reinforces and is reinforced by power structures that are at once social, psychic and symbolic, but it also underlines the danger of assimilating these forms of power into a single unified force: patriarchy. Illegitimacy marks the breach of the rule on which its existence depends; it is thus both constitutive and transgressive. The creation of a distinction between legitimate and illegitimate children is clearly central to both the definition and establishment of patriarchal power, of the ascendancy of the name and genealogy of the father over that of the mother, of the transmission of property and established power. Versions of the argument that the establishment of the legal codes of marriage (and thus, by implication, institutionalised heterosexuality) is central to the formation of 'society' (both material property relations and symbolic structures) have been central to the development of a range of social and anthropological theories since the eighteenth century. In the 1920s, for example, the anthropologist Bronislaw Malinowski developed his 'Principle of Legitimacy', arguing that the 'most important moral and legal rule concerning the physiological state of kinship is that no child should be born without a man ... assuming the role of sociological father', and this is often cited to maintain that most societies discriminate against those born outside a sanctioned marriage pattern, though the form it may take is historically and culturally specific (Malinowski 1930, 137). The 'Principle of Legitimacy' has been subsequently discredited, but it is important to remember that Malinowski himself advanced his theory reflexively, not as an immutable law but as a set of qualifying hypotheses that centred on the slippery status of 'fatherhood' itself .[6] And it is the slippery nature of paternity which recurs in work which seems to express the symbolic role of the father most forcefully, such as psychoanalytic and poststructuralist theories.

Freud's analysis of the establishment of the symbolic role of the father and with it the formation of a gendered social identity in the young child is tacitly based on the tenuousness of biological paternity. In his famous short essay 'The Family Romance of the Neurotic', he describes how the young boy initially sees his parents as perfect beings; how, on perceiving their imperfections, he invents the compensatory story that they are in fact humble substitutes for his own royal mother and father. Freud argues that this fantasy goes through two distinct stages – that of the Foundling and that of the Bastard – and that these are crucial to the effectiveness of the fantasy as an expression of the emergence both of sexual differences and of social divisions. The foundling stage represents a pre-social, pre-Oedipal moment in that the child is not aware of the details of sexual difference and of reproduction, and it implies that acquiring such knowledge involves a recognition of social hierarchies and legal codes. For in the 'bastard', Oedipal stage of the romance the child has both discovered sexual difference and has learnt, Freud writes, 'the old Latin legal maxim' and source of endless bawdy jokes: *'pater semper incestus est'* (Freud 1977, 223). The child has accepted his biological link with his mother, and sees his father alone as elevated but absent, and this confirms his sense of superiority even as it deprives him of formal legitimacy.

Yet the very process that seems to fix the power of the absent father and by extension to fix the mother in some pre-symbolic realm suggests an alternative story if one shifts frames and reads Freud as developing established conventions of nineteenth-century melodrama, which are in turn responding to shifts in the social significance of bastardy themselves. In Freud's story of the child's fantasy, the position of the mother is that of the working-class servant seduced and betrayed by the powerful master. She is beneath rather than beyond the shadow of the father's law, and occupies a place which is both displaced and supplemented by the position of the girl child of the family romance, who enacts the bastard story even more ambivalently, experiencing it as a double exclusion, mimicking and compounding her own 'illegitimate' place within the dominant symbolic structure, beneath the shadow of the absent father, yet still forming a symbolised space, albeit a negative one, for the mother. However, the 'bastard' stage also marks the subject's move into a set of specific social power relationships, and this means that it gains its psychic appeal precisely because it cannot be contained within this purely imaginary framework; it tacitly acknowledges the existence of a specific family structure within a legal code that is precisely *not* the one that, as fantasy, it is formed by – and which it is helping to form. As a trope it marks a crucial moment in Freud's story of individual psychic development because it introjects a set of power relations and material structures 'beyond' the child's negotiation and representation of the relationship with his real parents through fantasy. 'Bastardy' is thus a fantasy framed by the specific dynamic of the two-parent nuclear family, yet it also embodies the social frame which contains the psychic frame it is set in, and so on, *ad infinitum.*

That Freud universalised the experience of the nineteenth-century middle-class male in developing his theory of infantile sexuality – that he selected the myth that most closely tallied with this experience that then became a template to be imposed on different family scenarios – has become a familiar argument. In her study of the significance of illegitimacy in French personal narrative, for example, Marie Maclean is particularly critical of Freud's universalising tendencies, and like her I object to the ways in which 'the bastard' is pressed into the service of consolidating the 'legitimate' family rather than providing a standpoint that questions the naturalness of the form itself (Maclean 1994, 33–5). But here I want to take a stand beyond either the acceptance or rejection of Freud's model, and emphasise that while the fantasy of bastardy lies at the heart of social identity, historical shifts in the social and cultural significance of bastardy mean that at certain moments it can open up a particular kind of symbolised and social space for the mother – albeit one which is never straightforwardly oppositional. Fantasies of bastardy help shape its cultural meaning but are themselves shaped within the specific historical conditions. One significant way in which the 'real' conditions of illegitimacy question Freud's narrative is that they challenge the distinction between 'foundling' and 'bastard' altogether (since many foundlings were bastards) and they offer a potentially far more complex and ambiguous space for the single mother than that suggested when 'mother' is seen as one term in the 'mother/father' dyad. All this suggests that fictions of bastardy are not only ambiguous but embody epistemological ambiguity, and this is one of the sources of illegitimacy's extraordinary range of narrative possibilities.

Illegitimacy is embedded in particular narratives of origin, but always as an element which questions its constitutive terms, and thus can be implicitly or explicitly central in various poststructuralist accounts which question the very idea of origin itself. But these too bring their own set of problems which hinge initially on illegitimacy's peculiar status as metaphor. For example, in Derrida's essay in *Disseminations*, 'Plato's Pharmacy', writing is itself seen as a kind of bastardy, an *aporia* which repeatedly returns to a set of meditations on the instability of metaphor and meaning itself.[7] Derrida's starting-point is Socrates' argument in Plato's *Phaedrus* that 'spoken truths are to be reckoned a man's legitimate sons' and the distinction which is drawn between the written shadow speech (the legitimate son) and writing itself, the bastard. He describes a process of metaphoric transference between the *logos* and the paternal position, between speech and writing, suggesting not a fixed set of relationships between father and son, legitimate and illegitimate, but an endless dance of *différance* which hinges on the tenuousness of legitimate paternity. Yet in emphasising the equivocal position of the father (the mother remains a shadowy figure) Derrida provisionally holds in place the paternal position that he is breaking down; the symbolic figure of the father endlessly recedes, yet remains resonant in his very inconsistency. 'The specificity' is 'thus intimately bound up with the absence of a father', but it is a significant absence, while the 'bastard' figure is at once 'the father's other, the father and the subversive movement of displacement. The god of writing is thus at once the father, his son and himself. He cannot be assigned a fixed spot in the play of differences' (Derrida 1981, 93).

Bastardy here is analogous to the 'feminine' position as it is analysed in the different approaches of Hélène Cixous and Luce Irigaray; femininity 'cannot be assigned a fixed spot in the play of differences', it is a performative identity *par excellence*. Illegitimacy and femininity can both mutually construct and displace each other; bastardy is formed through the simultaneous repression and affirmation of a maternal genealogy that is always fractured. The illegitimate child's traditional use of the mother's surname is always ambiguous – it is condoned, quasi-legitimated by being the *grandfather's* name – but it nonetheless connects the child to the mother both socially and symbolically, always disrupting patrilinear continuity. The illegitimate son replaces and displaces both mother and daughter, and can replicate and repress the feminine in a homosocial world; it both opens up and closes down possibilities for the illegitimate daughter.

This raises more specific issues about the role it plays in the formation of dominant forms of authority – political legitimation in the general sense – and the ways in which that authority might be subverted or sustained. For in many ways the bastard is the precise embodiment of the idea of transgression which Michel Foucault outlined in his *History of Sexuality* and elsewhere, where the very act of subverting the dominant order simultaneously undermines and strengthens the rules of exclusion which create it (Foucault 1980). Yet it is always risky to impose other paradigms of 'otherness' on to illegitimacy; its very fictiveness suggests that it can both underpin and undermine other fictions of identity, always marking their limit. Moreover bastardy does not easily provide the basis of what Foucault termed a 'reverse discourse', that space which can be opened up within a movement or subculture in which dominant definitions can be inverted and appropriated to become the basis of a collective opposition. While historians have debated the existence of 'bastardy-prone sub-societies', the illegitimate have rarely emerged as a cohesive group with their own sense of a cultural identity.[8] Their existence is not determined by bastardy alone, but is always shaped by their class, gender or ethnicity, though illegitimacy may seep into these identities and transform them. Bastards have rarely had a movement, a manifesto of their own; as social subjects they have often been muted by the liberal discourse of individual rights which as fantasy they have been so crucial in helping to form, and, while the abolition of illegitimacy as a legal category has often been a revolutionary demand, it has rarely been implemented. It was, for example, abolished by the 12th Brumaire during the French Revolution, but under the Napoleonic Code of 1803 the position of bastards and their mothers became far worse than it had been under the *ancien régime* in ways which correspond and contrast with changes in England (Brinton 1936).

'VICTORIAN' BASTARDY

There are certain crucial ways in which illegitimacy's meaning shifts in England during the first part of the nineteenth century. Certainly there is a sense in which it now becomes 'stigmatised' in a new kind of way.[9] The shame of illegitimacy is internalised to a greater degree, as the illegitimate child is doubly perceived as both bearing and being the mother's 'mark of shame', and is increasingly felt by the working as well as the middle class, becoming one of the key markers of working-class respectability. But it is not helpful to see this simply as an aspect of a stereotyped 'Victorian' moralism, for illegitimacy above all struck at the heart of the meaning of 'morality' itself, revealing just how contested a term this was. For it was during the nineteenth century that it became the screen on which particular processes of marginalisation and social exclusion were reflexively debated and dominant meanings resisted and reformed in new kinds of ways. Moreover, the opprobriousness of illegitimacy was not purely the outcome of utilitarian and Evangelical attempts to regulate the working class and reform manners and morals throughout society; it was also the product of broader economic and cultural changes. Marriage itself had always been a slippery thing in English common law, and the attempt to regulate it under the auspices of the Church of England by Lord

Hardwicke's Marriage Act of 1753 had actually increased the number of unofficial unions; it was economic dependency as much as legal and religious proscriptions that consolidated the relationship of many working-class couples.[10] But, while illegitimacy rates peaked in the 1840s, by the mid-nineteenth century marriage by civil, church or chapel ceremony had gained widespread ascendancy. The Owenite utopian socialists had based their analysis of society on a critique of marriage as a bastion of arbitrary patriarchal power in their early radical years, but by the 1840s this had lost its impact as women of all classes rationally perceived their own interests to lie within monogamy, the alternative being even greater vulnerability to sexual exploitation. This is reflected in the hegemony of both marriage and motherhood as the moral, social and spiritual centre of society, not only in early Victorian evangelical reformism, but as one of the foundations of emergent feminism during the middle of the century. Ironically, as actual single motherhood for working-class women becomes increasingly outcast and marginalised, single middle-class women legitimise their entry into the public world of philanthropy by becoming 'social mothers'.[11]

The rise of domestic ideology, the increasing sexual division of labour and the separation of the workplace from the home, masculine from feminine spheres, also determined the ways in which illegitimacy was perceived and understood, yet the ways in which it did so are not always straightforward. For one of the factors both arising from and contributing to the growing stigmatisation of bastardy is that it becomes 'feminised'; the illegitimate child becomes increasingly linked to the mother as women become increasingly economically and socially marginalised and positioned within marriage, as the centre of the home. Before the late eighteenth century bastardy had overwhelmingly masculine connotations (still lingering in the term of abuse today). It was the visible product of an unstable paternal narrative, and at the same time the sign of patriarchal power and sexual prowess over both wives and concubines. It thus helped to underpin the patrilineal genealogy which it subverted (it was the bastard *eigné*, the eldest but illegitimate son, whose relationship to inheritance based on primogeniture was most problematic), while also opening a space for a 'modern' masculine self that could move beyond this 'feudal' patriarchy, as Derrida's metaphors reflect.[12] As wives women were the 'frame' of legitimacy and one of its possible points of rupture; as female subjects they were in a sense 'beyond' illegitimacy; they both replicated and cancelled it. But while emergent economic and social structures do not mean that 'older' forms wither away, these meanings undergo important modifications during the nineteenth century. A new space is simultaneously opened up and closed down for the single mother, who becomes the embodiment of clashing discourses on femininity and maternity, while the illegitimate girl or woman emerges as a potential, though profoundly problematic identity.

There are various ways in which illegitimacy is shaped through different kinds of discourses which give it particular cultural meanings during the nineteenth century. I would like to suggest three possibilities, which are not directly commensurate and do not fit into neat historical periods, although they broadly emerge toward the beginning, the middle and the end of the century.

The first – a passionate and melodramatic moment which plays a crucial part in shaping the complex and contradictory character of early Victorian ideology – is shaped through the specific social conditions which surrounded the single mother and her child and the debates about them: on the role of the state, pauperism, gender and class during the 1830s, 1840s and 1850s. They are most visible in the discussions surrounding the Bastardy Clauses of the (pre-Victorian) Poor Law Amendment Act of 1834 though they are not confined to it .

A second focuses more narrowly on the processes of debate and contest in specific novels during the 1850s and 1860s; particularly the sensation novels of Dickens and Collins. Sensation novels offered the widest range of narrative possibilities for exploring how the concept of illegitimacy throws legitimacy itself into question, in particular 'legitimate' marriage and the position of the 'lawful wife', who, like the bastard, is constructed as a 'legal fiction'. Hingeing on secrecy and disguise, on the disclosure of unsanctioned origins, on the instability of names and on the performativity of identity, sensation narrative connects secrets at the heart of the family to the exploration of social and psychic inheritance, the transmission of property and power.

A third, 'post-Darwinian', moment questions how changes in ideas about origins and evolutionary social development shifted the perception of the legitimacy/illegitimacy distinction during the latter part of the century. These had new implications which intersected with ideas about 'race' and national identity, about gender and 'natural' sexuality. Although there was no real challenge to marriage as a social institution beyond the arguments and activities of a relatively small group of intellectuals, the family became denaturalised as both a social and a biological unit with the development of anthropological and evolutionary theory, and these alternative accounts of kinship formed a crucial aspect of contemporary debates on natural and human law. One of Darwin's significant hypotheses had been that new species come into existence not through linear genealogies but as hybrid, bastard beings. Henry Maine's *Ancient Law*, published in 1861, two years after *The Origin of Species*, explicitly placed the patriarchal family as the basic unit of human society, while emphasising the historical variability of legal and social institutions, seeing the family itself as 'complex, artificial and strange', based on essentially fictional codes, paradoxically providing the premises by which patriarchal theories could be challenged.[13] Books as different as Bachofen's *Das Mutter-reight*, Tylor's *Primitive Culture*, Lang's *Social Origins* and Schreiner's *Woman and Labour* each tended to suggest unilinear accounts of human development, to see 'matriarchy' as a fixed point of origin, to equate 'primitive' cultures with earlier stages of human development, but their arguments have the effect of recasting the family in a less monumental form. At the same time illegitimacy becomes constructed as an object of scientific knowledge with the publication of Albert Leffingwell's *Illegitimacy and the Influence of Seasons upon Conduct* in 1892, while demands for changes in the position of illegitimate children culminated in the formation of the Legitimation League in 1890, whose manifesto pamphlet, *The Bar Sinister and Licit Love*, arguing for the abolition of bastardy and transformation of marriage, holds a significant place in *fin-de-siècle* feminism and sexual radicalism (Dawson 1895).[14]

The status of the bastard as *fillius nullius* had been established in civil and in common law in England since the early middle ages. This defined the bastard as literally nobody's child, a 'stranger in blood' who had neither automatic right of inheritance nor legal claim on either of his parents for support (Hooper 1911, 24–6). That contradiction in terms, the 'fatherless poor man's child', became the responsibility and 'property' of the parish under the Elizabethan Poor Laws, but the drain that this placed on the Poor Rate meant that whenever possible maintenance was actually placed at the door of both parents. 'Bastard-bearing' was chastised by whipping and imprisonment under the Old Poor Law and while women bore the brunt of punishment – an Act of 1607 committed them to the house of correction for a year for a first 'offence' – the aim of the church and civil courts was to control both male and female sexuality. As visible bearers of the children, women drew most censure, but men were also answerable for their actions, and fathers, real or reputed, were in practice made responsible for maintenance. A woman was encouraged to name the wealthiest man who could reasonably be assumed to be the child's father, and stories of false paternity suits abounded. Under legislation of 1732 and 1809 justices of divisions were empowered to imprison alleged fathers on women's evidence unless they could provide security, and if a woman could not name the father she was able to claim out-relief from the parish. Life was not easy for the single mother under the Old Poor Law who faced public humiliation, imprisonment and being hustled from parish to parish as each tried to shake off the responsibility of having the child born within their boundaries. But those who were able to claim out-relief did so with a small measure of freedom.[15]

The 1834 Poor Law Amendment Act and the enormous changes it brought about in the definition and state treatment of poverty were prompted by fiscal crisis as much as by the utilitarian desire to regulate and discipline the poor; yet it was this circumscribed independence, particularly the power of mothers to name the reputed father of their children, that particularly appalled the Commissioners in the sections on bastardy in the Poor Law Report of 1834. 'If there were no other objection to these laws than that they place at the mercy of every abandoned woman every man who is not rich enough to give security', they wrote, 'we should still feel it our duty to urge their immediate abolition. What can be more revolting than a law which not only authorises but compels this oppression?' (ed. Checkland 1974, 260) But this was not its worst aspect. 'The mode by which they oppress the innocent, revolting though it is, is far less mischievous to society than that by which they punish the guilty', the Report argued. 'To the woman a single illegitimate child is seldom any expense, and two or three are a source of positive profit …'(ed. Checkland 1974, 261). The Report and its appendices bulged with stories of women deliberately producing children in order to claim from the parish. 'Witness mentioned a case within his own personal cognisance of a young woman of four-and-twenty with four bastard children; she receives 1s. 6d. for each of them. She told him herself that if she had one more she should be very comfortable. Witness added, "they don't in reality keep the children; they let them run wild and enjoy themselves with the money"' (ed. Checkland 1974, 267). The commissioners recommended that firstly, unmarried mothers should no longer be imprisoned; and secondly, that all illegitimate children should follow the mother's settlement. This was partly aimed to stop the hounding of pregnant women from parish to parish; it had the effect of consolidating the material and symbolic connection between the child and the mother. Finally it recommended that fathers be absolved from all responsibility for their bastard children. These measures, with the stopping of out-relief for the poor as a whole, meant that the unmarried mother was in the same position as the destitute widow (as she was meant to be), and she was faced with the choice of 'farming out' her child and working if she could, or of being forced into the workhouse and sep-arated from it. The Poor Law Amendment Act thus consolidated the connection between mother and child with one hand, and broke it with the other.

The Bastardy Clauses reflected the rhetoric of the Act as a whole with its use of Malthusian Evangelical and utilitarian discourse, de-ploying notions of 'natural' checks and balances to reinforce moral discipline, and legitimising these measures through reference to a combined divine Providence and natural law. 'If our recommenda-tions are adopted a bastard will be what Providence appears to have ordained that it should be, a burden on its mother', stated the Report. 'If we are right in believing the penalties inflicted by nature to be sufficient, it is needless to urge further objection to any legal punishment.... In affirming the inefficiency of human legislation to enforce the restraints placed on licentiousness by Providence, we have implied our belief that all punishment of the supposed father is useless' (ed. Checkland 1974, 482). 'Perhaps we ought, in peni-tence and submission, to fall back on that simple law of nature, which has most sensibly decreed, that a woman after all is the best guardian of her own honour, and that the high rewards and the severe punishments which naturally attend its preservation and its loss are the beneficent means of securing our happiness, and of maintaining the moral character of our country', commented *The Quarterly Review* in April 1835, half-sardonically reporting the view of the Assistant Commissioner (Anon. 1835, 505). The woman's body is circulated as the guardian and symbol of national legit-imacy in the face of an unaccountable and predatory male sexual-ity, and women are positioned as custodians of national morality even when trangressing its rule.

The Bastardy Clauses met a massive tide of protest from working-class organisations and from middle-class philanthropists and were defeated by an Act of 1844 which removed affiliation and maintenance from parish control, allowing women to claim from fathers through Petty Sessions. But the criticisms often counterpoised an alternative model of femininity to the predatory one of the Commissioners; the language which both positions employed at once deployed and helped to form the melodramatic rhetoric that was so central to the discourse of class exploitation in radical writings, centring on the poignant image of the innocent working-class girl preyed upon by the upper-class rake.[16] The fury levelled at the Bastardy Clauses focused on its double standards, on the perception that removing all restraints on male sexuality would be more likely to increase illegitimacy rates than reduce them. But it was expressed as outrage against such unmanly, un-English treatment of the weaker sex, which not only reinforced the placing of the female body as the collective property and passive moral guardian of the nation, but did so by reinforcing the notion of male sexuality as a natural, irresistible force. Moreover, this rhetoric tended to be amplified by both the opponents of the Act, and also in a strange way by its half-doubtful supporters, who incorporated these melodramatic conventions into their own discourse in order to legitimise their countervailing arguments indirectly. 'To relieve the man from punishment, and to leave his unhappy victim to shame, infamy and distress, is a law discreditable to our national character, impious, cruel, ungenerous, unmanly and unjust', wrote *The Quarterly Review*, summarising the debate (Anon. 1835, 502), while Edward Hughes' 'compendium' of the Act emphasised that while the 'natural law' argument 'might instil a greater degree of caution on behalf of the woman, the other sex would, from an increased impunity, feel proportionately reckless, with an enlarged determination to effect his propensity to evil' (Hughes 1836, 15). He drew a picture of 'a poor, distressed woman...deserted in the midst of abject poverty – uncared for, nay reprimanded, and morosely treated by those from whom she would fain hope for solace and assistance; mourning the loss of her suitor (for she yet loved him), a heavy load of duty resting on her, for the maintenance of herself and her babe, and withal a conscience troubled by vice and exposure...' (Hughes 1836, 15).

I do not want to trivialise the appalling situation that faced single mothers under the New Poor Law, but rather emphasise how the shaping of this cultural icon drew on and reinforced a set of meanings which circulated in both fictional and political discourse. Much has been written on representations of the fallen woman and on the need to sanctify her in order to gain the sympathy of the liberal middle class during the mid-nineteenth century. The shaping of this figure through the codes of melodrama cut across both cultural and political hierarchies, not only enabling a tactical convergence of middle-class philanthropy (particularly that of dissenting Christianity) and radical working-class rhetoric, but also incorporating them into the very debates to which they were counterposed. In 1892 Albert Leffingwell would open his study of illegitimacy by conjuring up an endlessly repeated, familiar trope: 'Against the background of history, too prominent to escape the observation from which it shrinks, stands a figure, mute, mournful, indescribably sad. It is a girl, holding in her arms the blessing and burden of motherhood, but in whose face one finds no trace of maternal joy and pride. ... Who is this woman so pitiable and so sad? It is the mother of the illegitimate child. By forbidden paths she has attained the grace of maternity; but its glory is for her transfigured into a badge of unutterable shame' (Leffingwell 1892, 1–2).

But while the figure of the mother continually circulated there is a sense in which the children become impossible to represent, in both senses of the word; they are cross-category, 'transfigured' figures. They articulate the contradictions often repressed in the representation of the woman, seen as redemptive forces, as embodiments of innocence, as stigmatised by their parents' sin and as the signifier of the sin itself across various debates; at times the language in which they are imagined enacts the very process of bastardisation, enslavement and obliteration which is ostensibly being deplored, at others the child forces a revaluation of the rhetoric of natural law; despite the growing influence of the post-Romantic notion of the rights of the child and the relatively new sense of these children's vulnerability to exploitation and infanticide, they are never quite 'legitimate' subjects; they are either cut free from their origins and seen as being without subjectivity and thus completely subjected, slaves, or they are drawn back into being positioned as the product of their mothers' narrative.[17] In the early nineteenth century 'parish apprentices' had been sold individually or in batches as factory or agricultural labour; and while this gave rise to widespread outrage an article discussing infanticide in *The Magdalen's Friend and Female's Home Intelligentsia* as late as 1863 cited a reader's letter that suggested (and whether this is ironic is left open), that 'in slave states, every little black babe is worth ten dollars at its birth, and are white ones more worthless, less teachable than they? Might they not be reared to man our fleet, to cultivate our colonies – the fact of their illegitimacy giving the government a claim on them and their services for life, or for a stated term?'(Anon. 1832, 40). The article is primarily about infanticide, and it at once re-enacts the moral structure that gave rise to the crime and ambivalently ponders on this process. Discussing the specific history of Anne Pedfield ('It is a time-worn, pitiable, monotonously melancholy story of seduction, abandonment and crime ...'), it argues: 'It is an injustice and a scandal that while Anne Pedfield is sentenced to be hanged ... the father of that child, who tempted her into the path that led to the crime, suffers no penalty whatever. ... If anyone in this case deserves to suffer, it is that Society which, by her unequal treatment of the offender ... is virtually responsible for half the cases of infanticide in our land...'. Yet it continues: 'We should be very sorry to see Foundling Hospitals multiplied, thus affording an *unnatural* means of escape for the terrible retribution of maternity, to those whom nature has branded with this just mark of shame' (Anon. 1832, 29). The article goes on to support temporary mother and child refuges, and a fascinating process of continually deferred responsibility is at work here, from the mother to the father to Society, then back to the mother through the child, who is once more transfigured into an innocent 'badge of shame'.

These ambivalent perceptions presented novelists with particular possibilities and problems. Charles Dickens and Elizabeth Gaskell, Frances Trollope and George Eliot are variously writing from explicitly reformist positions; there is a very obvious sense in which *Oliver Twist* and *Ruth* are actively intervening in contemporary debates on the New Poor Law and the treatment of the 'fallen woman', and the innocence and purity of their central characters are clearly tendentious strategies to elicit their readers' sympathies. They, too, drew on and adapted melodramatic conventions in different ways in attempting to present the child as the product of an already-known yet poignant story, one that is at once familiar and unique. But in terms of its narrative structure and psychological appeal, melodrama tends to rely on a set of fixed oppositions and the disclosure of a fixed identity; it takes the form of a 'foundling' plot which follows a pattern of concealment and closure in which the legitimacy of the story of the past is a precondition for narrative resolution on the present.[18] The slipperiness of bastardy continually eludes this process of closure and this pulls the stories in different directions – back into the consoling 'foundling' fantasies of the family romance, into a legitimate position and a stable name, and at the same time forward into undecidability – and this involves various forms of splitting and displacement, and is always ambiguous. As narrative pattern, as uncanny social identity and in the tension between the two, bastardy exists at both the centre and margin of the cognitive framework through which it is defined, as three very brief examples show.

Oliver Twist opens with the death of Oliver's mother, and his unknown but undoubtedly elevated origins remain the underlying question as the layers of mystery are gradually built up and peeled away.[19] Oliver is initially an orphan, a foundling, and this position is paradoxically both reinforced and sabotaged by the conspiracies of his half-brother Edward Leeson (Monks) to make him internalise his social inheritance and become a criminal, and thus never be in a position to claim his paternal genealogy and patrimony. The sinister, epileptic Monks, Oliver's legitimate sibling, self-consciously enacts the role of envious, displaced bastard brother and inverts this structure, emerging finally as the polluted offspring of a corrupt marriage, and this produces a process of splitting and displacement which allows distinct and contradictory notions of bastardy – the best and the worst of the self – to co-exist, yet cancel each other out. At the same time the discovery of Oliver's origins involves the disclosure of his illegitimacy, and the impossibility of genealogical and ideological closure, so that while Oliver and Monks appear at opposite ends of the spectrum, as products of degenerate marriage and innocent love-child, Oliver can never completely operate as the positive to Monks's negative, despite the manichean rhetoric of the Preface. For it is in oscillating between the positions of foundling and bastard that the process of representing Oliver's social identity is revealed to be most provisional and indeterminate; he is, as he claimed he wished to be to Brownlow, always a seller rather than an author of books, of his own story.

Above all, Oliver's 'queer name' (as Brownlow puts it) implies his peculiar position at the centre of the narrative yet always, as a subject, absent (Dickens 1985, 30). It is an arbitrary signifier, a pet rather than a slave name (slaves tended to be given their masters' surnames even though they were never their 'own'). He is 'half-baptised' by the first of his three honorary grandfathers, Bumble the Beadle: '"I inwented it ... I Mrs Mann" ... "Why you're quite a literary character, Sir!"'; 'Oliver Twist' is as much a bureaucratic fiction as 'Tom White', the name provided by the magistrate's clerk (Dickens 1985, 51–2). 'Twist' carries some of the connotations of sinister 'bentness' that never sticks to 'Oliver', but it also adds a twist to it, implying that there will never be a moment when Oliver fits or discovers his 'real' name. And it is this dissociation of name and identity that contributes to Oliver's strangely blank liminality. He continually dwells in a 'borderland' state: his earliest moments are poised between life and death; his first workplace is a place of death, where he mutely enacts its rituals; he sees Fagin in the hazy state between sleeping and waking; he hovers between life and death on being rescued by Brownlow; on being reclaimed by Fagin and lying asleep, 'he looked like death; not death as it shows itself in shrouds and coffin, but in the guise it wears when life has just departed ...', and so on (Dickens 1985, 194). He is dazed and confused, he weeps frequently and often faints. And while his beauty, innocence and purity need to be seen in the context of the 'feminisation' of childhood in the early nineteenth century, it also has the effect of attenuating his gender, so that he comes increasingly to resemble his other apparently illegitimate counterpart, Rose Maylie (Nelson 1991). Oliver is finally socially legitimised through a fractured paternal narrative, through Brownlow's adoption, but behind and exceeding this hovers his mother, into whose image he continually blends, but as a ghost, a set of traces. The novel closes with a single name on a memorial, and with equivocation towards it: 'I believe that the shade of Agnes sometimes hovers round that solemn nook. I believe it none the less because that nook is in a Church, and she was weak and erring' (Dickens 1985, 480).

In Gaskell's *Ruth* (1853), Ruth's son Leonard is consciously moralised and idealised, and his existence focuses the formalised and didactic debate between dissenting and evangelical religious traditions. Like Oliver, he is the empty subject upon whom different discourses of redemption and retribution are projected, but the fact that his origins form part of the narrative rather than the history to be reconstructed raises a set of more complex questions about the process of stigmatisation and passing. It is passing which forms the central predicament of this novel and the performative nature of identity that it implies – the dilemma of whether Ruth should masquerade as a widow in order to create a fictionalised legitimacy for her son – and this performativity extends through the novel even as it is explicitly condemned in Ruth herself. It is Benson, Leonard's honorary grandfather, who bears the physical stigma which Leonard internalises, while his biological father has to take on a new patronym in order to inherit a property. And in a final displacement, a marginal character, Davis, the doctor, 'comes out' as a bastard, legitimising Leonard – after Ruth's death – by bequeathing him his name, his medical practice and a new professional middle-class identity. Until she is rescued by the Bensons, Ruth's own image could be Edward Hughes's 'poor distressed woman ... deserted in the midst of abject poverty...'; the novel's ideological framework cannot sustain an illegitimate maternal narrative and for her there is no future; but it is significant that Leonard is given a new masculine identity and legitimacy through an adoptive paternal narrative, by a bastard whose history is never told, but who has survived.

In George Eliot's *Silas Marner* (1861) a different process of displacement and 'transfiguration' is at work in which questions of illegitimacy are explored within a foundling narrative which takes apart its own conventions from within. Eppie, the abandoned child of an alcoholic mother and an irresponsible father, is structurally and socially in the position of a pauper bastard, and is metaphorically 'illegitimate' as the product of a cross-class relationship. The fact that Godfrey, her father, was actually married to her mother can in a sense be read as a way of anchoring his paternity, of highlighting his failure to acknowledge his daughter until it is too late; but concepts of paternity, maternity and parenting are transformed in Marner's nurturing of the child. Eppie herself is ambiguously positioned as a historical figure whose origins are present within the narrative and who has a future, and as a fantasy, a figure from Marner's past (she is 'legitimised' by being given his sister's name, Hepzibah, a 'Bible name') and from his unconscious, appearing during a cataleptic trance, and yet linking him with both a past and a future. The central form of metaphoric transfiguration in the novel, Marner's perception of Eppie as his gold returned to him, suggests that structurally and psychically, he is in the position of the single mother (his name, indeed, suggests 'mater' and 'martyr') while enacting a narrative of single parenting that it would not be possible to represent for the mother of an illegitimate child. Marner is a strangely genderless figure, a 'lone thing' who is betrayed, stigmatised by religious intolerance and cast out of his native commu-

nity by acquiring something illicitly, and who at first leads an
ostracised life in Raveloe. The arrival of Eppie, a redemptive
force who becomes a 'badge' of acceptance rather than shame at
once recasts and reverses these complex contemporary discourses.

Each of these novels pushes up against the limits of melodrama;
but it is sensation fiction, described by contemporary critics as a
bastard genre, a hybrid, which is able to fully elaborate illegitimacy's narrative complexity. As I suggested in relation to *Oliver
Twist*, in 'bastard' plots story time and narrative time (the order of
the story told and the order of the telling) are connected yet fractured – they disrupt and transform each others' meaning in a way
that shapes the performance of self in the very process of displaying its impossibility, and this is achieved above all in the illusive
and fictional nature of names. Dickens's use of illegitimacy can
never be detached from his explorations of class and gender, yet it
often remains the central metaphor of marginality that exceeds
others precisely by remaining marginal. In *Bleak House* Esther's illegitimacy becomes a means of exploring the construction of femininity at the edge of the law, with no identity within it, yet no
standpoint to speak outside it. Esther and Estella in *Great
Expectations* suggest countervailing sides of a dynamic in which illegitimacy becomes a complex trope for exploring the performance
of femininity, replaying, with a 'twist', dominant representations of
domestic self-effacement and manipulating sexuality. In *Little
Dorrit* Arthur Clennam is haunted by an incomprehensible sense of
lack that finally emerges in his own bastardy. But it is continually
prefigured in his sense of having no general legitimacy, of being
unable to function in the world either economically or psychically.
This is crucial to the process by which his central narrative position
echoes and counterpoises the other ineffectual forms of masculine
identity, of collapsed patriarchal authority, in the novel as a whole.
The central power of the book is maternal, yet maternity is denaturalised; Clennam's putative mother enacts a parody of patriarchal
evangelicalism, Amy and her father invert the father/child relationship even as the uncanny 'Little Dorrit' is known as a servant
through a diminutive patronym. Tattycoram is also a child with a
slave/pet name, named after the famous foundling hospital by a
mistress nicknamed 'Pet', and whose rage sabotages the consoling
myths of the foundling romance; a process pushed to its extreme in
the figure of Miss Wade, whose wholesale rejection of patrilineal
authority can only be presented as perversion.

Wilkie Collins's exploration of illegitimacy as a legal fiction which underpins other kinds of fictions of identity investigates the social foundations of difference itself; the illegitimacy/legitimacy divide – the most fictive difference of all – becomes the ground on which other kinds of distinctions rest, both literally and metaphorically. Above all, Collins's narrative structures themselves explore the forms of correspondence and analogy between the positions of the bastard and that of the 'lawful wife'; seemingly so opposed, but in fact both legal constructions which undermine legitimate subjectivity. 'There is no legal fiction in the Arabian Nights Entertainments, in the memoirs of the Baron Munchausen, or in the journey to the moon more wildly extravagant than some of the fictions in English law', maintained an article in *Household Words* in July 1855. 'Amongst them, few represent injustice pushed to the extreme of absurdity more vividly than that legal fiction – an English wife' (Anon. 1855, 598). Arguing in favour of married women's property rights many years before the final success of the legal campaign, the piece focuses on the complete obliteration of a woman's autonomous subjectivity on marriage: 'When she marries she dies, handed over to be buried in her husband's arms, or pounded and pummelled into the grave *with* his arms.' However, the rhetorical strength of the argument relies on contrasting the position of the wife to the relatively more favourable one of the mistress and her illegitimate children, a distinction which Collins takes to pieces in *The Woman in White* and *No Name*.

Although it is *No Name* that deals most explicitly with the performative possibilities and limits of illegitimacy and feminine identity, I would like to conclude this brief overview by pointing to some of the ways in which *The Woman in White* acts out the complexity of the notion of 'legitimacy' itself in the merging and substitution of the identities of Laura, the heiress and wife, and Anne, her working-class illegitimate half-sister. But while the substitution plot lies at its centre, there are two narratives of bastardy at work in the novel: that of the pauperised abandoned woman, the unacknowledged daughter of Philip Fairlie who bears her mother's name, and the apparent possessor of residual feudal power, Sir Percival Glyde, an excessively 'melodramatic' figure. It is through this dual narrative that bastardy becomes the central metaphoric structure as well as the double secret of *The Woman in White* through a continuous process of dislocation. At the 'Anne Catherick' end of the spectrum Anne and Laura are revealed to be related through their father, but Anne comes to identify with Laura though the bond with Laura's mother, one of the substitute maternal figures who replace her own mother who is 'a trouble and a fear to her'. Anne and Laura are each trapped within destructive paternal narratives: Anne, outside the law, can only, shadow-like, mimic the legitimate self she might have been; Laura, trapped within it, stripped of name, inheritance and finally sanity, becomes, too, 'socially, morally, legally – dead' (Collins 1981, 380). Laura's other half-sister, Marian Halcombe, also is formally legitimate but through her distaff connection with her sister becomes a kind of honorary bastard – this time a healthy hybrid who transcends gender divisions and embodies the energy of bastardy set free from an over-bred paternal genealogy. At the other end of the spectrum, Percival Glyde teeters on the brink of self-control in usurping the position of residual power from which he is formally debarred, and represents that point at which bastardy, as the exaggerated mimicry of exhausted forms of power, pushes them beyond their limits, to a crisis of legitimation.

Notes

1. Throughout this essay I'll be using 'illegitimate' and 'bastard' as contested and problematic terms but want to avoid the clumsy device of scare-quotes. A fuller version of the material discussed here will be appearing in my forthcoming book, *Illegitimate Fictions: Narratives of Bastardy in English Culture*.
2. The 1987 Family Law Reform Act removed the formal legal distinction between legitimate and illegitimate children in Britain.
3. Interview with Peter Lilley on the Child Support Act, *The World This Weekend*, BBC Radio 4, 7 March 1993.
4. Thersites is described by Shakespeare as a 'core of envy' and a 'damnable box of envy' (*Troilus and Cressida*, V. i. 5 and 22).
5. Jenny Teichman opens her account of illegitimacy with a brief discussion of these definitions, and goes on to point out that '"bastard" is derived from the old French "ba(s)t", meaning baggage. ... It thus literally means "baggage child", suggesting the temporary nature of the parents' union' (Teichman 1982, 1–2).
6. The interconnections and incompatibilities between anthropological and psychoanalytic explanations of these mythic and social structures emerged most clearly in the debate between Malinowski and Ernest Jones on the universality of the Oedipus complex (Malinowski 1927).
7. Thanks to Geoff Bennington and Henry Turner for discussing this point. Turner takes up Derrida's use of the bastardy metaphor as a

key term for writing in 'Illegitimacy in Early Modern Drama'; unpublished MA dissertation, University of Sussex, 1993.

8. See, for example, Peter Laslett, 'The bastardy-prone sub-society', in Peter Laslett, Karla Oosterveen and R. M. Smith (eds), *Bastardy and its Comparative History* (London: Edward Arnold, 1980), pp. 217–39; for a recent critique of the Laslett thesis, see also Andrew Blaikie, *Illegitimacy, Sex and Society: North-East Scotland* (Oxford: The Clarendon Press, 1994).

9. For a discussion of attitudes to bastardy in England in earlier periods, particularly its treatment by the church and civil courts during the seventeenth century, see for example, Keith Thomas, 'The Puritans and Adultery: the Act of 1650 reconsidered' in D. Pennington and K. Thomas (eds), *Puritans and Revolutionaries* (Oxford: The Clarendon Press, 1978)' pp. 257–82; G. R. Quaife, *Wanton Wenches and Wayward Wives: Peasants and Illicit Sex in Seventeenth-Century England* (London: Croom Helm, 1979); Martin Ingram, *Church Courts, Sex and Marriage in England 1570–1640* (Cambridge: Cambridge University Press, 1987).

10. See J. Scott and L. Tilly, 'Women's Work and the Family in Nineteenth-century Europe', *Comparative Studies in Sociology and History*, 17 (1975): 36–64; Barbara Taylor, *Eve and the New Jerusalem* (London: Virago, 1983), pp. 183–216; John R. Gillis, *For Better, For Worse: British Marriages, 1600 to the Present* (Oxford: Oxford University Press, 1985), pp. 190–231.

11. Thanks to Eileen Yeo for discussing this point with me.

12. The bastard *eigné* was the Norman legal term for the eldest son, born before the parents' marriage and illegitimate, but in some cases able to inherit the patrimony. Edward Coke, *The First Part of the Institutes of the Laws of England* (London, 1669), 246.6.

13. As Ros Coward points out, although Maine supported the idea of an originary patriarchy his arguments were finally self-defeating. He maintained that the patriarchal family was maintained by social power structures, 'not a biological unit, but a unity which creates a fiction of biological unity' (Coward 1983, 23).

14. The Legitimation League aimed to abolish the disabilities of illegitimacy and turn marriage into a regularly renewable contract, though Dawson argued presciently that this would not automatically abolish the stigma of bastardy.

15. See Ursula Henriques, 'Bastardy and the New Poor Law', *Past and Present*, 37 (1967): 103–29; for a recent discussion of the effects in Scotland, see Blaikie (1994, 158–84) and Gill (1977, 210–35).

16. One of the most forceful anti-New Poor Law tracts was G. Wythern Baxter, *The Book of the Bastille, or the History of the Working of the New Poor Law* (London: John Stephens, 1841).

17. An important recent study of infanticide and the debates about it in the nineteenth century, is Ann R. Higginbottom, '"Sin of the Age": Infanticide and Illegitimacy in Victorian London', in K. O. Garrigan (ed.), *Victorian Scandals: Representations of Gender and Class* (Athens: Ohio University Press, 1992), pp. 257–88. Higginbottom agues that the

degree of severity shown to women charged with infanticide depended on the length of time the child had been alive; the 'exposure' of new-born babies tended to be treated fairly sympathetically. See also Lionel Rose, *Massacre of the Innocents: Infanticide in Great Britain, 1800–1939* (London: Routledge and Kegan Paul, 1986).

18. The distinction between Foundling and Bastard narratives is central to Marthe Robert's *Origins of the Novel*, trans. Sacha Rabinovitch (Brighton: Harvester Press, 1980). Robert extrapolates from the developmental model in Freud's 'Family Romances' essay, seeing the founding/bastard distinction both as stages in a developmental process and as distinct ontological and epistemological paradigms which each have a crucial bearing on the narrative forms and social identities in the novel; her analysis is fascinating but procrustean.

19. Some of the works discussed here are examined from a very different perspective in Nicola Shutt, 'Nobody's Child: The Illegitimate Child in the Works of George Eliot, Charles Dickens and Wilkie Collins', Unpublished dissertation, University of York, 1991.

8

The Language of Control in Victorian Children's Literature

Robin Melrose and Diana Gardner

J. L. Austin's theory of speech acts proposes that all utterances should be seen as performing three acts simultaneously: a locutionary act (which roughly corresponds to the dictionary meaning of the utterance); an illocutionary act (the act the speaker intends to perform in making the utterance); and a perlocutionary act (the effect the utterance has on the listener). As Austin says, there are hundreds of different illocutionary acts, sometimes, but certainly not always, cued by particular verbs, like urge, advise, warn or request. As regards the language of control – we have borrowed this term from the sociologist Basil Bernstein – such illocutionary acts might include: urging, advising, exhorting, threatening, warning, requesting, and so on.

Jacques Derrida, however, has pointed out, in two papers of crucial importance to linguists, 'Signature Event Context' (Derrida 1982), and 'Limited Inc abc...' (Derrida 1977), what he sees as significant flaws in speech act theory. All signs, says Derrida – and this includes speech acts – are by their very nature iterable, and since they can be repeated, or quoted, they can be quoted out of context, and therefore misquoted. The intention of a speech act, for Derrida, is never really knowable, and once uttered, its effect, while not completely wild, is at least unpredictable (he calls this phenomenon 'dehiscence', or the 'law of undecidable contamination'). This is complicated by another phenomenon. Austin claims that speech acts uttered on stage, in a poem, and so on, are 'parasitic' upon 'ordinary' speech acts. Seizing on this, Derrida says that everyday speech acts are 'Societies', 'Limited Companies', liable to be sub-

143

verted by all kinds of parasites, including unconscious feelings, drives, impulses, and so on (1977, 216). In other words, speech acts may not simply be conventional, but may incorporate aspects of the unconscious; and if this can happen to the speaker, then surely it can happen to the listener as well.

In this context we look at the language of children's books from the second half of the nineteenth century in order to examine the overt and covert control that these works exercised, and continue to exercise, over their readers. We examine the kinds of language that Victorian writers used in children's books to shape the actions, behaviour and beliefs of their child readers, and the strategies they employed to persuade their readers to digest their messages. However, before we look more closely at this, we need to consider briefly how adults perceived childhood in the nineteenth century.

Two main views of the child co-existed through the nineteenth century: either children were naturally naughty and so in need of reform; or they were pure, and therefore required protection from evil influences; either way, guidance and teaching were considered necessary. These views were often linked to class. Children's books for the working-class child, according to Peter Hunt, seem to be 'a good deal more authoritarian and harsh than those for the sheltered middle classes' (Hunt 1991, 59). However, the Victorians had some unexpected notions about the relation between parent and child, and the teaching of children. In the 1860s Hesba Stretton suggested that 'children should not regard their parents as infallible, or even [feel] that it is their duty to obey them, if they are in the wrong' (see Kincaid 1992, 65). Catherine Sinclair, in *Holiday House*, complains that modern educational methods were stunting the creative development of children: 'the very mind of youth seems in danger of becoming a machine; and while every effort is made to stuff the memory, like a cricket ball, with well-known facts and ready-made opinions, no room is left for the vigour of natural feeling, the glow of natural genius, and the ardour of natural enthusiasm' (6).

This brings us to another consideration: that differing perceptions of the target audience may lead to differing ideas about the writer's role. Julia Briggs says about women writers of children's books, that they 'progressed from giving instruction to an identification with their readers, from proving themselves responsible adults to allowing themselves to adopt the subversive tones of childhood' (Avery and Briggs 1989, 222).

There is another aspect to writing for children, the writer's awareness that s/he is also writing for adults. This has direct consequences on the balance of the writer's relationship with the child reader and the adult purchaser, and we will look at how far selected Victorian children's books are shaped and modified by this relationship, as well as by the writer's perception of his/her role.

THE LANGUAGE OF CONTROL (1): CONVINCING THE AUDIENCE

Broadly speaking, nineteenth-century writers of children's books used one of two approaches to their audience: the 'I know better' approach ('giving instruction', as Briggs calls it) or the 'I'm one of you' approach, that is 'identification with their readers', in Briggs' words (*Alice in Wonderland* suggests a third approach, which we will examine later). It could be plausibly argued that these two approaches are the literary version of the two modes of control suggested by Basil Bernstein: the position-oriented mode (parent to child: 'Don't do that!' 'Why?' 'Because I told you not to'; bad behaviour is punished by an authority figure), and the person-oriented mode ('If you do that you'll make me very unhappy'; bad behaviour is punished by the loss of a valued friend). In our analysis, therefore, both speech acts and these two modes of control will be considered.

The first writer we look at is Hesba Stretton (Sarah Smith), and her early novel, *Enoch Roden's Training*, the story of a poor boy who works to support his family and resists various tribulations and temptations, to become a preacher. Stretton wrote a number of didactic books, including the highly successful *Jessica's First Prayer*, published by the Religious Tract Society, often for school presentations. What we might expect from such works would be a voice of authority, the 'I know better' approach. In fact, Stretton does not directly address her reader in *Enoch Roden*, but uses her characters to put forward her message, who in turn quote extensively from the Bible. Susan Roden sums up Stretton's guiding principle: 'Is there a verse in the Bible about everything?' The answer for Stretton was 'Yes', a case not of 'I know better', but 'The Bible knows better'; Stretton avoids giving her own opinions overtly. To convince her audience, she has relied on a kind of position-oriented threat or promise, an implied 'If you do that you'll be punished', or 'If you do that you'll be rewarded'.

In contrast to Stretton, Charles Kingsley, in *The Water Babies*, gives his opinions freely in asides which interrupt the narratives, often at length. However, like Stretton, he seems to fall squarely into the 'I know better' mode of address, with his exhortations to 'brave little English men'. His book presents arguments concerning the emotional and intellectual development of the child which, in spite of his patriarchal tone, suggest that he views boys at least as beings capable of creative thought and independence. As he says in Chapter Five: 'It's not good for little boys to be told everything, and never be forced to use their own wits' (96). He also stresses the importance of fantasy in the education of children:

> Some people think there are no fairies. Cousin Cramchild tells little folks so in his Conversations. Well perhaps there are none – in Boston, U.S., where he was raised.... And Aunt Agitate, in her Arguments on political economy, says there are none.... But it is a wide world, my little man, and thank heaven for it, for else, between crinolines and theories, some of us would get squashed. (37)

At this point, it seems that Kingsley, when he claims to share the child's belief in fairies, is adopting the 'I'm one of you' approach, though only to a limited audience that excludes girls and foreigners. However, his speech act (advice) seems position-oriented rather than person-oriented ('As your wise uncle, I advise you to...').

It is perhaps worth noting at this point that Catherine Sinclair, over twenty years earlier, shared Kingsley's concern for the education of children as whole beings, whose creativity should be developed. She complains that 'the minds of young people are now manufactured like webs of linen, all alike, and nothing left to nature' (5). In *Holiday House* she claims to have 'endeavoured to paint that species of noisy, frolicsome, mischievous children, now almost extinct ... when amidst many faults and eccentricities, there was still some individuality of character and feeling allowed to remain' (7). It seems that her philosophy is that real goodness cannot be learnt from a list of facts and rules, but grows out of the same impulses in the child which lead to 'naughtiness'.

Mrs Molesworth, in *The Cuckoo Clock*, the story of a little girl who goes to stay with two elderly aunts in an old house where she finds an enchanted cuckoo clock and becomes friends with the wooden cuckoo, also sees the importance of naughtiness in the development of the child. Griselda's learning experiences throughout the book are prompted by initial acts of disobedience. Although not given to the kind of sermonising that Kingsley favours, Molesworth certainly adopts the all-knowingness of the expert ('fairies, you know, children, however charming, are sometimes rather queer to have to do with'; 38). Like Kingsley and Sinclair, Molesworth stresses the importance of independent and creative thought, implicit in the final message of the story, where Griselda says: 'The way to the true fairyland is hard to find, and we must each find it for ourselves, mustn't we?' (164). At times Molesworth pretends to have less knowledge than her child readers; for example, in Chapter Six, she ponders disingenuously why we speak of a cold getting better, and seeks help from her readers:

> Children, I feel quite in a hobble – I cannot get my mind straight about it – please think it over and give me your opinion. (79)

Her reason for doing this is presumably to stimulate the child reader's interaction with her as narrator, reinforcing their active role in the narrative construction. Moreover, by adopting a person-oriented mode of control, and by seeking advice as well as giving it, Molesworth is more likely to win the sympathy of her child reader.

In general Mrs Molesworth avoids overtly advising her reader, since she uses a well-known device, a magically transformed inanimate object as the expert advice-giver (in her book it is a wooden cuckoo; another notable example is Francis Browne's *Granny's Wonderful Chair*, in which an old armchair is the little girl's comforter and mentor). Interestingly, such guides are almost invariably given a male persona, and even a certain sexual glamour (the chair is really a prince under a spell). The chair indirectly guides the little girl towards adolescence, by transporting her to a castle where every night it tells stories to the king; he rewards the little girl with scarlet satin shoes, gold-clocked stockings, and a white satin gown, and with each successive tale allows her to progress in status from eating kitchen scraps to dining at his table. It is only at this stage that the chair regains human form.

George Macdonald, in *The Princess and the Goblin*, takes on the role of all-knowing narrator, in the fairy-tale tradition. He employs the techniques of oral story-telling, carrying on a pseudo-dialogue with the child reader, asking questions for them for which he provides answers. An example of this occurs when the Princess meets her magical great-grandmother for the first time:

> Perhaps you will wonder how the Princess could tell that the old lady was an old lady, when I inform you that not only was she beautiful but her skin was smooth and white. I will tell you more. (121–2)

There follows a description of the old lady, then the comment:

> That is not much like an old lady, is it? Ah! but .... (122)

Macdonald as storyteller teaches mainly through the actions and development of the characters, in the way fairy-tales work, as symbolic images of struggle. As might be expected from such an approach, the language of control (giving advice, in this case), tends to be position-oriented (princesses always keep their promises), but can also be person-oriented (parents and children do things for each other because it gives them pleasure).

Other books seem to align themselves more fully with the child's point of view. In *Treasure Island*, Robert Louis Stevenson uses a child narrator, thereby winning an instant rapport with child readers, and side-stepping adult-style debates about morality. The danger of using a child narrator is that the child may end up sounding like an adult; but Stevenson reminds us from time to time that Jim is only a boy, inexperienced and vulnerable:

> I was drinking in his words and smiling away, as conceited as a cock upon a wall, when, all in a breath, back went his right hand over his shoulder. Something sang like an arrow through the air. (231)

Stephenson's identification with Jim may seem complete, but one is aware that Jim's self-knowledge is supplemented by the sort of experience that only an adult can bring. The adult reader is also aware, as we show in the next section, that Stevenson is exercising subtle person-oriented control and implicitly offering some sophisticated advice to his child reader.

If in Stevenson's work we are aware of an adult trying to speak through an adolescent boy narrating in the first person, in Lewis Carroll's *Alice in Wonderland,* the narrative is in the third person; yet we are aware of Alice's thought processes. Moreover, we see that Carroll shares in some way in the girl's vision of the world. Here is an example of this dual identity:

> 'Come, there's no use in crying like that!' said Alice to herself, rather sharply. ... She generally gave herself very good advice, (though she very seldom followed it), ... for this curious child was very fond of pretending to be two people. (19)

Here we seem to hear two voices – those of Alice and the narrator – almost engaged in a dialogue, with the narrator both outside and inside Alice's head. If Carroll is exercising any control at all in this extract, it is only to give some rather quirky person-oriented advice ('Do this and you'll make *yourself* happy'). This may perhaps be linked to Kincaid's view of Alice as a 'false child', who 'vacates the position of the true child, leaves it for us' (1992, 289).

THE LANGUAGE OF CONTROL (2): GETTING THE MESSAGE ACROSS

Children are notoriously selective readers when left to their own devices. While many of them will happily re-read a favoured text until they know it line by line, they are quick to spot any overt teaching or sermonising, and are likely to skip over it. A random questioning of adults who read *The Water Babies* in childhood but not since reveals they have no memory of his moralising monologues, but remember vividly Tom's adventures. By the same token it is easy to find books given as school prizes which show little evidence (fingerprints, stains, loose pages) of being frequently handled by their child readers. This illustrates the problem that what children want to read, and what adults want them to read, may be two different things; and it is how adult writers attempt to bridge this gap that concerns us here.

Just as there could be said to be two different approaches to the audience, so it could be argued that there are two ways to get a message across to the child reader: overtly and covertly. (We are, for the moment, discounting messages that the writer may not be aware of, but which we as readers consciously or unconsciously receive.)

Hesba Stretton uses *Enoch Roden's Training* overtly as a vehicle for evangelical teaching, but she dresses up themes from the Bible (for example, the prodigal son) in modern costume for her young readers. The main characters are an orphan child Lucy and her father's apprentice Enoch, who prove themselves able to help the weaker adults in the story, and overcome severe hardship and near-starvation to succeed. The narrative therefore has a number of elements designed to capture a young audience; however, these are equally balanced, and arguably outweighed, by those designed to please the book-buying adult. In *Enoch Roden*, Stretton clearly disapproves of feckless behaviour, and condones self-sufficiency and self-help. Mr Drury, the weak father, who is deeply in debt, optimistically comforts his worried daughter by saying:

> 'The Lord knows how to provide for us. Do not let us trouble about next Wednesday; we may not be living then.' (18)

His daughter replies:

> 'I don't expect God will let us die just to get out of a trouble we ought to have foreseen.' (18)

But Enoch, the hero, learns to support himself and his family properly:

> 'Granny told me this morning that I must be diligent in business, if I am a Christian.' (25)

The main message of this book is that charity begins at home, as this quotation illustrates:

> 'It's just the right sum, father; it is what grandmother left me...'.
> He did not ask Esther any further questions; the money had been provided for him, and he did not stop to discover at what pain or loss to her but took it as easily as if silver and gold came direct from Heaven, without labour or care. Esther brushed his coat

and buttoned his overcoat for him, and [...] he went at once and discharged his debt; but upon returning he called to see a poor woman who was a widow, and emptied his pockets of all the loose silver he carried in them. (35–6)

His family are finally bankrupted by his actions before he dies.

Another concern of Stretton's is that her characters should know their place. The Rodens, a respectable working-class family, neither wish to mix with those beneath them, nor behave as equals to the master's orphaned daughter, whom they adopt: 'We shouldn't like the master's child to go among those rough children; and nobody'll do me any harm with their low ways and talk' (72), says Granny as she elects to go to the workhouse. Stretton uses her narrative action and the dialogue of her characters, particularly the children, to give open instruction. However, Stretton's speech acts – Mr Drury's plea, his daughter's reproach, Granny's advice – whether intended as comic or serious, are now subject to dehiscence, and strike us a satire or spoof, recalling situation comedies like *Absolutely Fabulous*, where the child is serious and responsible while the parents are frivolous and irresponsible.

Kingsley is interested in reforming, or rather moulding, his young readers too, but he also directs a great deal of criticism at the adult world. Kingsley chooses a child from the lowest stratum of life to be the hero of his tale, and there is the usual fairy-tale progression from vulnerable ignorance and weakness to mature reflection and empowerment through knowledge. Kingsley, however, differs from Stretton in breaking into his narratives at regular intervals to present mini-lectures. These often require such a knowledge of contemporary figures of the period and their theories that it suggests Kingsley hoped that the child and adult would read the book together. His main concerns include education, punishment, cleanliness, honesty and spiritual purity. *The Water Babies* reads almost like a manual for rearing a child, with an emphasis on perseverance, a 'bulldog spirit', and a questioning mind, which still embraces fully the Christian religion. Here is Kingsley on honesty:

So when you grow to be a big man, do you behave as all honest fellows should; and never touch a fish or a head of game which belongs to another man without his express leave; and then people will call you a gentleman and treat you like one. (74)

And on perseverance:

> you must expect to be beat a few times in your life, little man, if you live such a life as a man ought to live. (31)

> But Tom was always a brave, determined little English bulldog, who never knew when he was beaten. (75)

Kingsley also set great store by spiritual purity:

> you will believe the one true doctrine of this wonderful fairy-tale; which is that your soul makes your body just as a snail makes its shell. (50)

He also had definite ideas about punishment:

> And so, if you do not know that things are wrong, that is no reason why you should not be punished for them; though not as much, my little man ..., as if you did know. (103)

And here is Kingsley's final moral, on obedience and the role of the English man:

> Do you learn your lessons, and thank God that you have plenty of cold water to wash in; and wash in it too, like a true English man. And then, if my story is not true, something better is; and if I am not quite right, still you will be, as long as you stick to hard work and cold water. (180)

Where Kingsley differs widely from Stretton is in his use of a fantasy world which lies hidden within the real world, and with which he seeks to convince the reader precisely by calling on the child's knowledge of the real world (an example of this is when Kingsley asks: 'What is more cheap and plentiful than sea-rock? Then why should there not be sea-toffee as well?' [101]). Tom learns his lessons in a place which is at once removed from normal experience, yet mirrors and is reinforced by the child's everyday world. This is the most satisfying part of the book, for the admonitions and advice that Kingsley offers are 'contaminated' by images of well-meaning but boring old uncles and Colonel Blimp-ish figures.

Mrs Molesworth, in *The Cuckoo Clock*, uses a similar technique, with her blend of magic and reality. In fact she uses a number of skilful strategies throughout what is essentially a very moral tale. One strategy stems from her obvious belief in the value of play in the learning process. Griselda has no one to play with at the beginning; therefore, she learns nothing until she meets the cuckoo, who promises to play with her. What she learns through play is the value of obedience and self-discipline. The cuckoo says to Griselda: 'I have to obey orders like other people' (30). As the cuckoo explains (140), this is just part of a natural cycle of life in which not only little girls but the sun, moon and stars obey and fulfil predestined roles.

But Molesworth never loses sight of the fact that in order to persuade her reader to accept the Cuckoo's advice (a speech act is not successful unless taken up), her book must tap into the desires and wishes of her child readers. She calls on their experience of smells, colours, textures, and tastes, and as in many children's books, food plays an important and symbolic role. Thus at Lady Lavender's boring tea party Griselda is given 'highly spiced, rather musty gingerbread', which she 'couldn't bear' (21); but in Mandarin Land boys give her 'trays filled with the most delicious fruits and sweetmeats' (59). Food is used here as an indicator of Griselda's state of mind, and many children could relate to her experience of being forced to eat something disgusting. The relationship between eating and reading for children is an interesting one, which we haven't space to look at fully here. However, it seems a common phenomenon that children like to eat something pleasurable as they read, possibly as a bridge between the everyday physical world they inhabit and the fantasy world they seek to enter, and as a source of reassurance, a symbol of parental protection; and the vast majority of enduring children's books contain frequent references to food, as if the writers were aware of its importance.

Molesworth does not rely solely on exciting narrative to make her message more palatable, but focuses on the slightly ambiguous relationship between Griselda and the cuckoo. The cuckoo himself is not a particularly pious character; he sulks at times, and responds irritably to Griselda's questions. He is also inclined to pomposity, which Molesworth quickly deflates (an example of this is when he begins to say '"Griselda, you have a very great [deal to learn]"', which Griselda interrupts with '"If you say that again, I'll jump out

of the palanquin and run away home to bed"' [52]). These imperfections make him a more approachable spirit guide. But there are
other ways in which his role is not entirely that of a paternal
adviser. There are many instances where close physical contact
with him is described as pleasurable to Griselda:

> 'Put out your hand. There, do you feel me?' 'Yes,' said Griselda,
> stroking gently his soft feathers, which seemed to be close under
> her hand. 'Yes, I feel you.' 'Well then,' said the cuckoo. 'Put your
> arms round my neck, and hold me firm. I'll lift you up.' (132–3)

She is then taken for a flight on the cuckoo's back, and her feelings
are described:

> Griselda shut her eyes and lay still. It was delicious – the gliding,
> yet darting motion, like nothing she had ever felt before. It did
> not make her the least giddy, either, but a slightly sleepy feeling
> came over her. (135)

We are not claiming that Molesworth knowingly set out to present
overtly erotic sensations, but she is interested in producing an emotional charge between the male figure, the little girl and, by proxy,
the child reader. *Granny's Wonderful Chair* uses a similar covert sensuality dressed up as romance to put across its message: the chair is
a male figure, who, like the cuckoo, carries the little girl where she
wants to go, and who tells her stories when she lays her head on its
seat cushions. Contemporary readers are certainly 'contaminated
undecidably' by such seductive invitations, which may explain in
part why *The Cuckoo Clock* still makes pleasurable reading.

Such an emotional charge is also present between Curdie and the
Princess in Macdonald's *The Princess and the Goblin*. Early on, the
Princess promises Curdie a kiss and finally consummates her
promise in the last chapter:

> The Princess reached down, threw her arms round Curdie's neck,
> and kissed him on the mouth, saying – There Curdie! There's the
> kiss I promised you. (296)

Like the cuckoo and the chair, Curdie carries the Princess in his
arms, protectively and apparently effortlessly:

He caught her up in his arms and set off at full speed ... Irene clung round his neck, and he ran with her like a deer. (292)

Apart from the importance of keeping promises, Macdonald's main messages seem to be the mutual obligations of parents and children ('if Curdie worked hard to get [his mother] a petticoat, she worked hard every day to get him comforts' [124]), and the value of integrity (Macdonald notes that it is a 'low and contemptible thing to refuse to confess a fault' [255]). But it is the Princess's promise (a sincere promise, as the kiss on the mouth proves), coupled with the emotional charge between the Princess and Curdie, and the dark threat from the cave-dwelling goblins (surely a symbol of the unconscious), that makes this book very readable.

When we turn to *Treasure Island*, the obvious link it has with the previous books is the importance of keeping promises (Jim refuses to flee with Dr Livesey because Long John Silver 'trusted me; I passed my word, and back I go' [269]). True, Dr Livesey does emphasise the importance of duty (293), but this is undermined by the code of the pirates, and by the attractiveness of Silver. This code, as expressed by Israel Hands, seems to be 'Him as strikes first is my fancy; dead men don't bite' (224). But it operates more subtly than that, by strategy and deceit; for Hands, when threatened by Jim, says: 'I'll have to strike [a bargain]' (231), then proceeds to pin him to the mast with a dagger. Jim is forced to practise deceit himself, and he learns to negotiate, for example, when he says to Silver: 'Kill another and do yourselves no good, or spare me and keep a witness to save you from the gallows' (247). Doing one's duty may be a suitable aspiration for a middle-class professional in Victorian England, but for a pirate or for a child, strategy is more likely to win rewards.

Alice also learns to use strategy, as in the episode when she is about to criticise the Queen but, noticing her nearby, hurriedly changes her sentence into a compliment. This is interesting given that in Wonderland, speech acts do not fulfill their normal function, and imperatives or other utterances that might count as commands in the context of adults and children, become nonsense. For example, the Duchess says: 'If people minded their own business, the world would go round a lot faster' (71). And later:

'And the moral of that is – O, 'tis love, 'tis love, that makes the world go round!' 'Somebody said', Alice whispered, 'that it's done by everybody minding their own business.' 'Ah well, it means much the same thing', said the Duchess.... 'And the moral of that is – Take care of the sense, and the sounds will take care of themselves.' (107)

In a world of such wild and disobedient signifiers, no orders need be obeyed and strategies of deceit are redundant; perhaps the only constant in Alice is rebellion:

'No, no!' said the Queen. 'Sentence first – verdict afterwards.'
    'Stuff and nonsense!' said Alice loudly. 'The idea of having the sentence first!'
    'Hold your tongue!' said the Queen, turning purple.
    'I won't!' said Alice.
    'Off with her head!' the Queen shouted at the top of her voice. Nobody moved.
    'Who cares for you?' said Alice, (she had grown to her full size by this time). 'You're nothing but a pack of cards!' (145)

RESISTING THE LANGUAGE OF CONTROL

One of the basic principles of speech acts, including speech acts used to control children, is that they are conventional, and can only be successful if certain conditions are satisfied. So, to adapt Austin's words slightly, control can be exercised only because there exists an accepted conventional procedure which includes the uttering of certain words by a person who has the authority to do so, and utters the words correctly and completely, and with sincerity. This is problematic enough in 'real-world' interactions: how do we know whether a speaker is sincere or not? is it enough that a child *thinks* an adult is sincere? But when we come to fictional interactions, the problems multiply. Obviously sincerity is difficult to judge in a fictional work; we cannot always know when a writer, even in an aside, is being sincere, and the notion is meaningless when applied to a character, unless we use some crude measure of 'sincerity' such as the extent to which a character's speech acts are clearly endorsed or undermined by the fiction. On the other hand, a writer can draw on conventional procedures to dispense advice, guidance, and so on, just as s/he can either adopt a voice of authority, or lend this voice to a character in the story. It is here that the unconscious 'parasites' referred to earlier intervene; the writer may, unconsciously perhaps, lend authority to an 'unsuitable' character, or modern readers may invest this character with authority. Or a speech act which 100 years ago might have seemed 'correct and complete' may now strike us as inadequate, thereby losing its effect. There are numerous ways to resist the language of control, and some of these can be illustrated through the books already examined.

When it first appeared in 1865, *Enoch Roden's Training* may well have satisfied all the conditions for successful speech acts, at least among those who purchased books published by the Religious Tract Society. The writer is apparently sincere, the characters are apparently 'sincere' (the narrator leaves us in no doubt as to the 'rightness' or 'wrongness' of a character's speech acts), and, most importantly, the writer invests authority for the language of control in what her readers must have seen as the ultimate authority, the Bible and the teachings of the Church. And that, of course, is the problem for many modern readers (and even, perhaps, for some earlier readers): the Bible has lost its authority, and without this underpinning, the language of control has become meaningless or even absurd. So when Enoch says that he 'must be diligent in business, if I am a Christian', or Lucy says that she does not 'expect God will let us die just to get out of a trouble we ought to have foreseen', we are either uncomprehending or amused, because we no longer accept the network of moral imperatives (expressed in Enoch's 'must' and 'Lucy's 'ought') which permitted such speech acts to be uttered 'in all sincerity'; and, what is more damaging for *Enoch Roden*, we are infected with 'parasites' like our suspicion of the so-called Protestant work ethic which turn us against Enoch's 'diligence'.

Like *Enoch Roden*, *The Water Babies* appears to be a 'sincere' work, but Kingsley based the authority of his speech acts on a number of sources, including Christian Socialism, science, enlightened educational theories, and English nationalism. While a contemporary reader is likely to accept, more or less, the validity of the first three (Christian Socialism is still an important force in the British Labour Party), the last, English nationalism, is likely to be resisted by some readers. Thus, when we read an assertion such as 'Tom was always a brave, determined little English bulldog', which seeks indirectly to control the reader, the 'parasites' are likely to intervene (suspicions of nationalism, associations with Fascism, memories of English football hooligans), and we cannot escape a feeling of unease or annoyance, or at least an ironic laugh. And there is another process at work here, related to the condition that speech acts must be 'correct and complete'. As previously implied, Kingsley's language of control is apparently directed at upper-middle-class English boys, so an injunction like the one previously quoted, 'when you grow to be a big man, do you behave as all honest fellows should...' seems in a real sense incomplete, since it excludes both women and anyone who doesn't go hunting; it may have been a conventionally complete exhortation in Kingsley's day, but for many modern readers this status is lost.

In *The Cuckoo Clock* Mrs Molesworth invests authority for the language of control in the seductive power of fantasy, and in a scientific paradigm that we still recognise and accept (that all beings, animate or inanimate, have to conform to certain natural laws and have a particular role to play in what we now call the ecosystem). There are certain unimportant 'parasites' which might make our reading of the story different from that of a hundred years ago ('I have to obey orders' is reminiscent of excuses offered by minor functionaries in Nazi concentration camps). But of greater interest than this are two strategies that Mrs Molesworth uses to control her child readers: in the first strategy, Mrs Molesworth pretends to seek help from her readers, in a narratorial gesture we all know to be 'insincere'; in the second, she sets up an emotional, almost erotic charge between the cuckoo and Griselda (and, therefore, the reader). Both these strategies remind us that the authority to exercise control is acquired not only through institutions, but through techniques of cunning and seduction.

As far as the language of control goes, *Treasure Island* and *Alice* are the most complex of the children's books studied here. In *Treasure Island*, it is noticeable that not all the conditions for successful speech acts have been met. There is certainly a conventional procedure, in the sense that Stevenson is using a recognised genre (one that includes *Robinson Crusoe*, *The Swiss Family Robinson* and *Coral Island*) and Stevenson is invested with the authority bestowed by the genre. But against this, his narrator, Jim, is clearly fallible, so that his speech acts can never be accepted as fully reliable; the fiction never clearly endorses the speech acts of Jim's adult friends like Doctor Livesey, nor does it fully undermine the speech acts of the pirates, in particular those of Silver. This emerges most strongly when we look at two key concepts in the last part of *Treasure Island*, entitled 'Captain Silver': *duty* and *bargain*. Towards the end of the book Livesey remarks that he 'did what I thought best for those who stood by their duty; and if you were not one of those, whose fault was it?' (293). Earlier, when Jim was a prisoner of the pirates, Livesey had said to him 'As you have brewed, so shall you drink, my boy' (268). And earlier still Silver had alleged that 'the doctor himself is gone dead again you, "ungrateful scamp" was what he said' (244), and had further quoted the doctor as saying 'As for that boy, I don't know where he is, confound him [...], nor I don't much care. We're about sick of him' (245–6). This apparent dismissal of Jim contrasts with Silver's invitation to Jim to 'jine with Cap'n Silver' (244), and Silver's later 'bargain with Jim: 'I'll save your life [...] But, see here, Jim – tit for tat – you save Long John from swinging' (251). It is no wonder that Jim later says, of the sleeping Silver: 'my heart was sore for him, wicked as he was, to think of the [...] shameful gibbet that awaited him' (261). No wonder, too, that the average reader is attracted by Silver, and slightly repelled by Jim's adult friends, and more ready to accept Silver's speech acts, at least for the duration of the fiction.

In *Alice* it almost seems as if Carroll had set out to subvert all the conditions that make speech acts and the language of control possible, let alone successful. If we are to judge by the poem that precedes Chapter One, and the dream of Alice's sister at the end, Alice is framed as a conventional children's story, from which we would expect advice, guidance and the like. Yet our expectations remain unfulfilled, for Carroll refuses to adopt a position of authority, or to invest with authority any character in the story, except perhaps Alice herself (this corresponds with Kincaid's view of Alice as a 'false child', representing the voice of logic). However, no character in Alice is in the least 'sincere'; arguably, not even Carroll is sincere, given the apparent gap between the introductory poem and the contents of the fiction. Carroll's subversion of speech acts and the language of control operates throughout the book, and only a few examples can be given which illustrate with particular force the ways in which Carroll plays with speech acts:

(1) 'Come, there's no use in crying like that!' said Alice to herself, rather sharply; 'I advise you to leave off this minute!' (p. 19)

(Does the act of advising carry authority when the 'I' giving advice is the same as the 'you' being advised?)

(2) 'Now tell me, Pat, what's that in the window?'

'Sure, it's an arm, yer honour!' [...]

'Well, it's got no business there, at any rate: go and take it away!'(p. 45)

(Is there a procedure for removing a very large arm from a window?)

(3) 'Have some wine,' the March Hare said in an encouraging tone. Alice looked all round the table, but there was nothing on it but tea. 'I don't see any wine,' she remarked.

'There isn't any,' said the March Hare. (p. 80)

(Can an offer be sincere if it cannot possibly be granted?)

(4) 'Talking of axes,' said the Duchess, 'chop off her head!'

Alice glanced rather anxiously at the cook, to see if she meant to take the hint; but the cook [...] seemed not to be listening. (71–2)

(Can a command be valid if nobody carries it out?)

(5) 'Off with her head! Off –'

'Nonsense!' said Alice, very loudly and decidedly, and the Queen was silent. (p. 95)

(And can a command be valid if the authority of the person uttering the command is challenged?)

Alice is possibly the first children's book which comes complete with its own built-in subversion. A work like *Alice* may not appear to be openly didactic in the way those of Hesba Stretton or Charles Kingsley were, but nevertheless, in presenting even an inverted topsy-turvy model of social control, it reinforces the very existence of this control.

CONCLUSION

Treasure Island and *Alice* both contain subversive elements and point the way to books for children that appeared at the turn of the century, which seemed not only to conspire with the child reader, but also to undermine the foibles of the adult world. Hilaire Belloc in 1899 produced *A Moral Alphabet* (*Cautionary Tales* not appearing until 1907) which parodied children's primers of the period. In the first poem, 'A stands for Archibald who told no lies,/And got this lovely volume for a prize', we have an ironic reworking of the theme of goodness rewarded. Archibald is repulsively good, and his reward is the very *Moral Alphabet* which is making fun of him. The moral to this poem, as with all the others, is as close to a real moral as those of the Duchess in *Alice*: 'Learn from this justly irritating youth,/To brush your hair and teeth and tell the truth'. The moral for 'F for a Family taking a walk' provides even less guidance: 'A respectable family taking the air/Is a subject on which I could dwell;/It contains all the morals that ever there were,/And sets an example as well.' Just as with Carroll's sequel, *Through the Looking-Glass*, Belloc appropriates a children's book genre and uses it to make sophisticated comments about adult life.

Also it would be difficult to ignore the contribution made by E. Nesbit, and her book *Five Children and It*. Roger Lancelyn Green, in his introduction to the 1964 edition, suggests a relationship between Molesworth's cuckoo and the Psammead in this story. Both are slightly grumpy companions with magical powers, who encourage the children to learn from their own mistakes. But Nesbit's Psammead is a more comical figure. Much of the humour of her stories relies on presenting the adult world as if viewed by a rational child, and though it would be wrong to suggest that she mocks the concepts of the family and home in the way Belloc does in *A Moral Alphabet*, Nesbit certainly presents them in a more ironic light. Her children often aspire to be what they believe adults want to them to be, but find out to their cost, as in *Five Children and It*, the disadvantages of being 'rich beyond the dreams of avarice' or 'beautiful as the day'; they end up being rejected by the very adults they hoped to impress.

The last writer looked at is not strictly a children's writer at all; but Saki wrote stories about children which have perhaps influenced a new generation of children's books in which children's strategies of deceit overthrow adult tyrannies. Although not strictly within the Victorian period, he wrote in the years leading up to the First World War, evoking the same middle-class society as Belloc. Bertha, a little girl who is 'horribly good' (393), and is eaten by a wolf who discovers her when her good-conduct medals clink together (in 'The Story-Teller', published 1914) would not be out of place in a Belloc poem. But Saki's children have a more sinister quality; for example, Conradin, in 'Sredni Vashtar' (1911), indirectly murders his aunt; and in 'The Open Window' (1914), an adolescent girl terrifies a nervous male guest by persuading him that her family are all ghosts (the story finishes with the dry comment 'Romance at short notice was her speciality' [291]).

Saki's image of childhood appears to differ enormously from Stretton's portrayal of Enoch and Lucy, but are these images as different as they appear? Stretton's children are self-sufficient and possess a certain evangelical power which they use to guide the adults. Saki's children are a perverted mirror-image of this; they are self-sufficient and powerful, but able to exploit adult Christian 'morality' to their own ends, since they themselves have different moral values, which nevertheless rely on notions of justice and retribution.

But here we reach a uniting factor, for justice and retribution are at the heart of much biblical teaching of the Victorian era, which is not so very far from Kingsley's view that children should be punished for doing something bad even if they did not know it was wrong (it is simply that in the stories of Saki or Dahl adults and children swap roles). So children who respond to Saki's stories, or Roald Dahl's, in this century, are accepting moral teaching, disguised as rebellion; yet another adult strategy for presenting the language of control.

9

Watch This Space: Wilkie Collins and New Strategies in Victorian Publishing in the 1890s

Alexis Weedon

The 1890s were a difficult time for established publishers as old formats and price strategies were threatened by entrepreneurial publishers proposing innovative practices. It was a time of much discussion about net book pricing in the trade periodicals where fears were expressed that what had happened in Germany following failure of price control would also happen in Britain. If the system failed, the whole structure of the industry could be in jeopardy. There was, too, some uncertainty as to where the demand for print, and consequently the 'mass market' (Anon. 1881, 422ff.), was going to emerge.

This chapter looks at the cheapening of book prices, especially novels in the 1890s, with the perspective of a survey of book production costs. The statistics are contextualised through a discussion of contemporary perceptions of what was happening in the industry from the viewpoint of the author, the publisher and the printer as manifested in the trade press.

Contemporary accounts of publishing in the nineties stress the increasing diversity of publishers' lists. Novel subjects in new formats hit the bookstalls as the three-volume novel declined, for while the hold of the circulating libraries was still strong, a market was opening up beyond their traditional domain. Publishers and authors alike were aware of this new demand and the struggle to supply it revolutionised the relationship between them.

One of the authors most aware of this change was Wilkie Collins, a successful novelist from the publisher's as well as the critic's point of view. Collins was a keen observer of the publishing scene. He had good reason to follow it closely as he trod a tightrope between financial imperatives in his ordinary life. His many family commitments meant that he was often urgently in need of money, but he was also painfully aware that by publishing his works at a lower price – which meant initially accepting less – he would benefit in the long term from the gain in popularity and wider circulation of his novels.

Perhaps because of this, Collins was rarely happy with the contracts he negotiated with his publishers. In 1870 he considered a proposal from Cassell to buy up all his copyrights and issue a cheap edition of his works. He decided against it because he felt that they were not offering enough to justify relinquishing the rights for the ten-year term they demanded. The following year he toyed with the idea of issuing a novel – possibly *The Woman in White* – in weekly penny numbers. But his publisher at the time, George Smith, advised against this and he did not do it (Peters 1992, 368). In a dilemma, Collins felt:

> a very few years more will see a revolution in the publishing trade for which most of the publishers are unprepared. ... I don't believe in the gigantic monopolies, which cripple free trade, lasting much longer. ... (Robinson 1951, 368–9)

In November 1874 Collins agreed to hand over the copyright of all his books to Chatto and Windus, except three which were held by Smith and Elder (*No Name, After Dark* and *Armadale*). They were bought by Chatto after Collins's death and published in 1890. The 1874 contract stated that Chatto and Windus would republish all thirteen novels within twelve months.[1]

Chatto and Windus were well-known for republishing novels (which had proven their success) at a cheap price. They usually published editions of these novels at six shillings, three shillings and sixpence, and two shillings, with the most popular works being issued in long runs and sold for sixpence. Collins had been successful and it would be natural for Andrew Chatto to issue Collins's most popular novels in the sixpenny format. Indeed one would assume that Collins would have welcomed it; he had advocated low-priced fiction at many a dinner table, and argued that reasonably priced classics and fiction would open up a fresh market and not intrude on the existing predominantly middle-class one

(Robinson 1951, 368). As it was, he argued, prices were kept artificially high by Mudie's and Smith's monopolies. 'Capital and courage are all that are wanted to break down the library system ... the market is immense – but nobody here seems to know how to get at it' (Robinson 1951, 369), he wrote to Harper's, the American publishing firm. Andrew Chatto was one of the few attempting to 'get at' this immense market.

However, the advent of cheap fiction and classics was contentious in the trade, as the correspondence to the *Publishers' Circular* shows. On 16 September 1899 Charles E. Towers wrote to the editors complaining that:

> the retail trade are [*sic*] heartily sick of distributing our master pieces in exchange for the insignificant sixpence....to encourage the public to believe that they can sooner or later get almost any novel for a sixpence is a grand mistake. (Towers 1899, 273)

A week earlier Fred L. Shepherd had argued that the change in price 'from six shillings to sixpence is too extravagant a reduction' for the bookseller (Shepherd 1899, 250). It was a debate which had rumbled on through the trade press for the whole of the decade, with correspondents pointing the accusing finger at different links in the publishing chain. In April 1890 'Cyclops', an anonymous correspondent, suggested that the wholesalers were to blame. They had flooded the market with cheap reprints of standard works without first of all 'calling in' the more expensive editions and thus were the 'sole cause of the many evils which exist' (Cyclops 1890, 380). But the undercutting printer, the discount bookseller, even the starveling hack were also alleged to be the causes of increased competition and decreased profits. Everyone, it seemed, was to blame.

But how could the publisher afford to sell these books so cheaply? Was it simply 'ruinous discounting' – the product of increased competition – which would eventually lead to the financial collapse of the publisher? Or was it a calculated reaction to a fall in costs of production and a larger market? Certainly the price of raw materials fell during the nineteenth century as a result of industrialisation and the benefits of trade within the empire. But how did this affect the publishers? We know from Simon Eliot that the number of·titles published saw an early peak in the 1850s when the first attempt at cheapening the price of books was made, only to fall back in the 1860s and then rise again from the 1870s onwards (Eliot

1994, 9). The number of new titles increased most rapidly in the 1890s. It was a period of innovation and expansion as new price strategies were tried for popular genres (Eliot 1994, 60ff.). Eliot draws on external sources for his data, such as the listings of new titles in trade journals, copyright registration ledgers and paper production figures. By using internal sources such as publishers' accounts books, publication ledgers and letterbooks, I have been able to construct a complementary view of the costs of book production in the nineteenth century.[2]

One interesting anomaly I have encountered is the discrepancy between Eliot's figures of the number of titles published in the nineties and the average print-run which I have calculated from the publishers' internal accounts (Weedon 1993). While it seems that the earlier peak in titles published is paralleled with an increase in the average print-run, this is not true of the nineties (Table 9.1). The number of editions published increases rapidly from the 1840s but levels off in the 1860s only to rise again in the 1870s (see Eliot 1994, 9ff.). In general, publishers ordered editions of 1000 copies of their books, and only risked longer runs when sure of their markets or when the market was expanding rapidly. However, in the 1890s the average print-run fell below that of the preceding decade. There are many reasons why this might be so; the publishers I have surveyed are generally the older-established publishers who would be most likely to suffer at the hands of the new entrepreneurs. Indeed, in times of recession publishers are known to increase the range of titles available but reduce the quantity of books they print of each

Table 9.1 Eliot's *Publishers' Circular* figures for the number of editions published in Britain compared with the average and the most common quantity of books printed from a sample of 1679 books

	No. of editions published	Avg. no. of books per printing	Modal no. of books per printing
1836	–	1612	500
1846	3231	2576	750
1856	3939	3142	1000/2000
1866	4388	2118	1000
1876	4888	2404	2000
1886	5210	3221	1000
1896	6573	2555	1000
1906	8603	4086	1000
1916	9149	3406	1000

title, tickling the appetite of the public. It may be that this is what is happening here. Certainly the observation reinforces the contemporary perceptions of competitive pressure within the industry. But was it a leaner publishing industry which could afford to reduce the price of its books, or were other factors involved?

In the trade literature (*Books and Bookselling, The Bookseller, The Bookseller's Review, Bookselling, The Printing World, The Publishers' Circular, The Scottish Typographical Circular*) we can see a concern for the growing pressures on the industry. John Southward reflects upon the cheapening of printed materials and the fall in professional standards:

> As soon as one publisher brings out what is claimed to be the cheapest edition ever issued, his neighbour announces one that is cheaper still. Now, the publisher and the bookseller require their profits; how is this cheapening process to be carried on [except] by the use of cheap inferior materials and employment, and cheap cutting printers? (Southward 1898, 187)

On 31 January 1896, *The Printing World* reported on the problems of estimating the cost of machining on poorer-quality paper. Its fragility meant that the paper needed to be left before binding and sometimes required the press to be run at a lower speed affecting both machining and binding costs. It appears from the survey data that in the latter half of the century printers were able to use paper more economically, either by ordering paper to be made to size or by printing on larger sheets (Table 9.2).

Paper costs are notoriously prone to fluctuation (Spicer 1907). But calculating the average price per square foot for all weights of

Table 9.2   The average cost of paper per square foot from a sample of 1689 books

	Avg. paper size (sq. in.)	Cost (pence per sq. ft)	Rousseaux index	Cost-adjusted deflation
1836	405.4	0.159	1.23	0.195
1846	431.6	0.144	1.09	0.157
1866	641.7	0.134	1.2	0.161
1876	745.7	0.133	1.15	0.153
1886	700.4	0.108	0.83	0.090
1896	760.8	0.078	0.73	0.057
1906	1194.0	0.044	0.93	0.041

paper reveals a decrease in the cost for the book publisher. When this is adjusted for deflation using Rousseaux price index, we can see the actual and rather dramatic decline in the real cost of raw materials in the last quarter of the century (Mitchell 1988).

Whether this is solely due to greater efficiency or whether the use of cheaper-quality paper is the cause, as *The Printing World* implied, has yet to be ascertained. I think it is unlikely that the older publishers such as Bentley were compromising the quality of their three-deckers, and certainly George Bell and Sons was using standard-quality papers for approximately a third of their output until the turn of the century. But Chatto and Windus printed their sixpenny editions on larger papers than their three shillings and six pence or two shilling editions (Table 9.3). Consequently the paper cost per individual volume was reduced. A comparison with the previous tables shows that Chatto and Windus used papers well above the usual size and printed more copies than average. We cannot compare like with like as none of the other publishers employed Chatto's novel reprint formula. This was undoubtedly a good way of gaining a competitive advantage over other publishers and was a highly successful publishing format for the firm.

The Printing World also reported problems with estimating for machining costs. Clearly accuracy was vital in a competitive industry, and the time to make ready the press had been calculated by the number of illustrative cuts in a forme. But the journal pointed out that the type of paper and quality of ink also effected the cost

Table 9.3   The size and cost of paper in Chatto and Windus's editions of *The Moonstone* in the 1890s

Retail price or edition	Day	Month	Year	Print run	Paper size (sq. in.)	Paper cost	Paper cost per book (pence)
6d	1	4	1896	100 000	1728	£ 585.00	1.40
6d	19	5	1898	20 000	1728	£ 107.27	1.29
6d	26	10	1899	20 000	1728	£ 95.00	1.14
2s	10	11	1890	3 000	1064	£ 31.50	2.52
2s	7	5	1892	3 000	1064	£ 31.50	2.52
2s	12	12	1894	3 000	1064	£ 28.88	2.31
3/6	24	2	1891	1 500	1200	£ 21.00	3.36
2s 3/6	11	8	1892	1 500	1200	£ 14.18	2.27
3/6	4	1	1894	1 500	1200	£ 21.00	3.36
3/6	1	1	1897	2 000	1200	£ 22.50	2.70
DT	6	3	1899	3 000	1200	£ 26.78	2.14

and a job in a hurry could require more than one person to get the press running.

Machining costs did decline through the century as presses were replaced by larger mechanised machines. The fall in real terms is not as dramatic as the fall in paper prices. The decline is spread over several decades as printers bought new presses when they could raise the capital (Table 9.4). The most significant period is between the sample years 1866 and 1886; the reduction of costs in machining appears to have started in the 1860s, before paper prices began to fall in the 1870s.

In his article Southward was concerned that the standard of printing was falling. He praised contemporary founts and was enthusiastic about the mechanised press's ability to print delicate faces at speed, yet he was concerned about the design of the page and criticised the modern printer for failing to take account of the compositor's art. The publisher:

> ignores the fact that in two offices there may be used the same foundry, paper from the same mill, and yet the results will be as different 'as chalk from cheese'. Why? because in one office there is a trained staff of careful, skilful, tasteful employees, and there is in the other a corps of mere type 'lifters' and machine 'minders'. (Southward 1896, 186).

The root cause of this was 'the publisher who encourages or compels excessive haste in manufacture', putting pressure on his printers, who are then forced to compromise on quality. In 1890, the Printing and Allied Trades Association was established. At

Table 9.4 The cost of machine printing a square yard of paper (from a sample of 1582 books)

	Machining cost pence per sq. yd	Rousseaux index	Cost adjusted for deflation
1836	0.078	1.23	0.096
1846	0.098	1.09	0.107
1866	0.097	1.20	0.116
1876	0.081	1.15	0.093
1886	0.067	0.83	0.056
1896	0.064	0.73	0.047
1906	0.046	0.93	0.043

their first meeting the representatives set forth their aims, which included an appeal for more practical scheduling of contracts; government work had a tendency to come all at once and with unattainable deadlines (Anon. 1890c). Whether scheduling was markedly worse in the 1890s than it was in the previous decades is difficult to determine. The dates given in the publishers' and printers' ledgers are inconclusive, as clerks frequently waited until a number of printing orders had accumulated before entering them in the ledger. However, the statistics suggest that the average time to print was one month and stayed one month from the 1876 sample year until the turn of the century. There appears to be no 'excessive haste' in the nineties.[3]

The date of the order and of the delivery of Wilkie Collins' *The Woman in White* supports this conclusion (Table 9.5). The time to print the editions seems to vary between nine days and three months. But Chatto may not have been in any hurry, especially if he had established his corner of the market. The economics of the three editions reprinted in the nineties show the advantages of printing larger quantities of the sixpenny. The cost of machining this cheap edition in 1894 was under a halfpenny a copy; the two-shilling edition printed in 1890 cost just over one and a farthing; and the three shilling and sixpence edition cost a penny more than

Table 9.5 Chatto and Windus's editions of Wilkie Collins's *The Woman in White* in the 1890s

Edn	Ledger date	Print run	Comp.	Mach.	Date delivered	Date last binding
6d	22/4/94	100 000	63 00 00	180 00 00	23/4/94	29/6/95
6d	13/8/95	20 000		48 00 00	24/10/95	15/7/96
6d	30/7/96	20 000		48 00 00	28/8/96	26/8/97
6d	21/9/97	20 000		43 13 04	21/9/97	13/8/98
6d	5/10/98	20 000		43 00 00	14/10/98	23/11/99
2s	10/11/90	4 000		22 08 00	8/1/91	7/5/92
2s	7/5/92	4 000		22 08 00	15/6/92	15/11/93
2s	14/11/93	4 000		22 08 00	30/12/93	8/3/98
2s	2/3/98	1 000		12 18 00	2/3/98	17/4/00
3/6	12/7/90	1 500		14 08 00	2/10/90	15/7/92
3/6	15/7/92	1 500		14 08 00	19/8/92	25/8/95
3/6	25/8/94	1 500		14 08 00	25/8/94	22/7/96
3/6	29/9/96	2 000	55 04 06	17 17 00	20/10/96	8/2/99
3/6	24/12/96	2 500		19 02 06	10/3/97	10/3/97
3/6	6/3/99	3 000		20 05 00	15/3/99	24/4/01

that. Making ready the press always made it cheaper to print in long runs but the editions *were* selling. The last volume of the first sixpenny edition was bound fourteen months after printing, which is not a bad rate of sale. The other editions sold more slowly; the sixpenny edition hit the sale of the two-shilling edition in particular. Nevertheless the sale was steady and Chatto was still reprinting these editions of *The Woman in White* in the 1920s.

Chatto often printed his two-shilling and three-and-sixpenny editions from the same setting, thus saving the cost of resetting the whole of a novel again. The cost of setting was a considerable outlay before any return could be made from sales. However, the advent of composition machines promised considerable reduction in labour costs and they were gradually coming into use in the nineties. It was reported that Southward had claimed that six different kinds of typesetting machine were being used in the country in 1896 (Anon. 1896d, 508), though three were single examples. He was not impressed with the quality of the machines for book work and preferred the linotype matrix machine. The machines were seen as a considerable threat by the workforce. The London correspondent of the *Scottish Typographical Circular* reported the threat of strikes in January 1896 claiming that there is 'an evident desire on the part of master printers to fight the London Society of Compositors' (Anon. 1896a, 485). The Society argued that the printers were imposing 'unjust' and 'unfair' conditions on the workforce in the belief that machinery would eventually dispose of the need for compositors. Periodic unemployment added to the compositors' insecurity. The Royal Commission's report on the wages of union and non-union men showed that weekly wages were approximately five shillings higher for non-union men doing piece-work for Hansards between 1892 and 1894. Clearly the work was good if you could get it but the different payments meant that the printer could no longer safely charge composition 'at any fixed rate' (Anon. 1896c, 12).

From the printers' point of view, the fluctuations in work load and the need to invest in modern equipment were all part and parcel of being in the industry. But the demands of the publisher for cost-effective printing required the printer to make the best use of his machinery and workforce. The nineteenth century was a period of experimentation in methods of imposition and this must be one of the factors which contributed to the fall in composition costs (Table 9.6). Traditionally books were printed four pages on a side of paper or on larger presses in multiples of four, but as the presses were mechanised new methods were developed to lay out the pages more economically. Table 9.6 shows a fall in composition costs from 1866, but we really need to see these prices set against the average wage of the period (1850–51) in order to see the significance of these figures. The indexes do not go back as far as 1836, but the sample years of 1846 and 1866 are close to the mean wage, and the trend between these dates appears to follow the wage index. From 1866, however, there is a divergence which is more marked by 1896. The cost of composition no longer follows the average wage. It seems that typesetting was getting cheaper despite the fact that labour was becoming more expensive, and this must surely be the result of the employment of mechanical composition machines.

While the trade press bewailed the falling standards in book printing, competition from the growing periodical and newspaper market made the owners of capital question whether it was worth investing in the industry at all. Advising readers on whether to put money into the publishing ventures in the late 1890s, the *Investors' Review* judged that:

the English people are not a book-buying people, and not to any large extent really a book-reading people. They 'skim' trivial periodicals and light literature, which costs them a few pence a week or a subscription to a local library, or they can lean openly upon the free libraries now scattered plentifully throughout the country even in small hamlets. (Anon. 1899b, 263).

Table 9.6 Average composition costs per square inch of paper from a sample of 169 books

	Composition in pence	Average wage
1836	1.43	1.01
1846	1.09	0.98
1866	0.86	1.32
1876	1.00	1.52
1886	0.92	1.48
1896	0.97	1.63
1906	0.84	1.81

There certainly was a great deal of choice. *La Nature*, reported in *Publishers' Circular* on 1 February 1890, recorded that 'Germany can boast of the largest number of periodicals in Europe – namely, 5,500, of which 800 are dailies. England comes next with 3,000, of which 809 are dailies. Then France, Italy, Austria-Hungary, Spain, and Russia follow in the order here given ...' (Anon. 1890b, 111). The number of newspapers in Britain increased four times between 1846 and 1890 – the quantity of dailies rising from 14 to 185. According to the Newspaper Directory for 1890 there were 2234 newspapers published in Britain, and 1752 magazines. Publishers like George Newnes were producing attractive, affordable pictorial literature such as *The Strand Magazine*, launched in 1891. Four years later *Bookselling* reported on its success that: 'no magazine in this country [has] ever reached so large a sale, the present circulation being about 350,000 per month' (Newnes 1895, 31). Such successes gave rise to spin-offs and look-alikes, for example *The Strand Musical Magazine*, which sold 150 000 copies per month, according to George Newnes, and the *Picture Magazine*, which sold 30 000. *Titbits*, which was a news magazine rather than a picture paper, was Newnes's greatest achievement and had a circulation of 600 000 at this time. The demand for these magazines was sufficient for Newnes to invest in his own presses, and he used their spare capacity to print cheap double–columned paperbacks such as the *Oracle Encyclopaedia* issued in sixpenny parts, *Library of Useful Stories* and novels by Conan Doyle and Mrs Humphry Ward among others, also priced at sixpence, thereby providing a direct competitor for Chatto and Windus.

Newnes became a public company in 1891, the trade buying a quarter of its shares. This vote of confidence in the firm at a time when many publishers seemed to be withdrawing their capital is a tribute to its success.[4] Indeed Newnes was one of the 'cheaply popular' firms which the *Investors' Review* believed were undermining the old publishers (Anon. 1899b, 263). Mistaking the trade's networks for the propping up of financially insecure firms, the review offered a bleak judgement on the industry: 'Failing to get their money out of the retailer, suffering also from the effects of over-publishing, which have sometimes been extremely hurtful, publishers have in recent years fallen more and more into the hands of their printers, or printers and stationers, and struggle on in this manner amid many changes, absorbings of rivals and partings without open failure' (Anon. 1899b, 262). The tradition of reinforcing trade relationships between publishers and suppliers or distributors through placing a son in another firm to learn the trade was common in the nineteenth century. This way the leading generation learnt different aspects of the business; printing, marketing or paper manufacture and supply. Sometimes these 'apprenticeships' went hand in hand with financial deals; when George Bell bought the Bohn libraries he was financed by Spalding and Hodge, the paper manufacturers, and William Clowes, the printers. Bell took Spalding's son into his business. Such arrangements aided client loyalty and enabled publishers like Bell to buy the copyrights of a successful series.

Taking the example of T. and A. Constable, a Scottish printer who undertook book work, we can get a glimpse of how the trade networked in the eighties and nineties. Even before then the connections are evident: Thomas Constable was the youngest son of Archibald Constable, the ill-fortuned publisher of Walter Scott. Thomas was placed in his father-in-law's printing business, and in 1833 took over sole control. Six years later he was appointed Her Majesty's Printer and Publisher in Edinburgh and, in 1859, he became printer to the university. His modest career ended with his death in 1881 and his son, another Archibald, inherited the business. He took Walter Blackie as his partner in the firm, and between them they rapidly expanded the business. The anonymous author of *Brief Notes on the Origins of T. & A. Constable* relates how the partners made their business both more efficient by modernising the working practices and more up-to-date by buying new founts and presses (1939). They also added new customers to their client list. The surveying of the firm for the database of book production costs revealed a dramatic increase in the number of books printed between the 1886 sample year and 1896 (Table 9.7).

Table 9.7 T. and A. Constable's book customers

Sample year	Total book customers	Number of book orders	Book orders per customer	Maximum book orders per customer
1866	59	160	2.7	29
1876	40	118	2.9	18
1886	38	204	5.4	95
*1896	33	188	5.7	38

*Data from Jan.–Mar. and Oct. 1896

The 1886 sample year also shows that the repeat trade from customers averaged over five titles per year, an improvement on the previous years. In the sixties, when the ledgers begin, the main book customer was Edminston and Douglas. Thomas had dabbled in publishing in the fifties but, not achieving any real success, he had sold his copyrights to this firm. But the breakdown of subjects shows an emphasis on public administration and legal work as one would expect from a Royal printer near the legal hub of Scotland (Fig. 9.1). This type of work was still a significant part of Constable's turnover in 1876. However, the number of orders from Rivington and Macmillan made literature and religion the largest subject categories that year, a trend which is more marked in the 1886. By 1896 the number of books printed had increased substantially, so only four months of the year were surveyed. Nevertheless an analysis of Constable's book customers shows that the partners were picking up work from the entrepreneurial firms of the south in the eighties and nineties. These new clients included, J. M. Dent who began publishing in 1888, convinced of the demand for pocket classics, Archibald Constable, another grandson of Scott's publisher, who founded a new business in 1890 and his partner and nephew H. Arthur Doubleday who took over in 1893, and Arthur

Fig. 9.1 A subject breakdown of books printed by T. and A. Constable in 1866

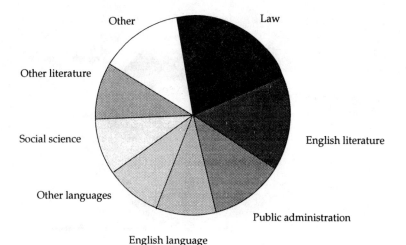

Stedman who set up Methuen in 1889. Of the older firms, Longman, Green and Co. was a regular customer, but business with the firm increased perhaps because it acquired Rivington in 1890. Thomas Stoughton had previously been with Nisbet and Co. So by 1896 Constable's were no longer dependent on their status as a royal printer and the majority of their book work was in the fields of Literature, Geography and History, and Languages (Fig. 9.2).

The tightly-knit networking of the trade was a concern to those who feared that the 'crash' of 1826 could happen again. When Archibald Constable's firm went under, landing Walter Scott with considerable debts, the repercussions in the industry took several other firms into the bankruptcy courts. A repeat of this experience in the 1890s was unlikely as the trade was not so reliant on post-dated bills and had much sounder billing and accounting systems. However, publishers were vulnerable. Unlike printers or paper manufacturers, their capital was invested in copyrights and stock which were notoriously difficult to value. Picking out a few companies' annual reports in the nineties and calculating the accounting ratios shows that the return on capital employed was generally low and liquidity very tight. Losses did occur and the *Investors' Review* was right to be concerned that 'As much as possible all details about these troubles are smothered up ... ' (Anon. 1899b, 262).

Fig. 9.2 A subject breakdown of books printed by T. and A. Constable in four months of 1896

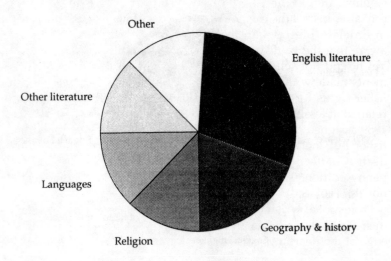

So how did the author fare? The *Publishers' Circular* agreed with the *Investors' Review* when they claimed that the author had never had it so good. The growth of the popular book market 'has forced the publisher to become more and more of a speculator, but one who must be capable of putting down his stake before the dice are thrown; the author takes no risk in such cases, the publisher takes all' (Anon. 1899b, 261). Naturally, the authors themselves did not agree. Walter Besant campaigned to establish the Society of Authors and was their vociferous spokesman.[5] The Society warned authors in a meeting in February 1890, that the cost of production stated in the publisher's agreement could be an underestimate – and reported instances when the final total was double the original figure (Anon. 1890a). Their complaints were not without foundation: copyrights were sometimes undervalued and the lump-sum payment given for a copyright was not the best way to sustain a writing career. However, reflecting on the nineties, Mumby relates how publishers were willing to take risks on unknown authors. T. Fisher Unwin began the *Pseudonym Library* which published the work of John Oliver Hobbes (Mrs Craigie) and Vernon Lee, among others. Heinemann made several discoveries for his *Pioneer Series* including publishing Robert Hitchens's *The Green Carnation* in 1894. From the 1850s authors were moving increasingly towards a royalty-type agreement and avoiding the outright sale of their copyrights (Weedon 1994).

So what did Wilkie Collins do? William Clarke has shown how Collins carefully prepared for the disposition of his literary property after his death. The novelist was concerned to exert his control in order to preserve an income for his dependants and he was aware that the value of his copyrights was falling (Clarke 1988, 4). Yet he did not sell his copyrights outright. In the series of agreements made with Chatto and Windus after 1874 he gave the publisher rights for seven years, specifying that no edition should be retailed at less than two shillings. The last agreement dated 2 April 1889 assigned the entire remaining rights of 24 novels to the publisher but included the same proviso. Five years after Collins's death Chatto published *The Woman in White* in his popular sixpenny edition. The ledgers tell a similar story for Collins's other novels (Table 9.8).[6]

Professional writers in this period were aware of the potential of their writings for resale and republication. Those who lived on the edge of their earnings collected their journal and newspaper articles

Table 9.8   First publication of Wilkie Collins's novels in Chatto's sixpenny edition

Year of 6d edition	Title	No. of impressions	Total copies
1894	*Woman in White*	10	290 000
1896	*Antonia*	5	85 000
1896	*Moonstone*	8	200 000
1898	*Dead Secret*	7	100 000
1900	*New Magdalen*	5	90 000
1902	*Armadale*	1	50 000
1908	*Law and The Lady*	1	25 000
1908	*Haunted Hotel*	1	25 000
1909	*Blind Love*	1	20 000
1910	*Man and Wife*	3	70 000
1912	*Poor Miss Finch*	1	25 000
1914	*Legacy of Cain*	1	25 000

into volumes for republication, rewrote novels serialised in the periodical press for the different formats available: the three-volume, or the one-volume reprint.[7] The correspondence between Wilkie Collins and Chatto and Windus shows that the author was aware of the value of his work when marketed in different formats; as serial fiction, as a three-volume novel, or as a cheap reprint. For example, in January 1878 he acknowledged the receipt of thirty guineas for 'The Duel in Home Wood' published in the *Belgravia* and the following month he received £650 for the serialisation and book publication of 'My Lady's Money' and 'another story'. But four years earlier he had held out for £1500 for the seven-year lease of copyright on *The Law and the Lady*. Clarke has shown that Collins did his own calculations to ascertain the likely return for his publisher on the sale of his novels and made his demands accordingly (Clarke 1988, 4). But these were usually over-optimistic. In 1874 Collins received £2000 for seven-years' lease of the copyright on 13 novels; by 1883 this had risen to £2500 for 19 novels but by 1889 the best he could do was £1800 on 24 novels. Although Collins's novels were worth more to Chatto, Collins was successful in negotiating a regular income. Over the 15 years covered by the correspondence Collins had negotiated agreements worth £13 480 with the publisher.

The 1890s are an interesting period in Victorian publishing history because the decade marks the beginning of modern mass-market publishing. Chatto and Windus's marketing of Collins's novels is only one example of the ways in which new book publishers were opening up the marketplace. They had their competitors who, like Newnes, were blurring the traditional boundaries between the newspaper, the periodical and the book press. This had an effect on the economics of the industry; from the nineties onwards the number of book publishers who became limited companies grew as the old partnership system became untenable in the increasingly competitive marketplace. As we have seen, the overall trends in costs show that cheapening of raw materials and the greater efficiency of the mechanised presses were more important in the cheapening of the costs of book production than the fall in the price of composition. The mechanisation of the industry meant that printers and paper manufacturers were the first to raise capital on the stock exchanges, but many publishers joined them in the first quarter of the twentieth century. The subsequent story of mergers and take-overs and the building up of large multinational media companies which is the history of twentieth-century publishing, has its origins in this period. The professionalisation of the writer, the mechanisation of production processes, the employment of cross-marketing in magazines and newspapers, and the syndication of fiction and news began earlier in the nineteenth century, but their convergence in the nineties broke down old boundaries and gave rise to recognisably modern forms of publication.

APPENDIX: MATERIAL QUOTED FROM THE CHATTO AND WINDUS ARCHIVE AT THE UNIVERSITY OF READING

(By kind permission of the publisher)

9 Sept. 1874. Memo signed by Wilkie Collins. £1500 for seven-year lease of *The Law and the Lady* for all editions down to 2/6d.
19 Nov. 1874. Agmt. States that copyright of the following thirteen works would be granted to Chatto and Windus for the period of seven years from 31 Mar. 1875. Collins would receive £2000. Chatto and Windus agreed to republish all works within twelve months from 31 Mar. 1875 and not to publish the novels for less than 2/-. Stereos, eight steel plates for six of the volumes and some wood cuts were bought from Smith and Elder for £650 (estimated by Mr George Bell of Bell and Sons). The novels were: *Antonia, Basil, Hide*

and Seek, Dead Secret, Queen of Hearts, Woman in White, Moonstone, Man and Wife, Poor Miss Finch, Miss and Mrs, New Magdalen, Frozen Deep, My Miscellanies.

16 Jan. 1875. Letter. Spottiswoode have stereoplates of *Woman in White, Hide and Seek, Man and Wife, Moonstone*.

8 Feb. 1875. Collins to Chatto and Windus. *Law and the Lady* received £1000.

12 Jan. 1878. Collins to Chatto and Windus. Received 30 guineas for 'The Duel in Home Wood' published in *Belgravia*. £150 for the cheap edition of *Two Destinies* on same terms as 'agreed on for cheap publication of my other novels'.

20 Feb. 1878. Agmt. 'My Lady's Money' *Belgravia* publication and Chatto and Windus book publication (not under 2/-, seven-year lease) with one other story (no title as yet) for £650. Copyright for both serial of new story and book form.

5 June 1879. Agmt. *Fallen Leaves*, seven-year 25th June 1879, not under 2/- for £600.

7 Apr. 1881. Collins to Chatto and Windus. Confirming receipt of bills: £200 at three, six and 29 months.

7 Apr. 1881. Agmt. *Black Robe* seven-year lease from 5 April. Terms: not to be retailed for less than 2/-. Pay Collins £600. If more than 1000 copies of three-volume edition, pay author additional £25 for each 100 sold.

1 Feb. 1882. Collins to Chatto and Windus. Thanks for £100 note for *The Law and the Lady* seven-year lease from 15 Feb. 1882. Terms: not retailed at less than 2/-. £300 for new collection of short stories plus £25 for each 100 over 750 of three-volume edition.

27 Mar. 1883. Agmt. *Antonia, Basil, Hide and Seek, Queen, Woman in White, Moonstone, Man and Wife, Finch, Miss and Mrs, New Magdalen, Frozen Deep, My Miscellanies*. £1000 for exclusive right seven years from 31 Mar. 1883. Terms: not to be retailed at less than 2/-.

28 Mar. 1883. Memo. Chatto and Windus. Written 'agreed' across top. 'Offered 2500£ for the entire remaining copyrights of 19 of W Collins novels including 13 contained in the agreement of this date and on the assumption that our unexpired interest in the 6 last was worth 500£ and that our interest in the stereos of was worth 1000£. Making the value of the whole of the stereos and copyrights 4000£. Mr Collins said he would accept this offer should the demand for his new story 'Heart and Science' in the 3 vol. form not greatly exceed that of his last two or three stories.'

3 Mar. 1883. Agmt. Collins get £600 for *Heart and Science* seven-year lease from 14 Apr. 1883. Terms: not to be retailed at less 2/- . If over 1000 of the three-volume edition sold pay Collins an extra £25 per 100.

20 Oct. 1884 . Agmt. Pay Collins £500 for *I Say No!* seven-year lease from 20 Oct. 1884. Terms: not to be retailed at less than 2/-. If more than 750 of the three-volume edition sold pay Collins £25 for each additional 100.

8 Feb. 1886. Agmt. Pay Collins £500 for *Evil Genius* seven year from 8 Sept. 1886. Terms: not to be retailed at less than 2/- . If over 750 of three-volume edition sold pay Collins £25 for each additional 100.

19 Feb. 1888. Agmt. Pay Collins £600 for *Jezebel's Daughter* for seven-year lease from 6 Feb. 1888. Terms: not to be retailed at less than 2/-. Statement of account: *Little Novels*

Number sold	£
3 vol. 400 @ 5/- royalty	100.0.0
840 @ 3/6 edn at 6d	21.0.0
2400 @ 2/- @ 3d	26.5.0
	147.0.0

23 Apr. 1888. Collins to Chatto and Windus. Received £250 due 26 July 1888 for printing *Two Destinies, Haunted Hotel, Fallen Leaves, Jezebel's Daughter, Black Robe* until April 1895.

4 July 1888. Collins to Chatto and Windus. *The Legacy of Cain* serialisation in newspapers ended 7 July 1888.

7 Aug. 1888. Collins to Chatto and Windus. Ask for £500 for exclusive right of publication book form for *The Legacy of Cain*. Terms: seven-year lease from 6 Dec. 1888. Same as agreement for *Evil Genius*, dated 8 Sept. 1886.

2 Apr. 1889. Agmt. Assign entire remaining rights of 24 novels to Chatto and Windus for £1800 *Antonia, Basil, Hide and Seek, Dead Secret, Queen of Hearts, My Miscellanies, Woman in White, Moonstone, Man and Wife, Poor Miss Finch, Miss and Mrs, New Magdalen, Frozen Deep, Law and Lady, Two Destinies, Haunted Hotel, Fallen Leaves, Jezebel's Daughter, Black Robe, Heart and Science, I Say No!, Evil Genius, Little Novels, The Legacy of Cain.*

30 Sept. 1889. Agmt. A. P. Watt, Collins's executor, agreement with Chatto and Windus. Paid £500 for the entire remaining copyright of

Blind Love, reserving Tauchnitz, translations and dramatisation rights.

1 Nov. 1889. Agmt. Chatto and Windus pay A. P. Watt £30 for *A Rogue's Life,* and Bentley £30 for copyright and stereoplates of story. Chatto and Windus will buy 950 copies of the work from Bentley at four and three-quarter pence each unbound. If published below 2/6 in cloth within four months from the date of the agreement, Chatto and Windus will recoup Bentley 'any allowance they may have to make upon copies recently sold'.

13 Oct. 1890. Smith, Elder and Co., to Chatto and Windus regarding Collins's works.

Notes

1. The contract dated 19 November 1874 stated that copyright of the following thirteen works would be granted to Chatto and Windus for the period of 7 years from 31 March 1875. Collins would receive £2000. Chatto and Windus agreed to republish all works within twelve months from 31 March 1875 and not to publish the novels for less than two shillings. Stereos, eight steel plates for six of the volumes and some wood cuts were bought from Smith and Elder for £650 (estimated by Mr George Bell of Bell and Sons). The novels were: *Antonia, Basil, Hide and Seek, Dead Secret, Queen of Hearts, Woman in White, Moonstone, Man and Wife, Poor Miss Finch, Miss and Mrs, New Magdalen, Frozen Deep, My Miscellanies.*

2. The database consists of 4163 individual records of book-production costs drawn from publishers' archives and 1261 records from printers' archives. The archives were sampled every ten years, and every book printed during the calendar year was entered. The only exception was the archive of George Bell and Co. Ltd. which was sampled every five years, and in the figures that follow Bell's data is shown separately. The publishers were: Richard Bentley, William Blackwood, Chatto and Windus, Oliver and Boyd, Bell and Bradfute, Chapman and Hall, Harris, Hodder and Stoughton, Jack and Macmillan. The printers were T. and A. Constable, William Clowes, MacFarlane & Erskine. An account of the methodology of the survey is given in Weedon, *Publishing History,* 33, 1993, and details of the archives surveyed in Weedon, *Leipziger Arbeitreis,* 1994.

3. More work needs to be done on this, especially as John Trebbel writes of the reprint trade in the USA: 'those who were successful in the competition learned to estimate publication schedules in hours instead of days or weeks' (Rosenbloom 1991, 58).

4. My thanks to Simon Eliot and Peter Martland for pointing out the sums withdrawn by the directors of Cassell and Co. Ltd in this period.

5. For the origins of Besant's involvement, see Eliot, 1989.

6. These figures are taken from the main series of publication ledgers held in the Chatto and Windus archive at the University of Reading. See S. Eliot and A. Weedon's transcription of the costs and print-runs of Chatto's editions of Walter Besant's and Wilkie Collins's novels in *History of the Book on Demand Series*. [For further information from the Reading archive referred to throughout this essay, see the appendix attached to this chapter – Eds]

7. For example, the journalist and novelist William Hurrell Mallock who wrote for *The Times* during the nineties. He published fictional and non-fictional works in periodicals and book form but never made a good living from his work. Towards the end of his life he was awarded a civil list pension.

Part IV
Quest(ion)s for Identities

10

Telling the Whole Truth: Wilkie Collins and the Lady Detective

Jessica Maynard

In a letter to William Roughead, Henry James outlined his aesthetic of the perfect crime. Roughead had recently sent him an account of the trial of Madeleine Smith, the Glasgow architect's daughter who had achieved notoriety in 1857 when she was tried for the murder of her lover, a Jersey shipping clerk named L'Angelier. But for James, the peculiar appeal of the case lay not so much in its un-doubted sensationalism – arsenic poisoning, a lover with a foreign name, unseemly love letters – as in its inconclusiveness. Aesthetic perfection here lay in imperfection itself, in a Scottish verdict of 'not proven' which enabled Smith to resume her place in society, albeit with a perpetual query above her name.[1] James recollects:

> I can still see the queer look of the 'not proven', seen for the first time, on the printed page of the newspaper. I stand again with it, on the summer afternoon – a boy of 14 – in the open window of the Rue Neuve Chaussée where I read it. Only I didn't know then of its – the case's perfect beauty and distinction. ... And what a pity she was almost of the pre-photographic age – I would give so much for a veracious portrait of her *then* face. (Lubbock 1920, 386–7)

It is, then, this 'queer look' – a failure in binary judgement, a refusal to decide one way or the other – that makes this 'the *type*', the perfect case, with nothing to be taken from it or added. James is here both literary practitioner and voyeur; indeed for James gratification in both cases rests on similar conditions, on the virtues of incompletion. In his Preface to *The Princess Casamassima*[2] James had discussed the challenge of registering the anarchist under-world, a world defined through its own obscurity and which, through its articulation in a novel, would thereby lose its essence. James raised an important contradiction here: that plausibility could be achieved only through omission, reality and the writer's renunciation of its pursuit.

Rather adroitly, James made a virtue of the writer's ignorance and inadequacy. This is not to say he dismissed the claims of reality. On the contrary, if his correspondence and his Preface are anything to go by, he seemed to rejoice in the role of peripatetic sociologist, the dutiful follower of Zola who visited Millbank prison with a notebook in preparation for one of his chapters.[3] Moreover, interpretation, James implied in the Preface, was bound up with the physiological act of seeing, which itself hovered somewhere in between the active and the passive:

> One walked of course with one's eyes greatly open, and I hasten to declare that such a practice, carried on for a long time and over a considerable space, positively provokes, all round, a mystic solicitation, the urgent appeal, on the part of everything, to be interpreted and, so far as may be, reproduced. (*PC*, 33)

The idea for the novel was, then, the natural issue of experience and exercise, of the senses and of the body; it was, James said, 'the ripe round fruit of perambulation' (*PC*, 33). Biological and literary inevitability even seemed to shade into one another in 'the urgent appeal, on the part of everything, to be interpreted and, so far as may be, *reproduced*'.

But at the same time, no matter how many sensations these walks round London yielded, they could not necessarily render a final account of the 'murky modern Babylon' (James 1960, 1), which only retained its force through impalpability. Given this sensory shortfall, how could the account be satisfactorily rendered? James answered the question thus. It was in this shortfall that perhaps the most intense realisation of the whole city for the urban connoisseur, and the most fertile terrain for the novelist could be found. It was to be found in what would always only be an intimation of the 'immense misery' of the city, which James spoke of in his essay 'London' (James 1960). Reality itself was authenticated and under-written by an *intuition* of 'that dark gulf' of destitution, poverty and crime. It was 'partly because we are irremediably conscious of that dark gulf that the most general appeal of the great city remains exactly what it is, the largest chapter of human accidents' (James 1960, 6)

So, when it came to *The Princess Casamassima* James would account for any 'sketchiness and vagueness and dimness taken by [the] picture' (*PC*, 48) by hailing it as authenticity. Shouldn't he find authenticity, said James, 'in the happy contention that the value I wished most to render and the effect I wished most to produce were precisely *those of our not knowing, of society's not knowing, but only guessing and suspecting and trying to ignore, what "goes on" irreconcilably, subversively, beneath the vast smug surface?'* (*PC*, 48; emphasis mine). His limitation as a social observer, it appeared to him, was something of a happy fault. I mention this because I see a similar contradiction in the 'queer look' of the Madeleine Smith affair. Just as James's art would capture the air of conspiracy in *Princess Casamassima* by simply honouring its impenetrability, so the typicality, perfection no less, that James sees in the verdict of 'not proven' suggests the epitome of criminality as lying in its irreducibility. And, I would argue, Doyle subscribes to a similar logic when he has Sherlock Holmes describe Moriarty as the 'Napoleon of crime' in 'The Final Problem' (Doyle 1993b, 252). Moriarty's supreme social delinquency is situated not so much in material acts as in intangible menace: in 'those undiscovered crimes' on which Holmes hasn't been consulted, in invisibility, in precisely not being designated 'criminal' by the authorities: '"Aye, there's the genius and the wonder of the thing!" says Holmes. "The man pervades London, and no one has heard of him. That's what puts him on a pinnacle in the records of crime"' (Doyle 1993b, 251). Holmes is right to wonder. By this sleight of hand, he succeeds in criminalising Moriarty without recourse to organised criminal justice. For him, the pinnacle of crime lies beyond official definition, in what hasn't yet come to light in what is always imminent. Perhaps crime is not so much the object of anxiety, as a symptom of anxiety without an object. Moriarty, the evil genius of late Victorian London, and as it were Holmes's genetic negative,[4] is rather more akin to the 'dark gulf' of human misery of which James spoke: at once a constituent of society, and a product it would rather be without, fascinating yet also dangerous. '"I tell you that I will never stand in the dock,"' Moriarty warns Holmes (Doyle 1993b, 255); his destruction can only apparently be achieved at the price of Holmes's. This is indeed what seems to happen at the end of 'The

Final Problem'. In their last confrontation, Holmes and Moriarty plunge over the Reichenbach falls, locked in a manichaean embrace.

'Art is essentially selection, but it is a selection whose main care is to be typical, to be inclusive', says James in 'The Art of Fiction' (Veeder and Griffin 1986). But, as we see with Madeleine Smith, or Moriarty, or James's realisation of London, to be typical can depend equally on omission as on commission, on something not being available to scrutiny. Similarly, the aesthetic of James the recreational consumer of true crime, corresponds to that of James the novelist. In each case, he locates typicality in what must remain unproven, in what, like Moriarty, will always evade conviction.

When James rues the lack of photographic record, therefore, he implies that a photograph would convey the mysterious totality of Madeleine Smith. In its immediacy, in its being a given that required no further gloss than 'This is Madeleine Smith', it would perfectly sum up the unresolved tension between guilt and innocence. This 'veracious portrait' would not provide physical symptoms of psychological dysfunction, whether explained in moral or biological terms. There would be no room here for criminological decoding. Rather, veracity would lie in the portrait's resistance to analysis. This would be its 'value' and 'effect'.

The manipulation of evidence in delivering a truthful account (of a person, an event) is also a concern of Wilkie Collins's *The Law and the Lady*.[5] But apart from that, there are also more specific correspondences between this text and the Madeleine Smith case (Maceachan 1950, 121–36; Bourne Taylor 1992, vii–xxv). The words 'not proven' provide the link between Smith, James and Collins, and point to a similarity between James's recipe for authenticity and the issues of this novel.

First, then, to the correspondences. While Smith was alleged to have administered arsenic to her lover in a cup of cocoa,[6] Valeria Macallan's husband Eustace in the novel is accused of murdering his first wife by similar means. And again, as with Smith, his reputation is left curiously in the balance, condemned to the perpetual irresolution of a non-verdict, neither guilt nor innocence. The truth of Sara Macallan's death remains undisclosed. This is the injustice his new wife sets out to rectify. Her husband's story, the 'story of the trial' which is contained within this story, has had no conclusion; judgement has been suspended. Valeria, on the other hand, demands conclusion and judgement as a condition for marital happiness. But by the end of the novel she seems to have dispensed with these, arriving at a decision which involves neither.

Valeria begins by reading the report of her husband's trial. Yet she finds such a reading increasingly inadequate as a road to the truth about the past. If this form of narrative failed to disclose an answer previously, then why should Valeria's re-reading, her retrial be any different? She sets out with a faith in the evidential reliability of the case transcription which, however, the following passage would appear to undermine:

> Turning to the second page of the Trial, I found a Note, assuring the reader of the absolute correctness of the Report of the proceedings. The compiler described himself as having enjoyed certain privileges. Thus, the presiding Judge had himself revised his charge to the Jury. And, again, the chief lawyers for the prosecution and the defence, following the Judge's example, had revised their speeches, for, and against, the prisoner. Lastly, particular care had been taken to secure a literally correct report of the evidence given by the various witnesses. It was some relief to me to discover this Note, and to be satisfied at the outset that the Story of the Trial was, in every particular, fully and truly told. (*LL*, 124)

But already doubts are sown as to whether this is a story 'fully and truly told'. How are we to read the fact that judge and advocates have 'revised' their speeches? Could they, in checking for errors, have also altered what they originally said, albeit inadvertently? With each 'revision', the distance between this transcription and the original speeches which it attempts to reproduce, only widens. A little later, we also hear that the evidence of a vital witness, being far too incoherent, has been transcribed into more intelligible English: '"The shorthand writers and reporters put his evidence into presentable language, before they printed it"' (*LL*, 199).

Valeria comes to recognise that the ordering and arrangement of the witness statements constitute a form of narrative, an argument. The statements do not simply reveal an event; they prompt its construction by the jury or the reader: 'Ignorant as I was of the law', Valeria says, 'I could see what impression the evidence (so far) was intended to produce on the minds of the Jury' (*LL*, 139). There is, in other words, a supplementary meaning beyond the mere facts testified to by the witnesses. Or, in terms of criminal evidence, what

Valeria has identified is the use of facts as evidence of *other facts* (Jackson 1988), the relationship of circumstantial evidence to the fact at issue (which might be considered: did Eustace Macallan poison his wife?). And it is, the judge tells the jury, the 'irresistible and just inference' (*LL*, 181) that bridges the gap between these two orders of fact. Successful narrative in this evidential context does not depend so much on proof as on plausibility, and in fact it comes into its own 'in the absence of truth based on observation' (MacCormick, cit. Jackson 1988, 19). It may not be able to produce what happened, but it can persuade the reader of what is *supposed* to have happened (Aristotle cit. Ginzburg 1992, 167).

At this point, Valeria chooses to add to the judge's direction, reminding us that inference may not necessarily depend on absolutes but on contingencies: 'Who is to decide what is a just inference? And what does circumstantial evidence rest on, but conjecture?' she demands (*LL*, 181).[7] If the absence of eyewitness testimony necessitates the construction of some kind of argument based on inferences, then its acceptability as a plausible account is more likely to rest on cultural and social norms, on shared values, on, for example, the assessment of witness credibility, none of which are measurable or universal. Could it be then that nothing in a criminal trial is ever proven as such but rather made to seem plausible? If the inference, or the reader's bridging of the gaps within the story, is a necessary part of judgement, then judgement itself is founded on incompletion. The inconclusiveness of the first trial was not then a matter of proof; it could be put down to its failure to present a plausible narrative.

Yet if Valeria has criticisms of this first attempt at narrative, and can see its problems, what does she propose to substitute it with? How can she avoid repeating its mistakes, since, in being part of nineteenth-century fiction herself, she would seem to contribute to that self-same trial/story process? As the title of the novel implies, she must play along with the narrative of 'the law', while at the same time challenging it as 'the lady'. Her legal difficulty is equally one of gender and class, a matter of her contradictory status as 'lawyer in petticoats'. In her re-reading of the trial, she rebels not simply against criminal law but also against social law. Her husband forbids her to pursue her investigations while her uncle, echoing Edmund Burke on Mary Wollstonecraft, regards her incursion into the law as tantamount to the reading of proscribed texts. Inappropriate participation in the male domain has its textual counterpart in the consumption of material not designated for women:

> 'You are conceited enough to think that you can succeed where the greatest lawyers in Scotland have failed. They couldn't prove this man's innocence, all working together. And you are going to prove it single handed? Upon my word, you are a wonderful woman.... May a plain country parson, who is not used to lawyers in petticoats, be permitted to ask how you mean to do it?'
>
> 'I mean to begin by reading the Trial, uncle.'
>
> 'Nice reading for a young woman! You will be wanting a batch of nasty French novels next.' (LL, 121)

What Valeria does in a sense is to move away from forms of reading that legislate for closure. In the end she demonstrates that there is nothing in the end to be proved, no fact in issue at all. Her story is about a non-event: that Sara Macallan wasn't murdered at all. In a strange way she retains the 'not proven' she set out to dispel. For one thing, she in turn refuses a proper ending for the story. Instead she presides over the suspension of revelation. She knows the truth, but it cannot be made public and it must be with-held from her husband. For the truth is not a binary one, a question of innocence or guilt, even after this reinvestigation. The first wife, Sara Macallan, unloved and neglected, has, it turns out, killed herself, after an overdose of truth: 'I have read your Diary. At last I know what you really think of me. I have read the confession of your loathing for me in your own handwriting' (LL, 391). Hence it seems that the written confession with its high truth value – Sara's reading of the story contained in Eustace's diary – must be associated with death and trauma. Valeria, on the other hand, writes from memory, 'unassisted by notes or diaries', she tells us (LL, 399). And she does so in order to explain how she survived a marriage that might have left her real name, her real identity in jeopardy.

In finding her own resolution Valeria avoids the kind of schedules she encountered in the trial report. Looking for clues as to her husband's past she will bypass the rank and file of historical narrative as arranged on Major Fitz-David's bookshelf – 'Walter Scott in green; the History of England in brown; the Annual Register in yellow calf' (LL, 82) – in favour of the more disordered higher shelves. It is through the apparent irrelevance of a broken vase that once stood on these shelves that Valeria advances closer to the secret of her husband's first marriage. Like her predecessor, Poe's Chevalier Dupin, she must use imaginative identification, not just inductive reasoning in order to reconstruct what happened in the past. Besides, there is another side to nineteenth-century history apart from scientific historiography; the kind of history that requires imaginative identification on the part of the historian to supply a gap between the document and the past reality to which it refers. And, W. David Shaw argues, it is an important element in Collins's *The Moonstone*:

> Just as Niehbuhr [author of *The History of Rome*] and his disciples insist that the historian must become a historical agent by exercising negative capability, so a reader of *The Moonstone* must empathize with each of Collins's narrators as he would with historical witnesses. (Shaw 1990, 288)

Valeria reminds us that there are several different models of truth, including both documentary and imaginative truth, and that these may be mixed up together. This is what she learns about narrative and the law in reading the trial, and this is what brings her to a second verdict of not proven.

It is better in the long run, the novel concludes, that Eustace be shielded from the truth of his first wife's suicide note, and this because of a still unresolved difficulty in assigning guilt. Eustace may be technically innocent, but who can ever measure the extent of his responsibility for Sara Macallan's death? It may be for these reasons, as much as for the sake of sparing his feelings, that the truth for him must remain in a sealed letter, the case unproven.

The other correspondence between the Smith and Macallan cases, mentioned earlier, was that of arsenic poisoning. What unites the fictional and the real here is the debate surrounding the cosmetic application of the poison, which, according to *Blackwood's Edinburgh Magazine*, exerted a beneficial effect on the complexion, if administered in judicious amounts (Anon. 1853, 678–95). Indeed, this is the expedient adopted by Sara Macallan in the novel in an effort to win her husband's love, but instead she uses the poison to kill herself. She might be viewed perhaps as Valeria's less successful sister, who, instead of recasting her marriage, attempts to recast herself: 'The poison will have its use at last,' she writes in her suicide note. 'It might have failed to improve my complexion. It will not fail to relieve you of your ugly wife' (*LL*, 392). Arsenic, in other words, at once indicates a cultural prescription of beauty and provides the pharmaceutical prescription for it: conformity or death. But with Madeleine Smith, the emphasis is slightly re-aligned. This time, arsenic becomes associated with nonconformity, and its poison lies in its power to dissemble, to mask blackness with whiteness. Cosmetics are Madeleine's defence (her counsel argued this was her reason for purchasing arsenic), her danger (it is impossible to finally declare the truth of her), and her allure (Henry James is fascinated by the idea of her photo). The point about arsenic here is that it sets up a disturbance in the relation between external symptom and internal ill. It nullifies such interpretation, it epitomises the suspended judgement of 'not proven'. As *Blackwood's* tells its readers, when the Styrian peasant girl takes arsenic, her transformation is no superficial deceit which will even-tually be exposed as fraudulent (as with the 'love philters, charms, and potions' of the east); it is substantial – 'Everyone sees and admires the *reality* of her growing beauty' (Anon. 1853, 689; empha-sis mine) – a profound yet simulated reality, real and not-real at the same time. How then does evaluation proceed, faced with such a compromised reality?

At the trial in *The Law and the Lady*, Sara Macallan's nurse does imply in her testimony a relation between Sara Macallan's 'muddy, blotchy' complexion and the violent temper tantrums to which she was subject. We see Valeria making similar inferences on the basis of a photograph of Sara: 'The woman's face was hard-featured and ugly, with the marking lines of strong passions and resolute self-will written plainly on it' (*LL*, 88). But Valeria must learn to avoid such rigidly inductive methods, and the novel later gives us several different views of Sara which cannot necessarily be reconciled.[8] Furthermore, in aspiring to be 'fair', to be pale and therefore both attractive and reasonable, Sara Macallan resigns herself to cultural codes which are of course thrown into crisis by Madeleine Smith, who quite clearly has not accepted them in her private life.

It is perhaps this disjunction, between Smith's youth, charm, class and gender, and the crime that she is said to have committed, that 'arsenic' comes to signify: something toxic, but fascinating nonetheless. Perhaps it is this disturbance in signifying codes that James alluded to with his 'queer look'. Somehow, in becoming a matter of press and public speculation, this detail acquires, in addi-tion to its forensic value, a discursive force. Eliding discourses of femininity and crime, it points not so much to legibility as to its reverse. Smith's supposed transgression – sexual and homicidal and racial?[9] – is not written on her face, which on the contrary according to contemporary reports would seem supremely amiable or bland (Altick 1970, 178). Nor can she ever be unmasked, for like the Styrian peasant girl, she is her deception. And this is precisely why Henry James regretted the lack of photographic record, because it captured the unclassifiable, because in being purely performative, it was pure evidence: 'If the Photograph cannot be penetrated,' says Roland Barthes, 'it is because of its evidential power … our vision of it is *certain* … I have the leisure to observe the photograph with intensity; but also, however long I extend this observation, it teaches me nothing. It is precisely in this *arrest* of interpretation that the Photograph's certainty resides' (Barthes 1993, 106–7; emphasis mine). This arrest of interpretation is often to be found in what may be socially unpalatable, for example, Eustace's relationship to his first wife and her suicide; the 'immense misery' of London; its imagined criminal potential as embodied in Professor Moriarty.

Madeleine Smith's correspondence with her lover adds to the sense of the unnaturalness, the foreignness of her conduct. In his address, the Lord Justice-Clerk stresses the unprecedented and 'fearful' nature of Smith's freedom of expression:

> she uses the word 'love' underscored, showing clearly what she meant by it; and in one letter she alludes to a most disgusting and revolting scene between them which one would have thought only a common prostitute could have been party to, and exhibiting a state of mind most lamentable to think of. Certainly such a sentence was probably never before penned by a female to a man. There are many other letters, all written in the same strain, and certainly exhibiting a strain of mind which it was fearful to contemplate. (Jesse 1927, 295–96)

So, for Smith, arsenic is part of a complex of associations that signals not simply illegibility but also unspeakability: the reading and the writing of forbidden texts, texts too 'fearful to contemplate' in their indeterminacy. A photograph of Madeleine Smith would certainly tell a story similar in some respects to that of Valeria Macallan: that to be perfect and complete must strangely be to remain incomplete, unproven. This is in the end a problem of modernity and cities, of people living on credit or trust, and not on the down-payment of knowledge. Hence it is trust, a willing suspension of definite knowledge, by which Eustace and Valeria's marriage is resolved. Suspicion, though, is the other half of trust, which is where Moriarty, Madeleine and James's writing deliver us. This is the particularly intractable experience James wishes to represent: that of 'our not knowing, of society's not knowing, but only guessing and suspecting and trying to ignore, what "goes on" irreconcilably, subversively, beneath the vast smug surface'.

Notes

1. See Richard Altick, *Victorian Studies in Scarlet* (New York: Norton, 1970); Mary Hartman, 'Murder for Respectability', *Victorian Studies* 16 (1973): 381–400; Jenny Bourne Taylor, 'Introduction', in *The Law and the Lady*, Wilkie Collins (Oxford: Oxford University Press, 1992), pp. vii–xxv.

2. Serialised in the *Atlantic Monthly* in 1885, and published in full in 1886; James added the Preface to the New York edition of 1909. All references to *Princess Casamassima* are taken from the Penguin edition, ed. Derek Brewer (1987; full bibliographical details in the Bibliography at the end of the book) and are cited parenthetically in the text, using the abbreviation *PC*.

3. 'I have been all the morning at Millbank Prison (horrible place) collecting notes for a fiction scene. You see I am quite the Naturalist'. Henry James, *Letters*, ed. Leon Edel, Vol. III (Cambridge Mass.: Harvard University Press, 1980), p. 61.

4. Compare his 'reptilian' physiognomy to Holmes's aquiline nobility. This is how Holmes is introduced in *A Study in Scarlet*: 'His eyes were sharp and piercing ... and his thin, hawk-like nose gave his whole expression an air of alertness and decision' (Doyle 1993a, 14). On the other hand, according to Holmes's description, there is something of the primeval about Moriarty, notwithstanding his highly developed cranium: '" ... his forehead domes out of a white curve, and his two eyes are deeply sunken in his head ... His shoulders are rounded from much study, and his face protrudes forward, and is forever slowly oscillating from side to side in a curiously reptilian fashion"' (Doyle 1993b, 254).

5. Serialised in the *Graphic* and published in full in 1875; references are cited parenthetically (*LL*) throughout, and are taken from Oxford University Press edition (1992). Full bibliographical details are provided in the Bibliography at the end of the book.

6. See F. Tennyson Jesse (ed.), *The Trial of Madeleine Smith* (London: William Hodge and Co. Ltd, 1927). William Roughead himself edited other trials in the series, including that of Mary Blandy, about which

James enthuses in another letter to Roughead: 'I devoured the tender Blandy in a single feast'. James, *Letters*, ed. Leon Edel, Vol. IV (Cambridge, Mass.: Harvard University Press, 1984).

7. This kind of scepticism regarding the nature of proof might be compared with Jeremy Bentham's epistemological stance in his *Rationale of Judicial Evidence*. He argues that the 'degree of connexion between a principal fact and an alleged evidentiary fact is strictly an "instinctive operation"' (Vol. VI, 216, cit. Postema); and, further, that 'probability and improbability, with their infinity of degrees are mere figments of imagination' (*Introductory View of Rationale of Judicial Evidence*, 46, cit. Postema). Probability for Bentham and Valeria alike is a matter of fictions, and not facts. See Gerald J. Postema, 'Fact, Fictions, and Law: Bentham on the Foundations of Evidence' in Twining and Stein (eds), *Evidence and Proof* (Dartmouth: New England University Press, 1992), pp. 25–7.

8. The nurse's evidence-in-chief, for example, characterises Sara as 'easily excited to fly into a passion, and quite reckless' (*LL*, 128). Yet, under cross-examination, she is forced to add another dimension to this negative portrait. Then, she concedes that at other times Sara 'spoke and acted like a well-bred lady' (*LL*, 140). This 'salutary counter-impression' (*LL*, 141) produced by the defence counsel emphasises the extent to which representations of Sara are coloured by cultural expectations of what becomes or ill-becomes a 'well-bred lady'. These are the same expectations that condemn Valeria as 'lawyer in petticoats'.

9. 'Racial' in the sense of a liaison between British and continental, Scottish and Gallic.

11

Dickensian Architextures or, the City and the Ineffable

Julian Wolfreys

The reader must not expect to know where I live. At present, it is true, my abode may be a question of little or no import to anybody; ... I live in a venerable suburb of London, in an old house which in bygone days was a famous resort for merry roysterers and peerless ladies, long since departed. It is a silent, shady place, with a paved courtyard so full of echoes, that sometimes I am tempted to believe that faint responses to the noises of old times linger there yet, and that these ghosts of sound haunt my footsteps as I pace it up and down. ... Its worm-eaten doors, and low ceilings crossed with clumsy beams; its walls of wainscot, dark stairs and gaping closets; its small chambers, communicating with each other by winding passages or narrow steps; its many nooks, scarce larger than its corner-cupboards; its very dust and dullness .... (*MHC*, 5–6)

this alien city ... (Ackroyd 1991, 680)

A town such as London, where a man may wander for hours together without reaching the beginning of the end ... (Engels 1988, 680)

'*The most distinctive cities,*' writes Paul Virilio, '*bear within them the capacity of being nowhere*' (Virilio 1994, 10). If this is true of London, where, then, do we imagine the City to be in the writing of Charles

Dickens? What is this city? What can we say about it, what do we think we know about it, what do we understand about it? If anything? Naming the city implies and even imposes both recognisable location and architecture: location *as* architecture. A structure is put in place, conceptually, geographically, figuratively, especially when associated with another proper name, such as that of Charles Dickens. Much criticism has been written about Dickens's London,[1] and the various biographies have also had their share in the discussion of Dickens's London. Indeed, the very phrase, 'Dickens's London' seems to deliver itself as a hieratic title, already armed with defensive and bullying quotation marks, marking off the subject of the city as one of which we can no longer speak; a subject which is, because of the volumes already spoken and written, ineffable. But if we can return to Dickens's London, shedding or erasing the quotation marks, even partially, it may be possible to witness Dickens as already writing the ineffable city, writing of a city which cannot be constructed simply and unproblematically, which cannot be expressed through words, a city which is unpronounceable, beyond description or expression; except, that is, through descriptions which speak of the unspeakability, informing us of the ineffable condition of the capital's architexture.

So, a proposition, with which to begin: the reading of 'Dickens's London' which this essay gestures towards, is built around an understanding of the novels and the city that they map as *events*. The term 'event' is drawn, in the particular sense that I am employing it, from its use in recent strands of architectural discourse. This is neither the origin nor the entire history of the use of 'event' in this context, however. The architectural situation or context neither exhausts nor monumentalises the construction of this particular definition, drawing the term itself from the language of the Situationists and the moment of 1968 (Tschumi 1994, 255). Before turning to Dickens's texts, a brief definition of the 'event' in architecture.

Architectural thinking, according to Bernard Tschumi, has relied in its classical and conventional stages on an implicit and reassuring received wisdom concerning what he calls the 'hierarchical cause-and-effect relationship between function and form' (Tschumi 1994, 255). Without going into lengthy analogy at this moment, it is possible to see how literary criticism relies upon similar relationships, especially in the case of the nineteenth-century novel and its interpretation. Contrary to such hierarchical relationships, the architectural – and, by implication, textual – event offers a 'combination of spaces ... and movements without any hierarchy or precedence amongst these concepts' (Tschumi 1994, 255). For Tschumi and other architects and architectural theorists, the 'event' takes place as part of an on-going, active definition, definition-astranslation, of a situation, space or, let us say, architectural narrative. Dickens's writing partakes of such a process through the development of the narrative of the city as event, while formally constructing the narrative – and thus the image of the city – from series of reiterated tropes, figures of speech, repeated syntactical structures, all of which, in certain ways, rely on negation or the impossibility of being able to describe a scene in full.

This can be seen in *Our Mutual Friend* when the city is deplored for its spring evenings:

> ... the city which Mr Podsnap so explanatorily called London, Londres, London is at its worst ... a black shrill city ... a gritty city ... a hopeless city, with no rent in the leaden canopy of its sky; such a beleaguered city.... (*OMF*, 144–5)

Despite the weary irony at Mr Podsnap's expense, an irony which reveals the inability to describe London through the paucity of Podsnap's own bilingual definition, Dickens is equally frustrated in his writing of the city. He resorts to repetition with an adverbial variation, the interminable description imitating the interminability of London in the springtime. The one break in the pattern comes when Dickens points to the absence of a break in the sky. This passage typifies the Dickensian architexture (or one aspect of it), with its combination of repetition, the failure of definition, the inclusion of negation and the collapse between form and content. The text fails to describe London with any sense of completeness, but becomes exactly what it fails to describe. In its movement this passage serves to introduce a sense or idea of the event, but the idea requires further elucidation.

To borrow from Tschumi once again, the architectural event involves the 'combination of heterogeneous and incompatible terms' and the 'questioning of multiple, fragmented, dislocated terrains' (Tschumi 1994, 255, 257). The passage from *Master Humphrey's Clock* which serves as an epigraph to this essay illustrates this definition, with its sense of spatio-temporal movement, its refusal to identify a single, frozen site or location, and its serial, fragmented detail which refuses to coalesce into an architectural whole. To go further, such an event is what Jacques Derrida has defined as 'the emergence of a disparate multiplicity' (Derrida, cit. Tschumi 1994, 257). Again, to refer to the passage – in both senses of that word, both literary and architectural – from and through *Master Humphrey's Clock*, the emergence of which Derrida speaks occurs through echoes, beams, stairways, passages, communications (between rooms and between the past and the present), lighting, nooks and dust. As this one extract demonstrates so eloquently, the 'event' goes beyond singularity and the invocation of a static monolith, whether that monolith be a building, monument or the very idea of the 'book' as a complete, discrete, and self-defining object, in which a narrative or textile weave is transformed and solidified through a process of reading. What the emergence of the concept of the event has done is to call into question and to 'open up', in Tschumi's words, 'that which in our history or tradition, is understood to be fixed, essential, monumental' (Tschumi 1994, 257).

Derrida, however, cautions that we question the possibility of imagining an architecture of the event, if only because architecture and the event cannot be spoken of, at least in the singular, without recalling both the classical and conventional and the desire in Western tradition for such fetishes. Events are so radically other, in their calling to mind space, movement, fluidity and the constant flux between non-fixed places, the notion of architecture in its classical sense, and all that is implied in the imminent history of such a term (Derrida 1987, 5), that the idea of an architecture of events can often only be considered either through what cannot be said and what is left unspoken, or through metonymic or metaphorical traces. Take for example certain passages in *Our Mutual Friend*. Dickens has no adequate positive language with which to describe Holloway, the home of Reginald Wilfer. He therefore names it alliteratively as a 'suburban Sahara', composed of a catalogue of tiles, bricks, bones, carpets, rubbish, dogs and dust (*OMF*, 33). The initial image of the desert as a figure for Holloway destroys any possible locatable referent. London is described by what it is not, by a term wholly inappropriate yet strikingly apposite. Furthermore, the lexicon of items following does nothing to add to the image of the desert. The figure is not given credence or authority, but is immediately displaced by a series of domestic details, refuse, animals and skeletal remains. These, we are asked to understand, figure Holloway. Yet they retain their disparate atomisation. They do not speak directly of London, they do not have a hierarchy, there is no fixed, essential or monumental image, and each term substitutes itself for every other in the serial itemisation of a North London suburb. Yet together they supposedly figure the city while not speaking of it directly.

We can read Dickens as having an understanding of this problematic condition through his narratives of the city. Dickens comprehends the city in terms of its spaces as having texture rather than being a series of fixed sites which are unproblematically defined and presented. And texture is indicated through lists of seemingly random elements. Hence my use of the term 'architexture' in the title, which suggests, among many other things, the desire to shake the solidity of the monumental, which desire is always present in Dickens. The history of meaning which the term 'architecture' puts into place and into operation every time it is used is so overdetermined that, like the phrase, 'Dickens's London', it cannot be evoked or announced without there being a certain return to particular understandings, a certain monumentalisation. Architexture, on the other hand, speaks of architecture without speaking it, privileging the narrative over the monumental, movement over the static, and informing us through the possible homology of structural resemblances between architecture and narrative, form and content. This is most immediately apparent in the phrase 'winding passages' in the excerpt from *Master Humphrey's Clock*, with its self-conscious reference to Dickens's own prose and to the details of the house. It is also apparent in the cataloguing of Holloway. We read the text listing the items as a substitute for description. The items comprise the list which simultaneously serves to imagine the particular area of London, while also constructing the text itself. Dickens builds his narratives out of such lists, the repeated presence of which mark the text as architextural event.

In writing London, Dickens clearly opens up the fixed, essential and monumental to a questioning and destabilisation, involving techniques which require the use of disparate multiplicity; he does so, furthermore, in an effort to be faithful to the ineffable labyrinth that is the modern city of London. While the novelist may well be 'very particular about street names', as Peter Ackroyd puts it (1991, 161), this strategy does nothing to counter the immanence of the abyss which Dickens conjures. In Ackroyd's words again, the city 'both is and is not the same' (1991, 679). Dickens happily substitutes, displaces, confuses and reduplicates elements which speak about London, his language being the register of an endlessly signifying process which is the city, and which mark the city as being structured like the unconscious (or like a language) while also revealing that the city is not to be spoken of directly or seen whole.

In *Oliver Twist*, a novel in which all of the neighbourhoods are, 'but for their names, mutually indistinguishable' (Schwarzbach 1979, 48), the Artful Dodger objects to entering London with Oliver until night; so, although Dickens names the streets around Islington, neither we nor Oliver can see the place (*OT*, 99–103). The street-names hover, like disembodied spectres in the chimerical text.[2] All we are told is that the streets are the dirtiest, most wretched streets, narrow, muddy and filled with filthy odours (*OT*, 103); any possible structural identification is lost, obscured in ephemera and effluvia. Mud, fog, rain all serve similar obfuscating and metonymic purposes through an open series of endless substitutions in *Bleak House*, while, in *Our Mutual Friend*, vessels appear to be 'ashore', houses 'afloat', the ceiling of a room is not the ceiling at all but the floor of the room above (seen from below), lacking the plastering necessary to conform to the architectural convention of defining a ceiling (*OMF*, 21). Roof, walls and floor are comprehensible only in the process of decomposition (*OMF*, 21). Stairs are little better than ladders because of 'inappropriate' construction (*OMF*, 21), while a building is described as having a forehead, marked by a 'rotten wart of wood' (*OMF*, 21). How this can be seen is literally not clear, however, because, as we are told, '*the whole* was very indistinctly seen in the obscurity of the night' (*OMF*, 21; my emphasis). While we can see details with poetic license, the architectural entirety is resisted, hidden, erased. Indeed the entire architectural meaning is brought into question, deconstructed as it is into a series of ambiguously architectural details. The eye is moved from piece to piece, but the gaze is ultimately refused an overall meaning, a monumental, organised presence on which it can fix.

Once again the scene of the event is clearly a scene which questions meaning and the possibility of its assertion. Dickens writes the event at every level, making fixed and essential meanings ambiguous, whether describing a single building, building materials, a street, structures such as Chancery or the Circumlocution Office, the sewer system of *Our Mutual Friend*, a district of London or what can appear to be the movement of the entire city at any given moment. Even fog is not a fixed element, not some essential or originary source of architectonic or structuring ability, capable as it is of being smeared by the 'light of kilnfires' in *Our Mutual Friend* (*OMF*, 33).

This all points in a certain direction. While Dickens is obviously an urban, rather than a rural writer, as Terry Eagleton has suggested (1976, 127) – and there is very much a sense for Dickens that to be urban means being part of London, as opposed to just any city – there is nonetheless an ambiguous, even ambivalent relationship between the writer and what is written. I raise this point because it is necessary to understand the continuous presence of this tension throughout Dickens's novels. There is not a shift between early and mature form, argued for by Terry Eagleton. He suggests that the 'anarchic, decentred, fragmentary forms of the early novels' come to be replaced by the 'unified structures of the mature fiction' (1976, 130), which forms and structures parallel the developments in capitalist modes of production, ideological state apparatuses and juridico-bureaucratic networks. In his Althusserian impersonation – he do the theorists in different voices – Eagleton argues that the later novels 'mime ... a set of [systematic] conflicts and non–relations' (1976, 130). Appealing as they are, such contentions are only partly accurate in their assessment, and for a very good reason: while recognising, in the words of Allon White, a 'certain homology between sentence structure and plot structure' (1993, 103), analyses such as Eagleton's do not take the recognition far enough. Such analyses do not comprehend the strategic use of the fragmentary situation of the city as a non-hierarchical counter-balance to the monolithic imposition upon the urban narrative of the juridic, capitalist, bureaucratic, ideological architectures.

One striking instance of the deployment of the city against an imposing structure (in this case the power of the Law), and the attendant ambiguity which such a scene uneasily articulates, comes with the scene of Oliver Twist's arrest. In Chapter Eleven, Oliver is arrested for having allegedly stolen a pocket handkerchief. The movement and events of the scene are notable in their precipitous violence, a violence of structure which acknowledges the force with which the Law is enforced, as Dickens works deconstructively between issues of justice and the Law.[3] We are told:

The offence had been committed within the district, and in the immediate neighbourhood of, a very notorious police office. The crowd had only the satisfaction of accompanying Oliver through two or three streets, and down a place called Mutton Hill, where he was led beneath a low archway, and up a dirty Court ... by the back way. It was a small paved yard ... [Oliver entered] ... through a door ... which led into a stone cell. ... The cell was in shape and size something like an area cellar, only not so light. It was most intolerably dirty. (*OT*, 118)

The passages down which Oliver is hurried also compose the passage in writing which hurries the subject to that place where he will be brought before the Law. Yet, where exactly is that place, the place of the Law? Can we even talk about the place of the Law? This seems unlikely, precisely because of the precipitation that marks the passage, and which the passage marks. Dickens talks of the 'district' and the 'immediate neighbourhood'; both are very domestic, urban descriptions rather than being specific names for the place of the Law. The Law is gestured towards but not indicated outright, such a si(gh)ting being impossible. And Oliver's passage is described, indistinctly, as being through 'two or three streets'. Mutton Hill is named, but this gives us no real sense of place. Furthermore, Oliver's access to the Law is very indirect, being through low archways, dirty courts and back passages. The overall sense is not one of precision but of the labyrinthine nature of the city, and of its indescribability. Given this, and the way in which Oliver is admitted to the unknown place of the Law, there is available to us a sense that the ineffability of place undoes or, at the very least, troubles, the structure and site within which the Law is supposed to operate.

There is something curiously illegal about Oliver's taking, and we read, I believe, that the Law is for Dickens illicit in its force and violence, both of which have little to do with justice. The Law is made to appear fragile and improperly situated by its being precariously placed in an unspeakable landscape. Even when Oliver is taken to the cell and placed in it, the details given are brief; they are the dirty court, a small paved yard, while the cell itself is described as being 'in shape and size something like an area cellar, only not so light. It was most intolerably dirty'. 'Something like' is hardly the most precise of analogical phrases, and this itself is negated by the fact that the cell is 'not so light' as an area cellar. None of the descriptive phrases used by Dickens invoke the Law; they belong instead to the taxonomy of working-class slum housing, the details being general enough to invoke a sense of any slum dwelling in London at the time of the novel.[4] This of course can be read as suggesting that all the poor are in a metaphorical jail. But Dickens's use of an architectural lexicon descriptive of poverty does nothing to uphold the sense that Oliver is either in the presence or the place of the Law. The play between cell and cellar is vertiginously ambiguous, while the Law is further reduced in power through the use of the term 'court' in its architectural and domestic, rather than judicial sense. When the Law does come to be represented in the shape of Mr Fang, its power is immediately unsettled by Fang's lack of power over proceedings, by Mr Brownlow's worrying interjections, and by the arrival of justice in the court of Law in the shape of the bookseller.

What we are witness to in Chapter Eleven – what in fact we are required to bear witness to – is a certain oscillation of architextural structures between the siting and citation of the city, and the place of the Law. The structure being described, to borrow from Derrida on justice and the law, is one in which 'law (*droit*) is essentially deconstructible, whether because it is *founded, constructed* on interpretable or transformable textual strata ... or because its ultimate *foundation* is by definition unfounded' (Derrida 1992b, 14–15). Derrida's language uses specifically architectural terms in order to demonstrate the Law's structure and the possibility of deconstruction. He continues: 'it is the deconstructible structure of law (*droit*) ... that also insures the possibility of deconstruction. Justice in itself ... is not deconstructible. ... Deconstruction is justice' (Derrida 1992b, 14–15). Dickens performs, in the passage above, the very deconstructibility of Law described by Derrida as imaginable. And he does so furthermore through the use of London's mobile structures which serve to produce justice for Oliver. Architexture *is* a condition of justice, its very possibility.

It can be seen then in this performance that, in all its immanence and ineffability, the architexture of the fluid, mobile, abyssal city is ranged against – and through – the solid architecture of whichever power structure is Dickens's target. Certainly, there is a 'certain homology'; but that homology is not necessarily between, say sentence structure and Circumlocution Office, or syntax and Chancery, even though there may very well be such elements available to our reading. The homology is more complex. In Mark Wigley's words (talking of Derrida's writing, though what he says is equally applicable to Dickens):

> the text, in a kind of strategic transference, assumes the form of
> what it describes ... it begins to shape itself according to the

spatial logic ... in order to articulate the somewhat uneasy relationship between a certain kind of thinking and a certain kind of
space (1992, xi; my emphasis)

Dickens's architextures assume the spatial logic of the city, rather
than the ideological logic of 'repressive institutional spaces' (1992,
155). The form being assumed is not that of Chancery or the
Circumlocution Office, but the streets, the houses, the sewer
system, the fog, the weather in general, the aleatory movements of
the city's inhabitants, whose wanderings constitute 'London' at any
given instance, yet which constitutions are always changing. The
uneasy relationship belongs to an effort to shape thinking and
writing in a manner faithful to the condition of London itself.

We can witness the beginnings of such a relationship in *Sketches
by Boz*. From this early text we can understand how Dickens begins
a process of writing the city which is continued throughout his
work, without there necessarily being the transition desired by
Eagleton. Of particular interest are the two sketches of the streets at
morning and night (*SB*, 49–61). Boz leads the reader through places
where there is an 'air of cold, solitary desolation' (*SB*, 49). The
streets are described as 'noiseless', as 'cold and lifeless', 'deserted',
'empty' and there is the 'stillness of death over the streets' (*SB*, 49).
Later, such descriptions are amplified, the scene being described as
a 'deserted prospect' with 'no signs of life, nor ... habitation' (*SB*,
51). At this hour even the trinity of the 'drunken, the dissipated,
the wretched have disappeared' (*SB*, 49). Only a solitary drunk and
a homeless person, victim of both 'penury and police' (*SB*, 49), that
is to say economics and the law, are left. This first description of
London impresses by the sense it gives of reiterated negation and
constant movement, a double movement throughout streets and
time, as Boz focuses our attention on yet another negation, while
calling to our attention the wearing away of another hour or half-
hour (*SB*, 51–3). London is a place without place, a place where
everything is not, and this repeatedly so. The city is never fixed.

Even when life does come half-hour by half-hour to the streets,
London is not so much a *tableau vivant*, as the place of 'decayed
cabbage leaves' (*SB*, 51) and a discordant 'compound' of sounds
(*SB*, 52). Both sound and decay speak (of) the event and the city as
event, through the Dickensian attention to the details of process
and a certain movement. And as people begin to fill the streets,
Boz's description of the streets becomes more sketchy, vaguely and

barely defined, as Londoners obscure and blur 'London', before its definition becomes too fixed. Description gives way to the image of a 'vast concourse of people' (*SB*, 54) engulfing the streets. Despite the fact that we can read a certain desire inscribed in the attempt to define the city, London clearly cannot be spoken of, except in the sketchiest of terms.

Boz seems to know the problem inherent in describing London; he appears to comprehend the way in which words will have already failed to capture a likeness, before that likeness is embarked upon, unless the writer resorts to cliché. The recognition of the problem is stated nowhere more lucidly than in the first sentence of the second sketch of the streets: 'But the streets of London, to be beheld in the very height of their glory, should be seen on a dark, dull, murky winter's night, when there is just enough damp gently stealing down to make the pavement greasy...' (*SB*, 55). That insistent objection with which the sentence opens registers the impossibility of writing the city in any full, simple manner; it also begins an attempt to justify the writing of the city otherwise; yet the ironic dimension is marked in the statement that, for the city to be viewed at its best, one should 'see' it through the atmospheric obstructions and lack of light that define a winter's night in London. The city can hardly be seen through the murk and the 'heavy lazy mist' (*SB*, 55), the 'cold, thin rain' (*SB*, 58) and the mud (*SB*, 59), the same mud which rises at the beginning of *Bleak House* and which is everywhere in *Our Mutual Friend*. All that does 'appear' to the eye is 'dirt and discomfort' (*SB*, 57), while glory, having departed, is only conspicuous by its absence (*SB*, 57). Even the lamps of the shops serve only to illuminate the enclosing and engulfing darkness (*SB*, 55). As in the daytime, discordant sound intrudes upon the 'melancholy stillness of the night' (*SB*, 58). What this scene and its companion piece illustrate is a city in process, in transition; a city, in short, composed of events, and London as existing as an architexture of events. Dickens can write only of a liminal city. What is glaringly absent in and between these two chapters is the city of the daytime, the city in full view. Such a city is clearly ineffable.

Instead we see fragments, fluid multiplicities of details which do not cohere, but which impress by their being so fragile, so tentatively drawn. And, to reiterate, Boz knows the difficulty; for, as he closes the night-time scene, he comments – defensively, wistfully – that scenes such as those we have been privileged to witness are so numerous, and replaced so endlessly by 'fresh ones', that 'a description of all of them, however slight, would require a volume' (*SB*, 60). Such a volume, we are assured, would be 'by no means pleasing' (*SB*, 60). So that which is unspeakable in and about London remains unspoken on the grounds of the author's reluctance to expend energy and the issue of the audience's aesthetic sensibilities.

But if Boz is unwilling or unable to go into greater detail, Dickens is not. Indeed, this reticence on Boz's part seems nothing less than the artist's coyness, given the already detailed performance of London's marginalia which entail the street scenes. If there is a perceptible shift between early and later Dickens, then that transition seems to be one where the verecund persona gives way to a performance-imbued with Pancksian relish.[5]

Dickens's architextures do not present us with a form – of a building, of the city – as a meaning, system or structure. Rather, we are presented with the textual event, the architextural event, as a means of exposing the limits of fixed meaning, and, by this, the limits of the utterable. The reiteration of structure is simultaneously concerned with the announcement of that structure's fragility and ambiguous meaning. The fixing of meaning, the imposition of the law of the absolute, is resisted through the spatio-temporal movement of the event. The architecture of meaning may well be desired, hence the seemingly infinite repetitions; but the Dickensian architexture of the event 'reinvents architecture in a series of "only onces" which are always unique in their repetition' (Derrida 1987, 13). In Derrida's words again, 'the dimension of the event is subsumed in the very structure of the architectural apparatus: sequence, open series, narrativity' (Derrida 1987, 5). It is not that there is what Steven Connor calls, in describing *Bleak House*, a '*problematic* excess of metonymy' (Connor 1985, 65; italics mine). The excess is not problematic, when regarded as belonging to the architextural event, as described in this chapter; it is merely part of the narrative structuring, part of a strategy to accommodate the modern capital in a writing which comprehends London, without seeking to apprehend it.

Those who do seek out the definite place in 'Dickens's London', seeking to apprehend or arrest the movable feast of the capital, should take as a salutary warning against such a desire certain passages from *Martin Chuzzlewit*. When Mr Pecksniff and his daughters arrive in London, the city is shrouded in fog, as though it were 'a city in the clouds' (*MC*, 180). The whole city is both afloat and insubstantial. One of the outsiders on the coach is pronounced parenthetically as mad because he chances to give a firm definition to some indefinable substance, calling it snow (*MC*, 180). Pecksniff's relationship to and knowledge of the city is highly ambiguous, verging between confidence and despondence, 'thinking he had lost his way, now thinking he had found it' (*MC*, 180), as he seeks Todger's. The city slips out of Pecksniff's grasp, leaving him in a perpetual state of 'perspiration and flurry' (*MC*, 180). Even when Pecksniff seems assured of his knowledge, and tells his daughters confidently where they are, our narrator is obliged to point out that

> at length they stopped in a kind of paved yard near the Monument. That is to say, Mr Pecksniff told them so; for as to anything they could see of the Monument, or anything else but the buildings close at hand, they might as well have been playing blindman's buff at Salisbury (180).

Absolute knowledge is subsumed by the dissolution of certainty. The paved yard cannot be defined except relatively, and Mr Pecksniff's arrogant authority is revealed as being its extreme limit. There is no truth to the city which can be fixed in place and the Monument[6] becomes a suitable figure and metaphor for architectural solidity and certainty undergoing deconstruction at Dickens's hand. Dickensian architexture clearly renounces any hierarchy or precedence, to invoke Bernard Tschumi once again, even at the moment in which it seems to have come to rest on a seemingly knowable, fixable feature. The text's architexture rejects any possible 'hierarchical cause-and-effect between function and form' (Tschumi's words already cited above) by making the certainty of the monument called the Monument merely an insupportable – and unsupported – assertion on the part of the perspiring Pecksniff, thereby placing the assertion at the level of one more contesting narrative strand, belonging to a general sequential structure.

When finally found, Todger's interiors are revealed; they are figured in a manner similar to other interiors already mentioned from *Our Mutual Friend* and *Master Humphrey's Clock* (*MC*, 182). And, as is revealed in the aptly-named Chapter Nine, 'Town and Todger's', with its alliterative exchange, the lodging-house is a figure of the event *par excellence* that is Dickens's London (and not 'Dickens's London' which is the fixation of a certain critical practice, most typically represented by a feature such as 'the Monument'). For London, as we are told, was worthy of Todger's (*MC*, 185). And yet for all its singularity, Todger's is resisted as a finite definition, being revealed as belonging to an 'odd family' of 'hundreds and thousands' (*MC*, 185). Todger's neighbourhood thus features as one of an undefined number of non-similar reiterations which make up the city. In this neighbourhood 'you' grope 'your way' 'through lanes and bye-ways, and court-yards, and passages; and you never once emerged upon anything that might reasonably be called a street' (*MC*, 185). Approximate definitions substitute themselves one for the other, indicating the principle of singular repetition which can mark the event, while it is noted that no one name can command definition, nor order the random movement into either a stable topographic feature or a taxonomic grouping. These are 'devious mazes' (*MC*, 185) belonging to a labyrinth 'whereof the mystery was known but to a chosen few' such as the postman apparently (although this is all told in a somewhat doxical and apocryphal register; *MC*, 185); and Todger's can never be found 'on a verbal direction, though given within a minute's walk of it' (*MC*, 185). Thus the city is never absolutely knowable, nor can one speak of its movements. But this is not a problem, for those who fail to find their way in the town around Todger's remain, in Dickens's words, 'tranquil and uncomplaining', and in a state of 'resigned distraction' (*MC*, 185). The city is ineffable, and only the Pecksniffs among us try to name it, to fix it and resist its constant re-figuring processes. For each figure is a figure for all other figures in the writing of the city. And this writing is what Allon White calls the 'insistent repetition' (White, 1993, 102) of the palimpsest, where the writing of the city figures the city as writing, or, in Derrida's words, the 'architectural experience of memory' (Derrida 1990, 11). And this is an apt approximation for Dickens's architextural memory of the ineffable city.

Notes

1. The standard studies are, of course, F. S. Schwarzbach, *Dickens and the City* (London: Athlone Press, 1979), Alexander Welsh, *The City of Dickens* (Oxford: Clarendon Press, 1971) and Raymond Williams, *The Country and the City* (Oxford: Oxford University Press, 1973). Perhaps the most important study of the figure of the city in nineteenth-

century fiction in recent years is that of Carol Bernstein, *The Celebration of Scandal: Toward The Sublime in Victorian Urban Fiction* (University Park: Pennsylvania University Press, 1991), which touches in several places on my own study, in its application of deconstructive theory to the trope of the city. Drawing also on Georg Lukács, Michel Foucault and Walter Benjamin, Bernstein works through readings of the immaterial city, producing a negative urban sublime and a failure to represent the modern city. Where our studies diverge most consistently and repeatedly is precisely over the question of 'failure'. In terms of the aesthetics of the study, Bernstein is markedly modernist in her reading of the failure of representation. My argument focuses more on a Dickensian celebration of provisionality and ineffability, as well as the architectural condition of writing.

2. F. S. Schwarzbach has also commented on the fact that Oliver and the Dodger wait until after dark (1979, 46). He observes also, in his chapter on *Oliver Twist*, that, despite the naming of streets as the two boys enter, Dickens does not heighten the realism; instead, naming serves merely to distance us even further, because no other details than names are provided (Schwarzbach 1979, 45–53). Schwarzbach's study is impressive in its attention to detail and the paradoxes and contradictions which arise out of the Dickensian concatenation of minutiae. The question of naming is one to which Schwarzbach repeatedly returns. One curiosity concerning street- or place-names is worth noting. When Oliver is arrested and taken to prison by the police, the one street named is a Mutton Hill (see the discussion of the arrest and its scene in the main body of this essay). As far as I have been able to ascertain from maps of London dating between 1813 and 1888 no Mutton Hill existed. In Clerkenwell, the district adjacent to Islington, there was a Mutton Lane leading on to Clerkenwell Green, and there still is a Muswell Hill. It would appear then that Mutton Hill did not exist, and Dickens's conflation of place-names only serves to heighten the ambiguity surrounding what we can say we know of 'Dickens's London' with any certainty.

3. On this subject see Derrida's reading of Walter Benjamin in 'Force of Law: The "Mystical Foundation of Authority"', *Deconstruction and the Possibility of Justice*, ed. Drucilla Cornell, Michael Rosenfeld, David Gray Carlson (London: Routledge, 1992), 3–68. This essay is of particular interest for the ways in which it counters arguments that deconstruction has no ethics, and for the difference which is opened up between notions of justice and the Law. Also of interest is the way in which the essay can be read as a scene of complication to the subject of the Law, which Derrida's earlier essay on the parable *Vor dem Gesetz* in Kafka's *The Trial* (Derrida, 'Before the Law', *Acts of Literature*, ed. Derek Attridge [London: Routledge, 1992], pp. 181–221; also in the same volume, see 'The Law of Genre', pp. 221–253) had instituted. 'Force of Law' complicates the discourse on the Law at many levels, not least in the ways in which it provides an implicit critique of certain (mis-)readings of 'Before the Law'.

4. Comparable passages from Engels are instructive and reveal the domestic, rather than carceral, context to Dickens's description:

    > These slums ... with cellars used as dwellings, almost always irregularly built. ... The streets are generally unpaved, rough, dirty, filled with vegetable and animal refuse ... foul, stagnant pools ... narrow, crooked, filthy, crooked streets. ... The houses are occupied from cellar to garret, filthy within and without ... dwellings in the narrow courts and alleys between the streets, entered by covered passages between the houses, in which the filth and tottering ruin surpass all description. Scarcely a whole window pane can be found, the walls are crumbling, door-posts and window-frames loose and broken, doors of old boards nailed together. ... Heaps of garbage and ashes lie in all directions, and the foul liquids emptied before the doors gather in stinking pools. Here live the poorest of the poor ... (Engels 1988, 70-1).

5. This is explored in more detail elsewhere, in my *Writing London* (Scolar Press, forthcoming).
6. The name of the monument – the Monument – serves as both proper name and generic definition, and this doubling seems to strain at the limits of what monumentalisation can achieve in terms of identification and fixity.

12

Inventing Social Identity: *Sketches by Boz*

Geoffrey Hemstedt

Mr Jennings Rudolph played tunes on a walking stick, and then went behind the parlour door and gave his celebrated imitations of actors, edge-tools, and animals. (*SB*, 250)[1]

A turn-up bedstead is a blunt, honest piece of furniture: it may be simply disguised with a sham drawer; and sometimes a mad attempt is even made to pass it off for a book-case; ornament it how you will, however, the turn-up bedstead seems to defy disguise. (*SB*, 177)

Sketches by Boz, the book we now have, is a collection of 56 short pieces, including a dozen (largely comic) tales, Dickens wrote between 1832 and 1836, when he was in his early twenties. They first appeared in *The Monthly Magazine*, *The Morning Chronicle*, *Bell's Life of London* and similar publications. They were brought together in two collections in 1836 and 1837, and Chapman and Hall ran them again in monthly parts from November 1837, to cash in on the success of *The Pickwick Papers*, which had just finished its run. They show Boz walking the streets of London as if beating the bounds of his domain, marking a writer's territory he was to hold for nearly four decades. 'We had been lounging one evening, down Oxford Street, Holborn, Cheapside, Coleman Street, Finsbury Square and so on, with the intention of returning westward, by Pentonville and the New Road' (*SB*, 231). He hangs around the river, or crosses it to the Borough (site of the Marshalsea). He favours the run from the slums of St Giles and nearby Monmouth Street with its dealers in second-hand clothes, across to the lawyers' districts: Holborn, Lincoln's Inn, the Law Courts, Newgate. Or he moves to the outskirts, the indeterminate spaces where the city is spreading itself, past 'a new row of houses at Camden Town, half street, half brick-field, somewhere near the canal' (*SB*, 264).

With its layerings and extensions this is a protean city, offering abrupt juxtapositions and inventories of things for which there seems to be no serviceable taxonomy, but the *Sketches* begin to cohere around reiterated thematic sets. The writer shows people making shift to survive, and like Mayhew a little later, an array of street traders who will be unassimilable in a mainstream economic history; London is not seen as a place of highly capitalised and technologically driven production. Even so, Boz has an eye for new fashions of behaviour in work and recreation, and his accounts of aspects of display, self-consciousness and socialisation prefigure his later writings about social change and modernity. Describing the Paris of Manet and his followers T. J. Clark has spoken of the bewildering density of the signals exchanged in the city's public life (1984). Manet's Paris was at a later stage of development than that of Boz's London, its map redrawn on the grid of Haussmann's boulevards. The citizen who, as a worker or for recreation, ventured from the familiar bearings of the *faubourg* into those modern spaces experienced both the risks and the pleasures of an identity exposed. London has never, even after the Blitz, been so purposefully remapped, but it has still changed continuously and dramatically. Such a process of change is made up of countless acts which rewrite the world we live in, always demanding new readings, and the citizen must be both writer and reader.

The most generative (and correspondingly problematic) point of vantage Boz adopts, the movement which repeatedly structures his narrative, is that of the *flâneur*, tracing an open movement of encounter, part chance, part quest, taking notice and taking notes. In fact, *'flâneur'* is not quite right. The writer may describe himself as 'lounging', but his energetic drive, the sheer pace of his movement from scene to scene, is something different from the display of self-at-leisure of the gentleman *flâneur*; and the history of his connection with the city denies him that quality of intoxication Walter Benjamin was able to recognise in Baudelaire. In *A Berlin Chronicle* Benjamin tells how he was himself, as the son of wealthy middle-class parents, guided to the 'wider expanses' (Benjamin 1992, 293) of that city by nursemaids. He further remarks: 'it is likely that no one ever masters anything in which he has not known impotence' (Benjamin

1992, 294). We may recall that Dickens had first made his way through the streets of London as a boy on the edge of puberty, wretchedly ashamed that gentlemen should have seen him through a window, working shoulder to shoulder with urchins at Warren's Blacking. As the writer of the *Sketches* he can display a different identity, becoming the observer, not the observed. Here he describes a character who lives in a back attic in Seven Dials:

> The shabby-genteel man is an object of some mystery, but as he leads a life of seclusion, and never was known to buy anything but an occasional pen, except half-pints of coffee, penny loaves, and ha'porths of ink, his fellow lodgers naturally suppose him to be an author; and rumours are current in the Dials, that he writes poems for Mr Warren. (*SB*, 74)

In the convolutions of this secret signature Dickens flirts with a confession of some sort, even as he ensures the seclusion of a self who has rendered Mr Warren other services than writing poems for him. Instead, proclaiming himself as Boz-the-author, he does what he sees Londoners doing all around him; he performs a social identity.

In 'The Streets – Morning' we see him again transforming recollection into a feature of the passing scene:

> Small office lads in large hats, who are made men before they are boys, hurry along in pairs, with their first coat carefully brushed, and the white trousers of last Sunday plentifully besmeared with dust and ink. It evidently requires a considerable mental struggle to avoid investing part of the day's dinner-money in the purchase of the stale tarts so temptingly displayed in dusty tins at the pastry cooks' doors; but a consciousness of their own importance and the receipt of seven shillings a week, with the prospect of an early rise to eight, comes to their aid, and they accordingly put their hats a little more to one side, and look under the bonnets of all the milliners' and staymakers' apprentices they meet. ... (*SB*, 54)

Here memory, displaced and cleaned up a little, produces an idiom which will pervade the *Sketches*. These lads are neither boys nor men, and tilt their large hats as if trying to tilt the balance. The moment-to-moment transactions which define their daily lives, being able to buy or not being able to buy, the glances, the self-display, take place on the streets, in the space between where they sleep and where they work. They are part of the social panorama, and there is a sense that they perform their part in the spectacle consciously.

It is characteristic of the street economy of the *Sketches* that the tarts should be stale. That is as near as you can get to second-hand food. There are accounts of second-hand clothing shops, marine store dealers, pawnbrokers' shops, gin shops, brokers' shops. A piece on 'Shops and their Tenants' plots the pathetic trajectory of failure that haunts petty commercial speculation. After dark the streets are still full of stallholders, or someone knocks at your door at nine in the evening and offers to sell you beer from a jug. There is the baked-potato man, and the kidney-pie man, 'with his warehouse on his arm' (*SB*, 58). Stalls lit by 'great flaring gas-lights, unshaded by any glass, display huge piles of bright red and pale yellow cheeses, mingled with little fivepenny dabs of dingy bacon' (*SB*, 58). Then, as the crowds disperse, the narrative cuts to a ragged beggar woman who clutches a child and sings ballads for pennies. The reader is caught up in the speed of this writing, the glare, the publicity, contrasts of light and dark, shifts from swirling activity to tableaus of isolation; then stopped short by a kind of discursive fracturing, a sudden confrontation with exposure and death. 'The feeble singer ... may turn away, only to die of cold and hunger' (*SB*, 59). This transition anticipates the description of Newgate, where we see 'the gibbet with all its dreadful apparatus' (*SB*, 195), but where the crowds passing the prison 'in one perpetual stream of life and bustle' (*SB*, 199) are 'utterly unmindful of the throng of wretched creatures pent up within it' (*SB*, 199), unaware that 'they stand within one yard of a fellow-creature, bound and helpless, whose days are numbered' (*SB*, 200). Such contrasts are starkly dialectic, seeming to allow for no middle ground. The last equation, the monumental presence of the condemned man at the heart of the living city, returns in the last section of the *Sketches*. 'The Black Veil' (*SB*, 359–69) tells of a mother who hires a doctor in a vain attempt to resurrect her hanged son. These are for Dickens the irreducible elements of a demotic eschatology, and will merge with others to fulfil the symbolic project of later writing. Think, for example, of Ralph Nickleby, before his suicide by hanging, passing a graveyard where the dead 'lay thick and close – corrupting in body as they had in mind – a dense and squalid crowd. Here they lay, cheek by jowl with life; no deeper down than the feet of the throng that passed there, every day, and piled high as their throats' (*Nicholas Nickleby* 1986, 902).

The misery of the slums, Boz says in the *Sketches*, 'can hardly be imagined by those (and there are many such) who have not witnessed it' (*SB*, 183). Dickens stresses this from the very beginning of his career as a writer (it is some vision of London, surely, that figures as a model for the provincial slum of the Sowerberry funeral in *Oliver Twist*). Even so, in *Sketches by Boz* the poorest districts are also picturesque and exotic, the site of fancy. In the journalism of the 1850s and 1860s (*Reprinted Pieces, The Uncommercial Traveller*), they are read in the manner of *Bleak House*, though necessarily without its apocalyptic register: as places to be cleansed, as the object of reformist anxiety, because they breed disease, misery and crime. By then the reformist rhetoric shows Dickens, in his journalistic mode at least, as an establishment figure, speaking a project that is both idealist and self-protective. Comparably, whereas in the *Sketches* we see for the most part marginal (because irregular) economic activity, the later journalism features enterprises of some scale, in an array which reflects the interlocking institutions of modern production: a nautical school which trains boys for the merchant service, a lead works, mass catering, a children's hospital, Chatham Dockyard, and so on.

The movement of perspective in the *Sketches*, deriving from the original conditions of their composition, is more volatile. Lost in the warrens of St Giles,

[y]ou turn the corner, what a change! All is light and brilliancy. The hum of many voices issues from the splendid gin-shop which forms the commencement of the two streets opposite; and the gay building, with the fantastically ordered parapet, the illuminated clock, the plate-glass windows surrounded by stucco rosettes, and its profusion of gas-lights in richly lit burners, is perfectly dazzling when contrasted with the dirt and gloom we have just left. (*SB*, 183)

Boz acts as a guide to the reader disoriented in a city that is at the same time old and modern, rotting and garishly exhilarating. I have tried to reproduce something of that disorientation by moving from the lads with their big hats to the graveyard; but the hanged man is an extreme case with which to urge a reading of the *Sketches* as some kind of existential panorama, lit by gas-flares under the walls of the prison-house, and indeed such a reading (however plausibly 'Dickensian') would be a misrepresentation. The cumulative plot follows a rhythm of dilation and contraction, the heartbeat of a living city. Boz knows that the whole functions organically, that in King's Cross the bread is pulled from the bakers' ovens an hour later than in Pentonville, following the clock of pedestrian commuters. By pulling back again and again to the slums, to the Dials and St Giles, and then reaching out to the growing suburbs, the narrative adumbrates a demography with edges and divisions that are sometimes sharp, more often uncertain. In a record of transitions and newness we see the plate glass, the new shop-fittings, the brick fields to service waves of new building. In the rookeries people still eat fast food – jellied eels and meat pies – if they can afford to, less as luxuries than because they have no means of preparing food at home. They eat in the streets. Some sleep in the streets. In Stamford Hill, or Clapham Rise, when the paterfamilias returns from his day's occupation in office or shop or warehouse, dinner is served.

There is a middle ground here after all, there is bound to be, and the people who inhabit it are shown to be always conscious of the boundaries defining the different social identities they might achieve, or fall into. What for some is a desired way of life is for others a kind of social death. Material and ideological effects are mapped on to each other. The beggar woman, who sings for food for herself and her child, may turn away to die of hunger. The 'young, delicate girl' (SB, 191) who is observed pawning a small gold chain and a forget-me-not ring 'given her in better times' (SB, 192) is exposed to public shame. 'What name shall I say? – Your own property of course? – Where do you live? – Housekeeper or lodger?' (SB, 191) The pawnbroker's catechism further marks the young woman as a person whose economic status denies her the right of privacy. She has become a person who can be written down. Boz mixes a number of discursive strategies to render such an event. He offers exact observation of the laws and degrees of personal disaster. 'There are grades in pawning as in everything else, and distinctions must be observed even in poverty' (SB, 186). What do you let go first, what do you hang on to until the end? What you pawn, the silver fork or the flat iron, further classifies you. He adds a sentimental and moralising register ('the coldness of old friends' [SB, 192]), and typologies from popular romance. The 'delicate girl' belongs to a type where youth, beauty and shame are combined in the shadowy menace of sexual exploitation; so 'in the next box' (*SB*, 192) at the pawnbroker's counter is a prostitute, and then a woman for whom there are 'but two more stages, the hospital and the grave' (*SB*, 192). This 'progress' articulates that condition of Victorian popular typologies whereby a whole sequence was potentially present in a single tableau.

These are established as key themes in the first sketches, 'Our Parish'. A widow appeals to the parish board for relief:

> 'Where do you live?' inquires one of the overseers. 'I rents a two-pair, gentlemen, at Mrs Brown's, Number 3, Little King William's Alley, which has lived there these fifteen year, and knows me to be very hard-working and industrious, and when my poor husband was alive, gentlemen, as died in the hospital –' (*SB*, 7)

Boz hears grammars which, in Miggs or Mrs Gamp, will be luxuriantly reworked for comic purpose, but here they register power relations and the idioms of ingratiation. The technical language of the broker's man carries grim metaphoric force; putting the distress in, possession, execution. Like the tableau at the pawnbroker's, his anecdotes encapsulate a style of realism intimately allied to popular romance. In transcribing and reconstructing these languages Boz enjoys the privileged position of the reporter, but he retains an investment in popular rhetoric:

> 'I used to think when I caught sight of her, in the clothes she used to wear, which looked shabby even upon her, and would have been scarcely decent on any one else, that if I was a gentleman it would wring my heart to see the woman that was a smart and merry girl when I courted her, so altered through her love of me. ... But if I ever saw death in a woman's face, I saw it in hers that night.' (*SB*, 34–5)

Clothes proclaim identity, and by the logic of the *Sketches* we may imagine that even these shabby clothes will be sold again when their wearer is dead. The second-hand clothes shops of Monmouth Street are 'the extensive groves of the illustrious dead' (*SB*, 76) where Boz reads in the garments hung out for sale the fortunes of their former owners. As the wearer speaks beyond the grave, perhaps a story of failed fortune, astonishingly these clothes are bought again. Where one life ends another begins, but this must surely be a figure not of renewal but of what had seemed an inconceivable prolongation of life. Or we have an inversion of the equation offered earlier. The dress that for one person would signal a kind of social death is for another the dress in which social identity may be sustained.

The dynamic of the *Sketches* lies in Boz's sense of the different potential meanings of the elements he observes. Commodities litter the text, and fascinate the writer partly because they are valued differently by different people, and partly because they challenge his ability to discover order where there seems to be only disorder. Objects are paraded in rolling inventories, pan-shots, kaleidoscopic tumbles. We have seen that the text is fractured by unassimilable elements, where the laws of the state or of getting and spending exact a death, but the rhetoric of these moments marks them off from this main exuberant flow. By and large the *Sketches* avoid the kind of tableau of domestic destitution that Charles Kingsley or Elizabeth Gaskell were to deploy in a reformist project. Those 'little fivepenny dabs of dingy bacon' are seen in the place where they are offered for sale, and stand as a sign of a condition of consumption, but the scene of feast is less likely to be a set at the limit of subsistence than a ceremony of working-class or petty-bourgeois recreation. In 'Miss Evans and the Eagle' we hear of 'quite a little feast; two ounces of seven- and sixpenny green, and a quarter of a pound of the best fresh; and Mr Wilkins had brought a pint of shrimps, neatly folded up in a clean belcher' (*SB*, 228). The limits of what can be had are defined, but people come together to transform lack into surplus. Things and the uses to which they are put form the raw material of a realist method which fills in the specific details of life in a specific time and place. The reader can add the information that hackney coaches cost a shilling a mile and so on to an accumulating sense of the tariff of daily living.

Much of *Sketches by Boz* is concerned with a residual or marginal economy. To play a part in the mainstream economic history of the years after the 1830s citizens would have to play by other rules. They would consume more than they needed. They might discard some of what they no longer needed, but the people who lived on this waste belonged to a secondary social order, unable to take part in the modern enterprise of capitalism, as both producers and consumers. Boz is interested in those who improvise in order to survive, but he is equally interested in the ways people set out to play as full a part as possible in an emerging modernity. To do so they must improvise institutions and performances, even invent styles of behaviour as they go along. In 'The River' (*SB*, 100–5) he describes the steamers that travel from St Katherine's Dock to Margate or Gravesend. These boats offer excursions, or a commuting service for men whose families are boarded at the seaside for the summer while they themselves keep working in London. The steamer moves off down the river.

> Telescopes, sandwiches, and glasses of brandy-and-water cold without, begin to be in great requisition; and bashful men who have been looking down the hatchway at the engine, find, to their great relief, a subject on which they can converse with one another – and a copious one too – Steam.
>
> 'Wonderful thing, steam, sir.' 'Ah! (a deep-drawn sigh) it is indeed, sir.' 'Great power, sir.' 'Immense – immense!' 'Great deal done by steam, sir.' 'Ah! (another sigh at the immensity of the subject, and a knowing shake of the head) you may say that, sir.' Novel remarks of this kind are generally the commencement of a conversation which is prolonged until the conclusion of the trip, and, perhaps, lays the foundation of a speaking acquaintance between half-a-dozen gentlemen, who, having their families at Gravesend, take season tickets for the boat, and dine on board every afternoon. (*SB*, 105)

To achieve conversation at all is to construct a small sodality which will make a frame of social identity for the speakers. Giving the conversation ceremonial form, ('Sir'), agreeing to operate in cliché (novel remarks, says Boz), the speakers tread the thin ice of collusion where convention lets ignorance show as knowledge. Are these 'gentlemen' clerks, cashiers, or men of some substance in the world of work? How are we to know? It does not matter, since the forms of exchange they adopt allow them to share some kind of right to the honorific 'gentlemen' whichever they are. These characters are well set to ride the wave of the full tide of Victorian bourgeois culture in the years ahead, when they will be called upon to learn on the job. Picture them, or their sons, having read Browning, dropping the names of Italian artists: 'Wonderful painter, this Andrea del Sarto, sir.' 'Ah! (a deep-drawn sigh), faultless they say, sir.' 'You may well say so. Great power, sir.'

Another instance. In 'The Ladies' Societies' (*SB*, 36–41), Boz anatomises systems of charity, but he is concerned less with more obviously public social effects, poverty, illiteracy and so on, and not even very much with the kind of satire aimed at charitable women in *Bleak House*. Rather he is fascinated by the invention of institutional practices which can serve to frame a collective identity. If the Ladies' Societies hire an orator they buy language-performance. If the speaker is a hot enough property they can hire Exeter Hall:

> He talked of green isles – other shores – vast Atlantic – bosom of the deep – Christian charity – blood and extermination – mercy in hearts – arms in hands – altars and homes – household gods. He wiped his eyes, he blew his nose, he quoted Latin. The effect was tremendous – the Latin was a decided hit. Nobody knew exactly what it was about, but everybody knew it must be affecting, because even the orator was overcome. (*SB*, 40)

The axis of the event is slung between oratory as a commodity at one end and the status it confers on the members of the Ladies' Society at the other ('the popularity of the distribution society among the ladies of our parish is unprecedented' [*SB*, 40]). Their original reformist agenda, poverty, is absent, and its more sensational substitute, Ireland, is broken into tags of rhetoric. The real action is to be found in the fleshing out of bourgeois identity.

The *Sketches* show a full spectrum of improvisations. Social Being is established, proclaimed, performed, and also tested and exposed, in public places. For the most part people enter this arena eagerly; the streets, the markets and drinking places, Greenwich Fair, Astley's, the theatre, music shows, tea gardens, Vauxhall, public dinners, excursions, 'societies' of all kinds. At the play the spectator is 'far more delighted and amused with the audience, than with the pageantry' (*SB*, 107), and the audience arranges itself accordingly; mamma directs the governess 'to pull the girls' frocks a little more off their shoulders' (*SB*, 107). When clerks and drapers' assistants take a river excursion, they turn up in nautical gear. They perform in private theatrical societies, paying a fee to play the more prestigious roles, and take elegant stage names, Belville and Melville, Byron and St Clair (*SB*, 123), to foreshorten the quest for genteel status. At dinners and testimonial gatherings people ape the orotund languages of parliamentary convention. While he was writing the *Sketches* Dickens developed this theme in the ceremonials and uniforms of the Pickwick Club. If men gather for the evening in a taproom, or Sam Weller is invited to dine with the valets and butlers of Bath, somebody is elected to the chair to ensure that due forms are followed. But these enterprises of self-fashioning entail risk too. Democracy is one thing when it holds a carrot to bourgeois aspiration under the terms of the 1832 Reform Bill, and a man can hold forth at a testimonial dinner as if he were in the House of Commons. It is something else when you are forced to rub shoulders with the wrong kind of person. A man who would dearly love to command a carriage, but travels by omnibus, may be publicly humiliated by the omnibus 'cad' (the fare collector [*SB*, 140]) if he gives himself airs. Boz delights to record such acts of insubordination, the revenge of the repressed, the social self the bourgeois fears and repudiates. Somebody should rewrite *Great Expectations* as *Trabb's Boy*.

The city is altogether insubordinate, in that it refuses our attempts to reduce it to a knowable form. It was stated at the beginning of this chapter that the city offers inventories of things for which there seems to be no serviceable taxonomy. Boz loves making lists. Here is part of one: '…about twenty books – all odd volumes; and as many wine-glasses – all different patterns; several locks, an old earthen-ware pan, full of rusty keys; two or three gaudy chimney-ornaments – cracked, of course; the remains of a lustre, without any drops; a round frame like a capital O, which has once held a mirror; a flute complete with the exception of a middle joint; a pair of curling irons; and a tinder box' (*SB*, 177). In lists such as this we can discern the shifting orders that together make up the formless organism of the city, with all its contradictions. The gas flares, the dingy bacon and the dying beggar woman are part of a grouping of phenomena, and the title of the sketch in which they appear furnishes a heading for them: 'The Streets – Night' (*SB*, 55–61). In an economy where a commodity circulates uncertainly, as a thing to be used, or as money or credit, 'pledged' in a sort of limbo, or brought back into use again, by the original owner or a new one, where it can be at one and the same time both rubbish and a thing of value, we may need to categorise things provisionally, as a holding operation. There is a scratch of irony when the pawnbroker is shown arranging 'cards of rings and brooches, fastened and labelled separately, like the insects in the British Museum' (*SB*, 188). In effect each inventory is its own taxonomy and, by collapsing the two, Boz exposes the inadequacy of any larger theory of categories. It is too soon to subordinate the city further. This London is phenomenal, and best seen phenomenally, as it exposes the insolence of any who would control its dynamism in some scheme of moralising explanation. Boz's lists help articulate the social themes of the book, even as he sees their absurd structure. Those quoted at the beginning of the paragraph are: things to be found in a law student's rooms; things sold to early-morning coach passengers; and (of course) things offered for sale in a second-hand shop: 'Our wonder at their ever having been bought, is only to be equalled by our astonishment at the idea of their ever having been sold again' (*SB*, 177).

This story of buying and selling, together with the motif of display and concealment, initiates a recalcitrant and subversive economic plot which Dickens will pursue for thirty years, culminating in *Our Mutual Friend*, which sets out the world of the Veneerings and mountainous dust-heaps, two kinds of recycling. In our own time the orthodoxies of postmodern explanation give yet another slant on recycling, making familiar and pervasive reconsumption, resurrection and imitation of older modes and styles. The eclectic opportunism of such reinscriptions was a particular characteristic of Victorian bourgeois culture. In both cases such recycling is a condition of the production, circulation and consumption of new commodities, in which we might trace a complex implication of desire through ideological investment in the values written in signatures of commodity style. Then and now, by emphasising these conditions of cultural practice, reading the surfaces of sign and referent, we miss something. In the grand plot of Victorian history what part is played by those citizens who largely consume what others throw aside, or who live on waste? The clothes one person casts off another buys, and we have seen how many life-stories might be traced from this juncture. In the array of commodities and social types, and the circulation of things, Boz finds modernity where we least expect to see it. In Britain, recent years have seen pawnbroking become a growth industry, along with second-hand dealing. At the same time commentators and legislators have paraded a new insolence by adding to their orthodox schemes of social categorisation the term 'underclass'. For Boz the phenomena of the city proclaim a crisis of classification that cannot be resolved by such a word, a fall-back category to which we are invited to consign those citizens who do not fit into the dominant order. We would be wrong to read in his account of the orders of detritus and indigence merely the (residual) other of an emerging capitalist hegemony. Rather we may read of the limits of that enterprise, in that these modes of living are still with us. In Dickens's later writing we might go on to see how as a society we fail to dispose of things, fail to bury them deep enough.

What has the theme of display and concealment to do with this? In the middle period Dickens writes about rich and powerful men who represent sharply defined political types: Dombey, Sir Leicester Dedlock, the Ironmaster Rouncewell. Whatever they represent, there is no suggestion that they are not the real thing. Dombey is the most complicated case. He believes in a world system, and knows himself in its terms: 'The earth was made for Dombey and Son to trade in ... ' (*Dombey and Son*, 2). He embodies Pride, but the allegorical dimension is congruent with a project of topical realism; it is important that he is a merchant capitalist, and his stiffness and coldness, like his obsession with male dynasty, may be read as ideological signs of the economic identity he fulfils. As capitalist he can acknowledge no bond with others, which cannot be somehow derived from the cash nexus, and he values 'son' or 'daughter' accordingly. He marks the human costs of such a system only when he is broken by it. This is a model of alienation. At no point, however, is he insecure about his own identity. Whatever he needs Joe Bagstock for, it is not lessons in etiquette. In later writing, Dickens develops a more expressionist mode, which has a mixed antecedent but owes something to pre-realist fabular styles (as indeed does *Dombey*) and to traditional satires on excess. Consider Merdle, old Dorrit after he comes into his fortune, and the Veneerings. Merdle, by one reading, is simply a monumental sham. Dorrit carries the ghost of his own concealed history, the social self he dare not show but which, like murder, will out. The Veneerings are named for their surface; they have life only through self-display, an extension of the commodities they own, among the other people-as-things whom they add like extra leaves to their table.

For Dombey, the things of the world cannot be made to mean what he calls them. The system fractures, and he breaks down. Merdle embodies a different kind of modern separation of things from names. On the one hand, straightforwardly enough, he is a sign of what he has never been, a sound man. He is also a modern man of new times and transactions, who understands, indeed is, the secret heart of a complex process of uses and transformations of money, harnessing the small agency of the uncomprehending citizen to the great power ('great power, sir') of capitalist enterprise. The investor is eager to put his money where his mind is. Merdle plays his part in a scheme whereby that abstract/material thing, money, must be cast adrift to circulate as an idea of wealth and power in Merdle's keeping. When the keeper has opened his veins in the warm-baths the money is found to exist no longer. This is a model not of alienation but of epistemological mystery. There is a shimmering effect, a double reading of Merdle as false sign and true sign. As false sign he is less disturbing; not a sound man, but a forger and robber. But in that narrative scheme another man might occupy Merdle's place whose prospectuses proved true, and who paid a sound return on investment. Merdle is false, not the system he abuses. But what of Merdle as a true sign? Here he embodies the dissolution of the relation between things and their names, where things vanish in the untrackable spaces of modern finance. For Merdle's investors this was not the heroic phase of capitalism, its workings laid out in the grammars of realism, and Dickens was not that kind of realist. As for old Dorrit, the motifs of the *Sketches*, deference, shabby-gentility, travel, display, the prison, dress, concealment, cluster around him. His fortune cannot cover him after all. He resembles Boz's shabby-genteel man, who also undergoes a seeming metamorphosis, but by the desperate means of painting the faded cloth of his suit with liquid reviver, to give it body and colour: 'It is a deceitful liquid, that black and blue reviver; we have watched its effects on many a shabby-genteel man. It betrays its victims into a temporary assumption of importance' (*SB*, 263). In these later books the most sensational representations of riches are coupled not with a celebration of the heroic Victorian story of progress and wealth creation, but with the themes of self-fashioning, instability and insecurity that are broached in *Sketches by Boz*, and Boffin's wealth, real wealth, is materially piled up in great heaps of dust and rubbish.

There is a moment where Boz speculates fancifully about the 'auto-biography of a broken-down hackney coach' (*SB*, 87) What kind of story would this be? A hackney coach is part of the machinery of the city, a shifting site of many contacts, and could thus take up snatches of other stories through brief and apparently unrelated encounters, or furnish the starting-point of innumerable and potentially interlocking life-stories. The actual or implied circulation of commodities in the *Sketches* reflects the possibility of such narratives. As we have seen, for example through the contemplation of clothes in Monmouth Street, commodities become the point of origin for narrative riffs. We are accustomed as novel readers to depend on the rendering of character, the human subject, as the focus of meaning, the essential element in any grammar of social or historical narrative. The phenomena of the world are defined in their relation to the human subject, the agent or receptor who lends them function and meaning, and whose presence determines any moral significance in their connection. Connections between person and person attain the greatest significance. We understand the dense returns of connection in such a novel as *Bleak House* in these terms, tracking the personal and institutional relations between people; but in that novel it is also possible to see contagion, circulating as a thing in itself, as the vector of connection. Through such a figuring Dickens can show that if the ideological conditions of modern life allow us to deny our connection with one another, something will be supplied after all to declare it. The very air we breathe is rewritten as miasma, passed in and out of many lungs, a disembodied medium of touch. The proposition of miasmal infection functions darkly as an idealist discourse which would proclaim an originary common humanity. Such a discourse might have the power to tear down the wall that obscures the condemned man from the consciousness of the passing crowd.

Notes

1. All quotations from *Sketches by Boz* are referred to parenthetically in the text. Full bibliographical details of this and other cited sources are given in the bibliography at the end of the collection – Eds.

Afterword: Diversity in Victorian Studies and the Opportunities of Theory

William Baker

All is fluidity and change.

In 1989, because of a feeling of general ignorance of what is called literary theory and a desire to counter that feeling, I began providing for *Style* an annual survey of publications that were appearing in the ever-expanding field of literary and critical theory. At the time, surprisingly, such a survey did not exist, perhaps because systematically it is difficult to arrange in subject categories the wealth of recent monograph material. Studies such as Valerie Sanders's *The Private Lives of Victorian Women* can easily be seen as feminist, historical or psychoanalytic criticism, to use just three of the diverse categories within which Victorian studies proceeds today. Indeed many of the papers given at the 'Victorian Literature, Contemporary Theory' conference in July 1994 at the University of Luton similarly resist narrow classifications.

The conference and the papers which were the basis for the chapters contained herein have made me, once again, only too aware of the areas to which my ignorance extends, an ignorance not helped by the proliferation of hybrid theories and approaches, many of which defy the categorisations I brought to my annual survey. Robin Melrose and Diana Gardner's fascinating essay in this collection belongs at least initially to the category of 'Semiotics, Narratology, Rhetoric' – a category from my survey – but again, as with all the other essays included in this volume, transcends or deconstructs the boundaries of categories that I and others such as M. H. Abrams or Jeremy Hawthorn have endeavoured to maintain. Mikhail Bakhtin has shown us why categories are there only to be broken. The literary work is a site of dialogic interaction of multiple voices or modes of discourse, and the same can be said to be true of the essays presented here. With the exception of Helen Debenham's fine readings of the early work of the neglected Rhoda Broughton, Bakhtin is not much in evidence, however (even Debenham brings Bakhtin to bear only inasmuch as he is useful to a feminist reassessment of the function of sensation fiction), even though he has been well-employed in the service of Victorian studies in recent years. Neither is there much hermeneutics or phenomenology lurking; budding Geoffrey Hartmans are not in abundance, although neither are nascent F. R. Leavises. By direct contrast, what this collection and other papers from the Luton conference have demonstrated to me is that finally we have got away from the lengthy sentence, the haughty judgement, the irony, the sarcasm and the assumption of superiority which went with *le théoricien malgré lui* of Downing College Cambridge.

In evidence repeatedly are the multitudinous effects of feminist thought on all manner of reading, although, yet again, feminist theory is not reified into a single, solid position. Jenny Bourne Taylor's essay sensitively illustrates the cross-boundaries, the dissolution of static positions and the awareness of the importance of cultural and historical context to narrative structures which today mark the diversity of Victorian studies. In doing so, she weaves a text imbued with an understanding of Victorian anthropology, along with the work of Raymond Williams and Sigmund Freud.

But I have written so far largely of the gaps, the absences, the transgressions and playfulness in which these essays indulge, in their uses of what we call theory. If there is a shared – although by no means homogenising – interest to be found, it is in the ideological interpretation of text, the pursuit of a reading against the grain of the politics implied by the practices of New Criticism. Particularly the discourse of the left is in evidence, as that discourse is influenced by the work of Terry Eagleton, Edward Said, Fredric Jameson, and, especially in Britain, Raymond Williams. In retrospect, some may view Williams's work and ideas as lacking in depth, resting on semantics, and having a certain absence of historical context; yet Williams did much to initiate an alternative tradition of in-depth reading of lengthy Victorian prose writers, such as Ruskin, Morris, Arnold and Carlyle, an alternative tradition which is perhaps the ghost in this collection's machine.

The essays gathered here are fascinating not least for the fact that they have their roots in the most interesting developments in critical and cultural analysis, developments which stretch back to the 1950s, to Walter Houghton and Walter Benjamin. The essays reflect a dual tendency: on the one hand there is a commitment to aesthetic criteria, and on the other to historical and cultural contexts. Furthermore, the writers of the present collection do not impose Lacan, Barthes, Derrida, Foucault, Kristeva *et al.* in an ahistorical fashion; they do reveal an awareness of the limitations and dangers of 'interpretation out of context', of the imposition of ideas from other cultures, traditions and generations. These essays resist the danger of imposing new theories on old strategies of reading. Diversity and differing, eclectic approaches are healthy and refreshing. Diverse readings of Victorian literature can only be in the spirit of Victorian literature itself. The dominant ideology behind the criticism of the late 1940s and 1950s which told us exactly *how* we should read Dickens or Eliot has been left behind. If there is continuity in this collection there are also breaks with the past.

Diversity has been present in Victorian studies from its modern incarnation, however, despite the centrality of Leavisite discourse. I have already mentioned Walter Houghton, whose *Victorian Frame of Mind*, in 1957, offered many diverse intertextual materials and insights across genres. Another such pioneering study was Asa Briggs's *Victorian Cities*, which drew in its analysis of the growth of the Victorian city from many different kinds of discourse. Because diversity was at the very roots of modern Victorian studies, the application of theory has not appeared as superficially radical as perhaps in other areas of activity such as Renaissance literature (New Historicism) or Romanticism (deconstruction), and there is still much to be done.

What then of the future? We live in the later age of print. Ours is the age of the electronic possibility; hypertext challenges the notion of copyright, while deconstructing the text. Even 'the text' can be said no longer to exist, only textuality, a web of traces, begot by other traces, through which the make-believe of a beginning is shown to be just that. Victorian studies, in all their complex diversity will flourish, and this with the help of electronic possibilities and radical reconceptualisations of the text in the form of hypertext. Although these essays revisit the past they do not perhaps look to the future enough. They celebrate a moment and mark what will perhaps, in future years, be considered the beginning of an end. For the future we should embrace the electronic possibilities before us, for Victorian studies can only be enriched.

All is fluidity and change.

Works Cited

Abrams, *et al. The Norton Anthology of English Literature:Volume Two*. New York: W. W. Norton and Company, 1962.

Ackroyd, Peter. (1983). *The Last Testament of Oscar Wilde*. London: Abacus, 1984.

Ackroyd, Peter. (1990). *Dickens*. London: Minerva, 1991.

Adorno, Theodor W. 'The Position of the Narrator in the Contemporary Novel'. *Notes to Literature*, Vol. 1. (1958). Trans. Shierry Weber Nicholsen. New York: Columbia University Press, 1991.

Almond, H. H. 'The Consecration of the Body', *Sermons by a Lay Headmaster*. Edinburgh: Blackwood, 1886.

Althusser, Louis. 'Ideology and Ideological State Apparatuses', *Critical Theory since 1965*. Ed. Hazard Adams and Leroy Searle. Tallahassee: Florida State University Press, 1986.

Altick, Richard. *Victorian Studies in Scarlet*. New York: Norton, 1970.

Anderson, Benedict. *Imagined Communities: Reflections on the Origin and Spread of Nationalism*. London: Verso, 1983.

Anon. 'A Legal Fiction', *Household Words*, 21 July 1855.

Anon. 'Article VII [Our Female Sensation Novelists]'. *Christian Remembrancer* NS46 (1863): 209–36.

Anon. 'Correspondent's Report on the Trade in London'. *Scottish Typographical Circular*, January (1896a): 485.

Anon. 'English Charity'. *Quarterly Review*. April 1835.

Anon. 'Government Printing Contracts. Report of the Select Committee'. *The Printing World*, 30 May (1896b): 117.

Anon. 'Not a New Sensation'. *All the Year Round* 9 (1863): 517–20.

Anon. 'Note on Estimating'. *The Printing World*, 31 January (1896c): 12.

Anon. 'Our Library Table'. *The Athenaeum*. (3 September 1880): 305/2.

Anon. 'Report of the Meeting of the Society of Authors'. *The Standard*, 28 February (1890a).

Anon. 'Report on John Southward's Lecture, "Machines for composing letterpress Printing Surfaces". *Scottish Typographical Circular*, March (1896d): 508.

Anon. 'Report on *La Nature*'. *Publishers' Circular*, 1 February (1890b): 111.

Anon. 'Review of the Condition of the Printing Trade Article'. *Publishers' Circular*, 2 September (1899a): 226.

Anon. 'Royal Commission Evidence'. *Scottish Typographical Circular*, 1 April (1896e).

Anon. 'The Condition of the Printing Trade'. *Investors' Review*, 26 August (1899b): 261–3.

Anon. 'The Narcotics We Indulge In'. *Blackwood's Edinburgh Magazine*, LXXIV, part III (July–December 1853): 678–95.

Anon. 'The Printing and Allied Trades Association'. *Publishers' Circular*, 15 November (1890c): 1499.

Anon. 'The Rise and Progress of the German Book Trade'. *The Bookseller*, 4 May (1881): 422ff.

Anon. *Brief Notes on the Origins of T. & A. Constable Ltd.* Edinburgh, n.p., 1939.

Anon. 'The Prevalence of Infanticide'. *Magdalen's Friend and Female Home Intelligensia*, 2, n.p., 1832.

Anon. [Review of *Encyclopaedia Britannica*, Vol. XIII]. *The Athenaeum.* (11 February 1882): 184/1

Anon. [Review of *Impressions of Theophrastus Such*]. *The Saturday Review.* 28 June 1879.

Arendt, Hannah. *Antisemitism, Part One of the Origins of Totalitarianism.* New York: Harcourt Brace Jovanovich, 1951.

Argyle, Gisela. *German Elements in the Fiction of George Eliot, Gissing, and Meredith.* Frankfurt am Main: Peter Lang Ltd, 1979.

Armstrong, Isobel. *Victorian Scrutinies: Reviews of Poetry: 1830–1870.* London: The Athlone Press, 1972.

Arnold, Matthew. *Selected Prose*, ed. P. J. Keating. Harmondsworth: Penguin, 1980.

Austin, Alfred. 'The Poetry of the Period'. *Temple Bar* 26. (1869): 179–94; 316–33; 457–74.

Austin, J. L. *How To Do Things With Words.* (1962). Oxford: Oxford University Press, 1976.

Avery, G. and Julia Briggs, eds. *Children and Their Books.* Oxford: Clarendon Press, 1989.

Baker, William. *George Eliot and Judaism.* Salzburg: Institut für Englische Sprache und Literatur, Universität Salzburg, 1975.

Bakhtin, M. M. *The Dialogic Imagination: Four Essays by M. M. Bakhtin.* Ed. Michael Holquist. Austin: University of Texas Press, 1981.

Barthes, Roland. 'The Death of the Author'. *Image – Music – Text.* Trans. and ed. Stephen Heath. Glasgow: Fontana, Collins, 1977. 142–8.

Barthes, Roland. *Camera Lucida: Reflections on Photography.* (1980). Trans. Richard Howard. London: Vintage, 1993.

Baxter, G. Wythern. *The Book of the Bastille, or the History of the Working of the New Poor Law.* London: John Stephens, 1841.

Beer, Gillian. 'Sensational Women'. *The Times Literary Supplement* (11 March 1994): 26.

Belloc, Hilaire. *Complete Verse.* (1954). London: Pimlico, 1991.

Benjamin, Walter. 'A Berlin Chronicle'. (1970). *One Way Street and Other Writings.* Trans. Edmund Jephcott and Kingsley Shorter. Int. Susan Sontag. London: Verso, 1992.

Benjamin, Walter. 'The Storyteller'. *Illuminations.* (1955). Trans. Harry Zohn. New York: Schocken Books, 1977.

Bernstein, Carol. *The Celebration of Scandal: Toward the Sublime in Victorian Urban Fiction.* University Park: Pennsylvania State University Press, 1991.

Blaikie, Andrew. *Illegitimacy, Sex and Society: North-East Scotland.* Oxford: The Clarendon Press, 1994.

Bloom, Harold. *Poetry and Repression: Revisionism from Blake to Stevens.* New Haven: Yale University Press, 1976.

Booth, Wayne. 'Freedom of Interpretation'. *The Politics of Interpretation.* Ed. W. J. T. Mitchell. Chicago and London: Chicago University Press, 1983: 51–82.

Boswell, John. *The Kindness of Strangers: The Abandonment of Children in Western Europe from Late Antiquity to the Renaissance.* Harmondsworth: Penguin, 1988.

Bourne Taylor, Jenny. 'Introduction'. *The Law and the Lady.* Wilkie Collins. Oxford: Oxford University Press, 1992. vii–xxv.

Bowden, W. E. *Edward Bowden: A Memoir.* London: Longman, 1902.

Boyd, John D. and Williams, Anne. 'Tennyson's "Mariana" and Lyric Perspective', *Studies in English Literature* 23 (1983): 575–93.

Boyle, Thomas. *Black Swine in the Sewers of Hampstead: Beneath the Surface of Victorian Sensationism.* London: Hodder and Stoughton, 1989.

Brinton, Crane. *French Revolutionary Laws on Illegitimacy.* Cambridge, Mass.: Harvard University Press, 1936.

Brontë, Charlotte. *Jane Eyre.* (1847). Oxford: Clarendon Press, 1969.

Brontë, Charlotte. *Villette.* London: Smith, Elder, and Co., 1853.

Broughton, Rhoda. *A Beginner.* London: Richard Bentley and Son, 1894.

Broughton, Rhoda. *A Fool in Her Folly.* London: Odhams, 1920.

Broughton, Rhoda. *Cometh Up as a Flower.* London: Richard Bentley and Son, 1867.

Broughton, Rhoda. *Not Wisely But Too Well.* (1867). Stroud: Alan Sutton, 1993.

Broughton, Rhoda. *Red As a Rose is She.* London: Richard Bentley and Son, 1870.

Browne, Francis. *Granny's Wonderful Chair.* (1857). London: Dent, 1963.

Buchanan, Robert. 'Society's Looking Glass'. *Temple Bar* VI (1862): 129–37.

Buckley, Jerome H. *Tennyson: The Growth of a Poet.* Cambridge: Harvard University Press, 1960.

Burke, Edmund. *Reflections on the Revolution in France.* (1790). Harmondsworth: Penguin, 1986.

Carlyle, Thomas. 'Characteristics'. *A Carlyle Reader.* Ed. G. B. Tennyson. Cambridge: Cambridge University Press, 1984.

Carlyle, Thomas. 'Chartism'. *Selected Writings.* Ed. Alan Shelston. Harmondsworth: Penguin, 1986.

Carroll, Lewis. *Alice's Adventures in Wonderland.* (1865). London: Penguin, 1984.

Carter, Angela. *Wise Children.* London: Chatto, 1991.

Checkland, S. G. and E. O. A., eds. *Report of the Royal Commission on the Poor Laws* (1834). Harmondsworth: Penguin, 1974.

Chitty, Susan. *The Beast and the Monk: A Life of Charles Kingsley.* London: Hodder, 1974.

Christ, Carol. *The Finer Optic.* New Haven: Yale University Press, 1975.

Clark, T. J. *The Painting of Modern Life: Paris in the Art of Manet and his Followers.* Princeton: Princeton University Press, 1984.

Clarke, William M. *The Secret Life of Wilkie Collins.* London: Allison and Busby, 1988.

Coke, Edward. *The First Part of the Institutes of the Laws of England.* London: n.p., 1669; 246.6.

Coleridge, S. T. *Works, vol. 10: On the Constitution of the Church and State According to the Idea of Each.* (1830). Ed. John Colmer. London/Princeton: Routledge/Princeton University Press, 1976.

Colley, Linda. *Britons: Forging the Nation 1707–1837*. New Haven: Yale University Press, 1992.

Collins, Wilkie. *The Law and the Lady*. (1875). Ed. Jenny Bourne Taylor. Oxford: Oxford University Press, 1992.

Collins, Wilkie. *The Woman in White*. (1860). Ed. H. P. Sucksmith. Oxford: Oxford University Press, 1981.

Connor, Steven. *Charles Dickens*. Rereading Literature. Oxford: Basil Blackwell, 1985.

Coward, Rosalind. *Patriarchal Precedents*. London: Routledge and Kegan Paul, 1983.

Crosby, Christina. *The Ends of History: Victorians and 'The Woman Question'*. New York and London: Routledge, 1991.

Culler, Dwight A. *The Poetry of Tennyson*. New Haven: Yale University Press, 1977.

Cyclops. 'Correspondence'. *Publishers' Circular*, 1 April (1890): 380.

Davidson, Arnold I. 'Sex and the Emergence of Sexuality'. *Critical Inquiry* 14 (Autumn 1987): 16–48.

Dawson, Oswald. *The Bar Sinister and Licit Love*. London and Leeds: n.p., 1895.

Derrida, Jacques. 'A Letter to Peter Eisenman'. Trans. Hilary P. Hanel. *Assemblage: A Critical Journal of Architecture and Design Culture* 12 (1990): 7–14.

Derrida, Jacques. 'Limited Inc abc ...'. Trans. Sam Weber. *Glyph 2* (1977): 162–254.

Derrida, Jacques. 'Plato's Pharmacy'. *Disseminations*. (1972). Trans. Barbara Johnson. London: Athlone Press, 1981; 61–173.

Derrida, Jacques. 'Point de folie – maintenant l'architecture'. Trans. Kate Linker. *La Case Vide La Villette 1985*. Bernard Tschumi. London: Architectural Association, Folio VIII, 1987. pp. 4–20

Derrida, Jacques. 'Signature Event Context'. *Margins of Philosophy*. (1971). Trans. Alan Bass. Chicago: University of Chicago Press, 1982.

Derrida, Jacques. (1980). 'The Law of Genre'. *Acts of Literature*. Trans. Avital Ronell. Ed. Derek Attridge. London: Routledge, 1992c. 221–53.

Derrida, Jacques. (1985). 'Before the Law'. Trans. Avital Ronell. *Acts of Literature*. Ed. Derek Attridge. London: Routledge, 1992a. 181–221.

Derrida, Jacques. (1990). 'Force of Law: The "Mystical Foundation of Authority"'. *Deconstruction and the Possibility of Justice*. Ed. Drucilla Cornell, Michael Rosenfeld, David Gray Carlson. London: Routledge, 1992b. 3–68.

Deutsch, Gotthard. 'Anti-Semitism'. *Jewish Encyclopedia*. 1901 edition.

Dickens, Charles. *Bleak House*. (1853). Ed. Norman Page. Introduction J. Hillis Miller. Harmondsworth: Penguin, 1971.

Dickens, Charles. *Dombey and Son*. (1848). Ed. Alan Houseman. Oxford: Oxford University Press, 1982.

Dickens, Charles. *Little Dorrit*. (1857). Ed. John Holloway. Harmondsworth: Penguin, 1967.

Dickens, Charles. *Martin Chuzzlewit*. (1844). Ed. P. N. Furbank. London: Penguin, 1986.

Dickens, Charles. *Master Humphrey's Clock* and *A Child's History of England*. Int. Derek Hudson. The Oxford Illustrated Dickens. Oxford: Oxford University Press, 1958.

Dickens, Charles. *Nicholas Nickleby*. (1839). Ed. Michael Slater. Harmondsworth: Penguin, 1986.

Dickens, Charles. *Oliver Twist*. (1837–39). Ed. Peter Fairclough. Int. Angus Wilson. Harmondsworth: Penguin, 1986.

Dickens, Charles. *Our Mutual Friend*. (1865). Ed. Martin Cotsell. Oxford: Oxford University Press, 1989.

Dickens, Charles. *Sketches by Boz and Other Early Papers 1833–39*. Ed. Michael Slater. The Dent Uniform Edition of Dickens's Journalism, Vol. I. London: J. M. Dent, 1994.

Dickens, Charles. *The Pickwick Papers*. (1837). Ed. Robert L. Patten. Harmondsworth: Penguin, 1976.

Dickens, Charles. *The Uncommercial Traveller and Reprinted Pieces*. Int. Leslie C. Staples. Oxford: Oxford University Press, 1987.

Dollimore, Jonathan. *Sexual Dissidence, Augustine to Wilde, Freud to Foucault*. Oxford: Clarendon Press, 1991.

Doyle, Arthur Conan. *A Study in Scarlet*. (1888). Ed. Owen Dudley Edwards. Oxford: Oxford University Press, 1993a.

Doyle, Arthur Conan. *The Memoirs of Sherlock Holmes*. (1893). Ed. Christopher Roden. Oxford: Oxford University Press, 1993b.

Eagleton, Terry. *Criticism and Ideology: A Study in Marxist Literary Theory*. London: Verso, 1976.

Eagleton, Terry. *Saint Oscar* . Derry: Field Day, 1989.

Eliav, Benyamin. 'Anti-Semitism'. *Encyclopaedia Judaica*. 1972 Edition.

Eliot, George. *Impressions of Theophrastus Such*. (1879). Ed. Nancy Henry. London: Pickering and Chatto, 1994.

Eliot, George. 'Miscellaneous Essays'. *George Eliot's Works*. New York: International Book Company, 1883.

Eliot, George. *Daniel Deronda*. (1876). Ed. Barbara Hardy. London: Penguin, 1986.

Eliot, George. *Daniel Deronda*. (1876). Ed. Graham Handley. Oxford: Clarendon Press, 1984.

Eliot, George. *Silas Marner: The Weaver of Raveloe*. Edinburgh and London: John Blackwood, 1861.

Eliot, Simon. 'Unequal partnerships: Besant, Rice and Chatto'. *Publishing History*, 26 (1989): 73–109.

Eliot, Simon. *Some Patterns and Trends in British Publishing 1800–1919*. Occasional Papers 8. Bibliographical Society. 1994.

Ellmann, Richard. *Oscar Wilde*. (1987). Harmondsworth: Penguin, 1988.

Encyclopaedia Britannica (11th edn, 1910–11, Vol. 2).

Engels, Friedrich. (1845). *The Condition of the Working Class in England*. Ed., with a Foreword by Victor Kiernan. London: Penguin, 1988.

Flint, Kate. *The Woman Reader, 1837–1914*. Oxford: Clarendon Press, 1993.

Foucault, Michel. 'A Preface to Transgression'. *Language, Counter-memory, Practice*. Trans. D. F. Bouchard and S. Simon. Oxford: Basil Blackwell, 1977.

Foucault, Michel. 'The Subject and Power'. *Art after Modernism*. Ed. B. Wallis. New York: New Museum of Contemporary Art, 1984.

Foucault, Michel. *A History of Sexuality*, vol 1: Introduction. (1976). Trans. R. Hurley. London: Penguin, 1978

Foucault, Michel. *Discipline and Punish: The Birth of the Prison*. (1977). Trans. Alan Sheridan. New York: Pantheon Books, 1977.

Freud, Sigmund. 'Family Romances'. (1908). *On Sexuality*. Trans. James Strachey. Ed. Angela Richards. Penguin Freud Library. Harmondsworth: Penguin, 1991; 217–27.

Fryckstedt, Monica Correa. *Geraldine Jewsbury's Athenaeum Reviews: A Mirror of mid-Victorian Attitudes to Fiction*. Uppsala: Acta Universitatis Upsaliensis, 1986.

Gagnier, Regenia. *Idylls of the Marketplace*. Aldershot: Scolar Press, 1987.

Gallagher, Catherine. *The Industrial Reformation of English Fiction 1832–1867*. Chicago: Chicago University Press, 1985.

Gaskell, Elizabeth. *Ruth*. London: Chapman and Hall, 1853.

Gaskell, Elizabeth. *The Life of Charlotte Brontë*. (3rd edn, 1857). London: Smith, Elder, and Co., 1871.

Giddens, Anthony. *Central Problems in Social Theory: Action, Structure, and Contradiction in Social Analysis*. Berkeley: University of California Press, 1979.

Gill, Derek. *Illegitimacy, Sexuality and the Status of Woman*. Oxford: Basil Blackwell, 1977.

Gillis, John R. *For Better, For Worse: British Marriages, 1600 to the Present*. Oxford: Oxford University Press, 1985.

Gilman, Sander. 'White Bodies, Black Bodies: Toward an Iconography of Female Sexuality in Late Nineteenth-Century Art, Medicine, and Literature'. *Critical Inquiry* 12 (Autumn 1985).

Ginzburg, C. 'Fiction as Historical Evidence'. *Yale Journal of Criticism*, 5. 2 (1992).

Giroux, Henry. *Theory and Resistance in Education: A Pedagogy for the Opposition*. Massachusetts: Bergin and Garvey Publishers, 1983.

Green, David. 'Preface'. Charles Murray, *The Emerging British Underclass*. London: The Institute of Economic Affairs, 1990.

Green, Joyce. 'Tennyson's Development', *PMLA* 66 (1951): 662–97.

Grey, Maria and Shirreff, Emily. *Thoughts on Self-Culture Addressed to Women*, 2 vols. London: Edward Moxon, 1850.

Hacking, Ian. 'Making Up People'. *Reconstructing Individualism*. Ed. Thomas C. Heller, Morton Sosna and David E. Wellbery. Stanford: Stanford University Press, 1986; 222–36.

Hacking, Ian. 'The Making and Molding of Child Abuse'. *Critical Inquiry* 17 (Winter 1991): 253–88.

Haight, Gordon S., ed. *The George Eliot Letters*, Vol. 6. New Haven: Yale University Press, 1955.

Haley, Bruce. *The Healthy Body and Victorian Culture*. Cambridge, Mass.: Harvard University Press, 1978.

Hall, Stuart. 'Culture, Community, Nation'. *Cultural Studies* 7.3 (October 1993): 349–63.

Hartman, Mary. 'Murder for Respectability'. *Victorian Studies* 16 (1973): 381–400.

Hawley, John C. 'Charles Kingsley and the Literary Theory of the 1850s'. *Victorian Literature and Culture* 19 (1991): 167–88.

Henriques, Ursula. 'Bastardy and the New Poor Law'. *Past and Present* 37 (1967): 103–29.

Higginbottom, Ann R. '"Sin of the Age": Infanticide and Illegitimacy in Victorian London'. *Victorian Scandals: Representations of Gender and Class.* Ed. K. O. Garrigan. Athens: Ohio University Press, 1992; 257–88.

Hill, Christopher. 'Protestantism and the Rise of Capitalism'. *Change and Continuity in 17th Century England.* London: Weidenfeld, 1974, 81–102.

Hobsbawm, E. J. *The Age of Empire 1875–1914.* London: Weidenfeld, 1987; New York: Vintage Books, 1989.

Homans, Margaret. '"Her Very Own Howl": The Ambiguities of Representation in Recent Women's Fiction'. *SIGNS* 9.2 (1983): 186–205.

Hooper, Wilfrid. *The Law of Illegitimacy.* London: n.p., 1911.

Hough, Graham. *The Last Romantics.* (1949). London: Duckworth, 1983.

Houghton, Walter E. *The Victorian Frame of Mind.* New Haven: Yale University Press, 1975.

Howe, Irving. 'George Eliot and the Jews'. *Partisan Review* 46 (1979): 359–75.

Hughes, Edward. *A Compendium on the Operation of the Poor Law Amendment Act.* London: n.p., 1836.

Hughes, Thomas. *Tom Brown's Schooldays* (1857). Oxford: Oxford University Press, 1989.

Hughes, Winifred. *The Maniac in the Cellar: Sensation Novels of the 1860s.* Princeton: Princeton University Press, 1980.

Hunt, P. *Criticism, Theory and Children's Literature.* Oxford: Blackwell, 1991.

Ingram, Martin. *Church Courts, Sex and Marriage in England 1570–1640.* Cambridge: Cambridge University Press, 1987.

Jackson, Bernard S. *Law, Fact and Narrative Coherence.* Boston: Deborah Charles Publications, 1988.

Jacobs, Joseph. Review of *Impressions of Theophrastus Such. The Athenaeum* (7 June 1879): 720.

James, Henry. 'London'. (1905). *English Hours.* Ed. Alma Louise Lowe. London: Heinemann, 1960.

James, Henry. *The Letters of Henry James.* Vol. III. Ed. Leon Edel. Cambridge, Mass.: Harvard University Press, 1980.

James, Henry. *The Letters of Henry James.* Vol. IV. Ed. Leon Edel. Cambridge, Mass.: Harvard University Press, 1984.

James, Henry. *The Princess Casamassima.* (1886). Ed. Derek Brewer, Notes Patricia Crick. London: Penguin, 1987.

Jameson, Fredric. 'Cognitive Mapping'. *Marxism and the Interpretation of Culture.* Urbana: University of Illinois Press, 1988. 347–57.

Jesse, F. Tennyson, ed. *The Trial of Madeleine Smith.* (1905). Notable British Trials. London: William Hodge and Co. Ltd., 1927.

Jewsbury, Geraldine. Letters dated July 2 and 3, 1866. Readers' Reports. Bentley Archive. British Library.

Jewsbury, Geraldine. *Zoë, or the History of Two Lives.* London: Chapman and Hall, 1845.

Johnson, E. D. H. *The Alien Vision of Victorian Poetry.* Hamden: Archon Books, 1963.

Joseph, Gerhard. *Tennyson and the Text: The Weaver's Shuttle.* London: Oxford University Press, 1992.

Josipovici, Gabriel. *The World and the Book*. Fourth edition. London: Macmillan, 1994.

Kincaid, James R. *Child-Loving: The Erotic Child and Victorian Culture*. London: Routledge, 1992.

Kingsley, Charles. 'Thoughts on Shelley and Byron'. (1853). *Literary and General Lectures and Essays*. London: Macmillan, 1890a.

Kingsley, Charles. *Alton Locke*. (1850). Oxford: Oxford University Press, 1983.

Kingsley, Charles. *Charles Kingsley: His Letters and Memories of His Life*. Ed. 'his wife'. London: Macmillan, 1890b.

Kingsley, Charles. *Hypatia; Or, New Foes with Old Faces*. (1853). John W. Parker and Son. 1856.

Kingsley, Charles. *The Water Babies*. (1863). London: Gawthorn, n.d.

Kingsley, Charles. *Yeast*. (1848). London: Macmillan, 1879.

Kohl, Norbert. *Oscar Wilde, The Works of a Conformist Rebel*. Trans. David Henry Wilson. Cambridge: Cambridge University Press, 1989.

Laslett, Peter. 'The bastardy-prone sub-society'. *Bastardy and its Comparative History*. Ed. Peter Laslett, Karla Oosterveen and R. M. Smith. London: Edward Arnold, 1980; 217–39.

Lawrence, George Alfred. *Guy Livingstone, or Thorough*. London: John W. Parker and Son, 1857.

Leavis, F. R. *The Great Tradition: George Eliot, Henry James, Joseph Conrad*. New York: George W. Stewart, 1949.

Leffingwell, Albert. 'Illegitimacy, a Study in Morals'. *Illegitimacy and the Influence of Seasons Upon Conduct*. London: Swan and Co, 1892.

Linehan, Katherine Bailey. 'Mixed Politics: The Critique of Imperialism in *Daniel Deronda*'. *Texas Studies in Literature and Language*, 34:3 (Fall 1992): 323–46.

Lubbock, Percy, ed. *The Letters of Henry James*. London: Macmillan, 1920.

Lukács, Georg. *The Theory of the Novel*. (1971). Trans. Anna Bostock. Cambridge: MIT Press, 1985.

Macdonald, George. *The Princess and the Goblin*. (1871). London: Blackie, n.d.

Maceachan, David. 'Wilkie Collins and the British Law'. *Nineteenth-Century Fiction* 5 (September 1950): 121–36.

Maclean, Marie. *The Name of the Mother: Writing Illegitimacy*. London: Routledge, 1994.

Malinowski, B. 'Parenthood, the Basis of Social Structure'. *The New Generation*. Ed. V. F. Calverton and S. D. Schmalhausen. London: George Allen and Unwin, 1930; 113–68.

Malinowski, B. *Sex and Repression in Savage Society*. London: Kegan Paul, 1927.

Mangan, J. A. *Athleticism in the Victorian and Edwardian Public School: The Emergence and Consolidation of an Educational Ideology*. Cambridge: Cambridge University Press, 1981.

Mangan, J. A. *The Games Ethic and Imperialism: Aspects of the Diffusion of an Ideal*. Harmondsworth: Penguin, 1986.

Mansel, H. L. 'Sensation novels'. *Quarterly Review* 113 (1863): 481–514.

Marcus, Stephen. *The Other Victorians: A Study of Sexuality and Pornography in Mid-Nineteenth-Century England.* (1966). London: Corgi, 1969.

Martin, Carol A. 'Contemporary Critics and Judaism in *Daniel Deronda*'. *Victorian Periodicals Review* 21:3 (Fall 1988): 90–107.

McCormack, Kathleen. 'George Eliot and Victorian Science Fiction: *Daniel Deronda* as Alternate History'. *Extrapolation* 27:3 (1986): 185–96.

Meredith, Owen, and Julian Fane. *Tannhäuser: or, The Battle of the Bards.* London: Chapman and Hall, 1861. (Published under the names of Neville Temple and Edward Trevor.)

Meredith, Owen. 'Last Words'. *Cornhill Magazine.* (November, 1860): 513–17.

Meyer, Susan. '"Safely to their own Borders": Proto-Zionism, Feminism, and Nationalism in *Daniel Deronda*'. *English Literary History* 60 (1993): 733–58.

Miles, F. H. 'Illustrated Interviews: Simpkin, Marshall, Hamilton, Kent and Co., Limited'. *Bookselling.* January (1895): 8–9.

Miller, Nancy K. 'Emphasis Added: Plots and Plausibilities in Women's Fiction'. *Subject to Change: Reading Feminist Writing.* New York, 1988.

Milnes, Richard Monckton. *Selections from the Poetical Works of Richard Monckton Milnes.* London: John Murray, 1863.

Minucius Felix. *The Octavius of Marcus Minucius Felix.* Trans. G. W. Clarke. New York: Newman Press, 1974.

Mitchell B. R. *British Historical Statistics.* Cambridge: Cambridge University Press. 1988.

Mitchell, Sally. *The Fallen Angel: Chastity, Class and Women's Reading, 1835–1880.* Bowling Green: Bowling Green University Popular Press, 1981.

Molesworth, Mrs. *The Cuckoo Clock.* (1877). London: Dent, 1963.

Moretti, Franco. *The Way of the World: The Bildungsroman in European Culture.* London: Verso, 1987.

Mumby, Frank Arthur. *Publishing and Bookselling.* London: Jonathan Cape, 1954.

Munro, H. H. *Complete Short Stories of Saki.* London: John Lane, 1930.

Murray, Charles. *The Emerging British Underclass.* London: The Institute of Economic Affairs, 1990.

Nassaar, Christopher S. *Into the Demon Universe: A Literary Exploration of Oscar Wilde.* New Haven and London: Yale University Press, 1974.

Nelson, Claudia. *Boys Will be Girls: The Feminine Ethic and British Children's Fiction 1857–1917.* New Brunswick: Rutgers University Press, 1991.

Nesbit, Edith. *Five Children and It.* (1902). Harmondsworth: Penguin, 1964.

Newman, John Henry. *Lectures on the Present Position of Catholics in England.* (1851). London: Longman, 1892.

Newman, John Henry. *Callista.* (1856). London: Burns, Oates, and Co., c. 1870.

Newnes, George. 'Illustrated Interviews: Messrs George Newnes, Ltd.' *Bookselling.* Christmas (1895): 27–41.

Newsome, David. *Godliness and Good Learning: Four Studies on a Victorian Ideal.* London: Murray, 1961.

Norman, Edward. *The Victorian Christian Socialists.* Cambridge: Cambridge University Press, 1987.

Oliphant, Margaret. 'Novels'. *Blackwood's Edinburgh Magazine* 94 (1863): 168–82.

Paley, William. *Natural Theology.* (1802). *Works.* Edinburgh: Nelson, 1844.

Palmer, D. J. 'Tennyson's Romantic Heritage'. *Writers and Their Background.* Ed. D. J. Palmer. Athens: Ohio University Press, 1975.

Patai, Raphael. 'Anti-Semitism'. *Encyclopedia Americana.* 1994 Edition.

Pater, Walter. *The Renaissance: Studies in Art and Poetry.* (1873). Ed. Kenneth Clarke. London and Glasgow: Collins Fontana Library, 1961.

Peltason, Timothy. 'The Embowered Self: "Mariana" and "Recollections of the Arabian Nights"', *Victorian Poetry* 21(1984): 335–50.

Peters, Catherine. *The King of Investors: A life of Wilkie Collins.* London: Minerva, 1992.

Platizky, Roger. *A Blueprint of His Dissent: Madness and Method in Tennyson's Poetry.* Lewisburg: Bucknell University Press, 1989.

Postema, Gerald J. 'Fact, Fictions, and Law: Bentham on the Foundations of Evidence'. *Evidence and Proof.* Ed. William Twining and Alex Stein. Dartmouth: New England University Press, 1992.

Pykett, Lyn. *The Improper Feminine: The Woman's Sensation Novel and the New Woman Writing.* London and New York: Routledge, 1992.

Pykett, Lyn. *The Sensation Novel from* The Woman in White *to* The Moonstone. Plymouth: Northcote House in association with the British Council, 1994.

Quaife, G. R. *Wanton Wenches and Wayward Wives: Peasants and Illicit Sex in Seventeenth-Century England.* London: Croom Helm, 1979.

Rabinow, Paul, ed. *The Foucault Reader.* New York: Pantheon Books, 1984.

Ragussis, Michael. 'Representation, Conversion, and Literary Form: *Harrington* and the Novel of Jewish Identity'. *Critical Inquiry* 16 (1989): 113–43.

Rance, Nicholas. *Wilkie Collins and Other Sensation Novelists: Walking the Moral Hospital.* London: Macmillan, 1991.

Ricks, Christopher, ed. *Selected Criticism of Matthew Arnold.* New York and Scarborough, Ontario: Signet, 1972.

Ricks, Christopher. *Tennyson.* New York: Macmillan, 1972.

Ricks, Christopher. *Tennyson: A Selected Edition.* Berkeley: University of California Press.

Ritchie, Anne Thackeray. *The Letters of Anne Thackeray Ritchie.* Ed. Hester Ritchie. London: John Murray, 1924.

Robert, Marthe. *Origins of the Novel.* Trans. Sacha Rabinovitch. Brighton: Harvester Press, 1980.

Robinson, Kenneth. *Wilkie Collins, a Biography.* Oxford: The Bodley Head, 1951.

Rose, Lionel. *Massacre of the Innocents: Infanticide in Great Britain, 1800–1939.* London: Routledge and Kegan Paul, 1986.

Rosenbloom, Joshua. 'Economics and the Emergence of Modern Publishing in the United States'. *Publishing History,* 29 (1991): 47–68.

Sadleir, Michael. *Things Past.* London: Constable, 1944.

Said, Edward W. *Culture and Imperialism.* New York: Alfred A. Knopf, 1993.

Said, Edward W. *The Question of Palestine*. New York: Vintage Books, 1979.

Saville, John. *1848: The British State and the Chartist Movement*. Cambridge: Cambridge University Press, 1987.

Schwarzbach, F. S. *Dickens and the City*. London: Athlone Press, 1979.

Scott, J. and L. Tilly. 'Women's Work and the Family in Nineteenth-Century Europe'. *Comparative Studies in Sociology and History*, 17 (1975): 36–64.

Sedgwick, Eve Kosofsky. *Between Men: English Literature and Male Homosocial Desire*. New York: Columbia University Press, 1985.

Seltzer, Mark. 'Statistical Persons'. *Diacritics* 17:3 (Fall 1987): 82–98.

Semmel, Bernard. *George Eliot and the Politics of National Inheritance*. New York: Oxford University Press, 1994.

Shannon, Edgar Finley Jr. *Tennyson and the Reviewers*. Cambridge: Harvard University Press, 1952.

Shaw, W. David. *Victorian Mystery: Crises of Representation*. Ithaca: Cornell University Press, 1990.

Shepherd, Fred L. 'Correspondence'. *Publishers' Circular*, 9 September (1899): 250.

Showalter, Elaine. *A Literature of Their Own: British Women Novelists from Brontë to Lessing*. (1977). London: Virago, 1978.

Shutt, Nicola. 'Nobody's Child: The Illegitimate Child in the Works of George Eliot, Charles Dickens and Wilkie Collins'. Unpublished dissertation. University of York, 1991.

Sinclair, Catherine. *Holiday House*. (1839). London: Ward, Lock and Co., n.d.

Sinfield, Alan. *Alfred Lord Tennyson*. Oxford: Basil Blackwell, 1986.

Smith, Paul. *Discerning the Subject*. Minneapolis: University of Minnesota Press, 1988.

Smith, Walter C. 'Obituary: "The Late Thomas Constable"'. *The Scotsman*, Saturday, 28 May (1881): 8.

Southward, John. 'Art in Book Printing'. *Bookselling*, April (1898): 186–7.

Spencer, Herbert. *Education: Intellectual, Moral and Physical*. London: Mainwaring, 1861.

Spicer, D. *The Paper Trade*, n.p., 1907.

Stanley, Arthur Penrhyn. *The Life and Correspondence of Thomas Arnold*. (1844). London: Murray, 1881.

Stevenson, Robert Louis. *Treasure Island*. (1881). London: Blackie, n.d.

Stretton, Hesba. *Enoch Roden's Training*. (1865). London: Religious Tract Society, n.d.

Sutherland, John. 'The Book Trade Crash of 1926'. *The Library*. Sixth Series 9. 2 (June 1987): 148–61.

Taylor, Barbara. *Eve and the New Jerusalem*. London: Virago, 1983.

Taylor, Jenny Bourne. *In the Secret Theatre of Home: Wilkie Collins, Sensation Narrative and Nineteenth-Century Psychology*. London: Routledge, 1988.

Teichman, Jenny. *Illegitimacy, A Philosophical Examination*. Oxford: Basil Blackwell, 1982.

Tennyson, Alfred. *The Poems of Tennyson*. London: Longman, 1969.

Terry, R. C. *Victorian Popular Fiction, 1860–80*. London: Macmillan, 1983.

Thackeray, Anne Isabella. *The Story of Elizabeth: A Tale*. London: Smith, Elder, and Co., 1863.

Thomas, Keith. 'The Puritans and Adultery: the Act of 1650 reconsidered'. *Puritans and Revolutionaries*. Ed. D. Pennington and K. Thomas. Oxford: The Clarendon Press, 1978: 257–82.

Thompson, E. P. *The Making of the English Working Class*. Harmondsworth: Penguin, 1968.

Timko, Michael. 'The Victorianism of Victorian Literature', *New Literary History* 6 (1974–5): 602–27.

Towers, Chas. E. 'Correspondence'. *Publishers' Circular*, 16 September (1899): 273.

Tschumi, Bernard. *Architecture and Disjunction*. Cambridge, Mass.: MIT, 1994.

Tschumi, Bernard. *La Case Vide La Villette 1985*. With essays by Jacques Derrida and Anthony Vidler. Interview by Alvin Boyarsky. London: Architectural Association, Folio VIII, 1987.

Tucker, Herbert F. *Tennyson and the Doom of Romanticism*. Berkeley: University of California Press, 1988.

Turner, Henry. 'Illegitimacy in Early Modern Drama'. Unpublished MA dissertation, University of Sussex, 1993.

Unwin, T. Fisher. 'Illustrated interviews: Mr. T. Fisher Unwin'. *Bookselling*, April (1895): 105–7.

Vance, Norman. *The Sinews of the Spirit: the Ideal of Christian Manliness in Victorian Literature and Religious Thought*. Cambridge: Cambridge University Press, 1985.

Veeder, William and Susan M. Griffin, eds. *The Art of Criticism: Henry James on the Theory and Practice of Fiction*. Chicago: University of Chicago Press, 1986.

Virilio, Paul. *The Vision Machine*. (1988). Trans. Julie Rose. Perspectives. Bloomington and Indianapolis: British Film Institute and Indiana University Press, 1994.

Waters, Michael. *The Garden in Victorian Literature*. Aldershot: Scolar Press, 1988.

Weedon, Alexis. 'A New Approach to the Survey of Book Production in Nineteenth-Century Britain'. *Leipziger Arbeitreis zur Geschichte des Buchwesens* (1994): 163–85.

Weedon, Alexis. 'A Quantitative Survey: George Bell and Sons'. *Publishing History*, 33 (Spring 1993): 5–35.

Weedon, Alexis. 'Reports fron S.H.A.R.P. Conference, 1993'. *Publishing History*, 34 (Autumn 1993): 88–90.

Welsh, Alexander. *The City of Dickens*. Oxford: Clarendon Press, 1971.

White, Allon. *Carnival, Hysteria and Writing: Collected Essays and Autobiography*. Int. by Stuart Hall. Oxford: Clarendon Press, 1993.

Whyte-Melville, G. J. *The Interpreter: A Tale of the War*. London: John W. Parker and Son, 1858.

Wigley, Mark. *The Architecture of Deconstruction: Derrida's Haunt*. Cambridge, Mass.: MIT Press, 1992.

Wilde, Oscar. *The Writings of Oscar Wilde*. Ed. Isobel Murray. Oxford and New York: Oxford University Press, 1989.

Wilde, Oscar. *The Selected Letters of Oscar Wilde*. Ed. Rupert Hart-Davis. Oxford: Oxford University Press, 1979.

Williams, Raymond. *The Country and the City*. Oxford: Oxford University Press, 1973.

Williams, Raymond. *The English Novel From Dickens to Lawrence*. (1970). London: The Hogarth Press, 1984.

Wolf, Lucian. 'Anti-Semitism'. *Encyclopaedia Britannica*. Eleventh edn, 1910–11.

Wood, Marilyn. *Rhoda Broughton (1840–1920): Profile of a Novelist*. Stamford: Paul Watkins, 1993.

Worth, George M. 'Of Muscles and Manliness: Some Reflections on Thomas Hughes'. *Victorian Literature and Society: Essays Presented to Richard D. Altick*. Ed. James R. Kincaid and Albert J. Kuhn. Ohio: Ohio University Press, 1984.

Yaeger, Patricia. *Honey-Mad Women: Emancipatory Strategies in Women's Writing*. New York: Columbia University Press, 1988.

Žižek, Slavoj. 'Eastern Europe's Republics of Gilead'. *New Left Review* (Sept./Oct. 1990): 50–62.

Index